THE UNIVERSITY CHALLENGE

Cardiff Papers in Qualitative Research

About the Series

The Cardiff School of Social Sciences at Cardiff University is well known for the breadth and quality of its empirical research in various major areas of sociology and social policy. In particular, it enjoys an international reputation for research using qualitative methodology, including qualitative approaches to data collection and analysis.

This series publishes original sociological research that reflects the tradition of qualitative and ethnographic inquiry developed at Cardiff in recent years. The series includes monographs reporting on empirical research, collections of papers reporting research on particular themes and other monographs or edited collections on methodological developments and issues.

The University Challenge
Higher Education Markets and Social Stratification

LESLEY PUGSLEY
University of Wales College of Medicine, UK

ASHGATE

Published by
Ashgate Publishing Limited
Gower House
Croft Road
Aldershot
Hants GU11 3HR
England

Ashgate Publishing Company
Suite 420
101 Cherry Street
Burlington, VT 05401-4405
USA

Ashgate website: http://www.ashgate.com

British Library Cataloguing in Publication Data
Pugsley, Lesley
  The university challenge : higher education markets and
  social stratification. - (Cardiff papers in qualitative
  research)
  1.Education, Higher - Social aspects - Great Britain
  2.Higher education and state - Great Britain 3.Education,
  Higher - Great Britain 4.Social classes - Great Britain
  I.Title
  378.4'1

Library of Congress Cataloging-in-Publication Data
Pugsley, Lesley.
  The university challenge : higher education markets and social stratification / by
Lesley Pugsley.
      p. cm. -- (Cardiff papers in qualitative research)
  Includes bibliographical references and index.
  ISBN 0-7546-3987-8
  1. College choice--Social aspects--Wales--Longitudinal studies. 2. Education,
Higher--Social aspects--Wales. 3. Higher education and state--Wales. 4. Social
stratification--Wales. I. Title. II. Series.

  LB2350.5.P84 2004
  306.43'2--dc22   2004010340

ISBN 0 7546 3987 8

Printed in Great Britain by Antony Rowe Ltd, Chippenham, Wiltshire

Contents

List of Figures and Tables

Preface

Significant changes have been made in both the structure and funding of higher education in the United Kingdom over the past two decades. Policy reforms have taken place within a quasi market framework, with efficiency, responsiveness and choice acting as the drivers seeking to justify this shift to a consumerist agenda. The expansionist agenda has seen the system shift from one of elite to mass provision, framed within a discourse of access, inclusivity and equity. However patterns of participation are relatively unchanged and working class groups remain under-represented in higher education. So how do young people engage with the highly competitive and differentiated university sector? How do potential students go about choosing a university? What key factors impact on and influence their choices?

This book provides a thought provoking and revealing account of the ways in which choices are made. It considers the complexities of the choice process and the multifaceted way in which choices are shaped, considered and negotiated. It argues that for many potential students choices are constrained by their differential access to information about university. Many young people are unaware of the crucial importance of making the right choice in terms of both the value of higher education and the influence it can have on career pathways and graduate opportunities. Consideration is given to the role of both the school and the family in order to explore the ways in which social class is transmitted and reproduced as it is played out in an engagement with this process. A unique feature of the book is that the findings are drawn from an innovative study of some of the last cohort of students to enter higher education, prior to the introduction of tuition fees. Their voices are heard and their stories told in order to theorize on the significance of social capital in the marketplace. The book argues that the real university challenge is to address the continued dominance of the middle classes access to higher education and the privileges that this confers.

Acknowledgements

Originally written as a doctoral thesis this study has now emerged as a monograph and I owe a debt of gratitude to a number of people who have either individually or collectively contributed to its completion. Firstly I am grateful to the Economic and Social Research Council for their sponsorship which enabled me to undertake the study. Thanks go to John Fitz for supervising the research with customary rigour and good humour and to Sara Delamont who continues to encourage my efforts, urging me to read widely and think laterally. Stephen Ball, Gareth Rees and Brian Davies offered critical comment on the study and I am grateful for their intellectual rigour and their interest in the work. Thanks also to colleagues at Cardiff University for their friendship and support especially Kate Stewart, Sarah Brown, Patrick White, and Trevor Welland for their collegiality and constructive comments during the fieldwork. Pia Towell has been a lifesaver, her skills and calm efficiency produced the camera-ready copy. I also want to thank Lynne Allery and Janet Macdonald for their encouragement and tolerance during the writing stage and to Roy for everything. My special thanks are reserved for the Class of '97 who allowed me to share their lives and tell the stories of their university challenges and triumphs. Any errors that remain are mine.

Chapter 1

Setting the Scene

Introduction

I have adopted a somewhat classical approach to the layout of this book moving from the macro to the micro, in order to consider the modern concern of higher education and markets. This historical overview of the sector is presented in order to locate the realities of choice that are explored later. Over the past four decades there have been considerable changes in the structure and governance of higher education in the United Kingdom. The elitist concept of access and participation has been re-examined and the manipulation of funding mechanisms has allowed for greater state intervention. In consequence the relationship between the academy and the government has undergone substantial transformation. While the Robbins Report in the 1960s promulgated an expansionist agenda Ainley suggests that by ignoring the power relations of gender, race and social class it merely 'reinforced the myth of disembodied meritocracy' (1994:11). Nevertheless the expansionist plans continued to gain momentum throughout the seventies and eighties, culminating in the 1992 Further and Higher Education Act. This saw the removal of the binary divide and created the framework necessary for a system of mass higher education. This marked a huge philosophical shift in the political perception of the role of higher education in the United Kingdom. It has been suggested that until late in 1990 British politicians had used the expression 'mass higher education' with 'apologies, embarrassment or distaste' (Daniel, 1993:197). However by mid-1991 the term was more readily accepted at all levels and had become assimilated into the cross-party political vocabulary.

Nevertheless the political commitment for expansion was not matched by a concomitant promise of increased levels of funding. Rather there have been major changes in the public funding regimes over the past three decades that have led to gradual reductions in government subsidies and grants for universities. Post Robbins expansion was fully funded both for recurrent and capital expenditure. By way of contrast more recent expansion has been accompanied by severe reductions in resources. Funding mechanisms have shifted from block grants to per capita funding allowing for a greater degree of state intervention in the sector. These changes can be seen as 'a deliberate intent to promote competition and cost effectiveness' (Wagner 1995:74). The populist agenda of the Thatcherite governments included the politics of choice and saw the introduction of a 'quasi market in education' (Le Grand and Bartlett, 1993). The market has continued to be a major influence for successive governments shaping and driving education policy in Britain (Pritchard, 1994a; Gerwirtz, Ball and Bowe, 1995; Glatter, Woods and Bagley, 1997; Ball, 2003). Researching school choice in education has become a well-established tradition. Studies have generally looked at the implications of policy changes in the compulsory sector and the political rhetoric of improved standards, accountability and parental choice (Gorard, 1996a; Gewirtz et al 1995; David, 1993; Fitz et al 1993; Whitty et al 1993; Deem et al 1994). The literature on school choice is extensive and Whitty (1997) provides an extensive review spanning the United Kingdom, the United States of America and New Zealand. All of this research has served to demonstrate the complexity of the choice process involving as it does both formal and informal factors.

Writing in 1992, Walford noted that despite significant changes in the structure and management of the university sector the sociology of British higher education remained an under researched area. The majority of the research looking at post compulsory pathways has focused on choices in relation to career decisions and citizenship (Banks et al, 1992; Bates and Riseborough, 1993, Hodkinson et al 1996; Bynner et al 1997). Research in higher education has seen the focus related to structuralist issues and the impact of government reforms on the management and organization of the sector. The interests of the research community have largely concentrated on standards and accountability (Salter and Tapper, 1994; Shattock, 1994; Mackay et al, 1995). Research on students themselves has centred on issues of gender, age, stress levels and graduate experience (Berry, 1995; Bryant, 1995; Dabney, 1995, Mallier and Rodgers, 1995). With the notable exception of Ball (2003) the few studies that look at choices in higher education are in the main retrospective surveys and hence conducted with a quantitative design focus (Weiler, 1996; Windolf, 1995; Wilson et al 1992; Barrett, 1996). Using a survey approach allows for claims of representativeness and generalizability of the findings and can also provide data on large cohorts of students. Survey based research studies can make important contributions to the corpus of knowledge around university choices They can, for example, provide data on the proportions of students who 'agree' or 'disagree' with a particular questionnaire item. What they cannot do is uncover the subtleties of the individual responses and make explicit the factors that informed and shaped the decision making process. Furthermore, a retrospective survey may lend itself to false accounting. Respondents may, with the benefit of hindsight, feel they have a need to rationalize their decisions in order to qualify the choices that were made. The use of retrospective surveys can only produce data that identify particular issues as problematic. Pre-coded responses can never allow the more fine grain complexities of a study to be explored and there remains a lacuna of empirical evidence on the ways in which a higher education market can impact on individual choices.

This book aims to fill some of these gaps in knowledge through the examination of individual accounts of the university choice process experienced by a group of pupils who were among the last cohort of undergraduates to enter university under the Robbins banner of 'free' education. In the chapters that follow comparisons are made between the ways in which individual choices are facilitated at the micro level of the family and the school. The data were collected in south east Wales, where sixth form pupils in ten different schools were tracked throughout the two years of their sixth form careers. The study used a mix of focus groups and open-ended interviews in order to explore the ways in which the higher education market has impacted on the choice process. This has allowed me to provide an account of the complex and multifaceted ways in which young people engage with a higher education market. The comparisons between individual families and the different levels of engagement that they have with the market are considered in terms of power relations, access to information and social capital. Access to information as a class based competency is explored and analysis demonstrates how working class families lack information about university application and choice. The information they have is often constructed in ways that relate to their cultural background and experience and so serves to disadvantage them in the market place.

The significance of 'place' to the research agenda is constantly reiterated and emphasized, (Gorard, 1996b; Rees et al, 1997; Gewirtz et al, 1995; Giddens, 1991). British studies often take England as their focus rather than one of the other countries in the UK. In contrast this research is located in Wales, more particularly it is concentrated in one specific part, the south east region, bounded to the west by the Vale of Glamorgan, to the north by the Brecon Beacons, and to the east by Offa's Dyke and the marshes. Burgess (1996) has likened researching in this area to 'working in border country' but has argued that Cardiff and its environs have given rise to 'considerable potential' for ethnographic enquiry (see Brown, 1987; Beynon, 1985; Salisbury, 1994). I would suggest that the patterning of findings in the local context while they inform and are informed by a Welsh culture are not merely an artefact of the region, but do have wider, transferable policy implications. Gorard (1996b:2) notes that, this approach would allow for the findings to be generalized to a national context more safely than with many wider ranging samples, 'since the merely local effects are now more clearly visible'.

Distinctions may be made between England and Wales, not merely in terms of geographic boundaries but also in relation to issues of language culture and demography. However, Wales, unlike Scotland, has, for the purposes of both policy and practice, been assimilated into the English education system. Delamont and Rees (1996:2) highlight, the 'For Wales see England' entry in an early edition of the Encyclopaedia Britannica, as providing an accurate description of the conventional approach adopted by many researchers when attempting to offer an analysis of the educational system in Wales. However, this enforced tandemisation of Wales and England has been seen to be inappropriate in many instances (Bellin, et al, 1994; Pugsley, 1995; Delamont and Rees, 1996; Betts, 1997). Historically, Wales has had a distinctive approach to higher education. Over time, though there has been a forced reduction in its national character in favour of an alignment with England. As Jones (1997:12) has noted 'not since the Welsh Intermediate Education Act of 1889 has there been any real attempt to recognize Wales as a national community'. He suggests, rather, that the 'London perspective on class, community and culture prevails and brooks little variation'. In response Phillips (1997:2) has identified the 'need to theorize systematically the origins, trajectories and outcomes of education policies in Wales and consider how they relate to the "bigger picture" outside it'.

An historical overview of the patterns of participation in higher education in Wales can be found in Rees and Istance (1997:50). They argue that 'currently there is a social integration into a Welsh and English system'. This view is supported by the study on the patterns of participation in post-compulsory education and training (POCET) in South Wales (Fevre et al, 1997:1) which notes that the region 'reproduces the characteristic UK pattern'. The specific issues relating to the recent changes in the structure and governance of higher education in Wales and in the rest of the UK are considered and are compared with international higher education systems in the following chapter. However it is important to note that the patterns of participation among Welsh and English students are very similar (Rees and Istance, 1997). Policy changes have resulted in a transformation of the education system in the UK since 1988. However, allowing for some variations of comparisons across nation states when different agencies are used to collect and collate data, Parry (1997) found that it is still possible for similar trends towards mass higher education to be identified in Wales, Scotland and England.

The introduction of market principles has marked a dramatic shift towards consumerism in education and has brought with it the rhetoric of choice. These changes have generated considerable interest in the policy analysis community. However as Phillips (1997) notes the boom in policy analysis has consistently taken England as its focus. He argues that there is a need for researchers in Wales to focus on the distinctiveness of the region and to produce the quality of policy analysis here, which has already emerged with Ball in England, McPherson and Raab in Scotland and O'Buachalla in Ireland. By focusing on Wales and conducting qualitative research in the region, this book sets out to address, in part, the omission which has occurred in this area of policy analysis. It aims, in so doing, to contribute to the limited body of knowledge which currently exists in the sociology of higher education in the UK.

Adopting a qualitative focus to researching the choice process enables the participants to provide their accounts in their own words. Such studies can explore assumptive worlds and lived realities. Researching in 'real time', as choices are explored, or unconsidered and then decisions made, can add a richness and authenticity to the accounting. The complexities of engaging with choices can be uncovered and crucially the levels of facilitation and degrees of influence which family and school can bring to the decision making can be made visible. Families and family negotiations are generally private, studying in depth the ways in which family units engage with the choice process can add a new perspective on the ways in which the higher education market is operating. Throughout this book I will argue that while free market principles espouse equality and opportunity, choices at higher education levels are social constructed, determined by social class rather than academic ability. Also the accounts of family lives and family negotiations are of themselves intrinsically interesting and significant. There is a range of literature documenting family life in Wales in the 1960s and 1970s (Rosser and Harris, 1965; Barker, 1972; Leonard, 1980;). The evidence presented here represents a valuable addition to the accounts of the social history of some of the families in south east Wales in the latter part of the twentieth century.

The study described in this book encompasses several aspects of sociological interest; these include the durability of social class inequalities and educational access, the diversity of family relationships and parental roles and the ways in which knowledge, values and beliefs are socially determined. For young people now, going to university can be seen as an unproblematic, taken for granted rite of passage. In the 1960s fewer than seven per cent of eighteen-year-olds went into higher education. Currently with a political agenda promoting mass participation and with levels of entry in excess of 60 per cent of the age group, going to university is the norm and there is an assumption that for many eighteen-year-olds that university is the next and obvious stage. Certainly there has been a commonly held perception that the only issue is simply that of getting the required grades. The suggestion that an education market is simply a mechanism to ensure that standards are improved and selection is a straightforward and equitable process can and is bolstered by political rhetoric. However as was noted earlier the considerable amount of research on school choice has indicated that the process is complex and multifaceted. The theorising for this study has been eclectic 'since social action inherently denies all efforts to produce a broadly acceptable unifying theory' (Cohen, 1996:112). Rather as Ball (1994:14) suggests 'diverse concepts and theories are required in order to deal with the complexity and scope of policy analysis'. However, there are key theorists and areas that have been most influential in informing this study and providing a theoretical underpinning to the work. In consequence much of the remainder of this introductory chapter will focus on a discussion of the theoretical and methodological strategies that underpin the work, and will map out the way in which the book is ordered.

Exploring Choice

Social structures serve to define boundaries of both knowledge and experience and clear links can be made between social class and differential access to information and social provisions such as education. From a sociological perspective, class contextualizes the lives of individuals and impacts on the opportunities that they have and the choices they make. Sociologically, theorising allows an opportunity to make the familiar strange, to challenge the taken for granted order and to offer different perspectives on every day occurrences. Theories can help to locate narrative accounts and allow for commentary on social practice. The work of Bourdieu is widely recognized for its contribution to sociology and social anthropology and his contribution to the structure action debate has 'consistently been framed by an engagement between systematic empirical work and reflexive theorising' (Jenkins, 1992:10). His work places an emphasis on social practice and his focus is very much on individuals and how they live their lives. Crucially however it is neither the sum of individual actions nor social structures per se which shape and determine individual practices. Rather Bourdieu argues that the key to understanding social action is intrinsically linked to issues of 'intangible wealth'. Central to this are his theories of cultural capital and habitus. He suggests that cultural capital is inculcated in children as part of the socialization process within the family. Since societies 'privilege' certain styles of language, behaviours, activities and artefacts, those children who are born into families which possess the valued assets inherit a familiarity with and an appreciation of 'high' culture, for example the arts and foreign travel. In consequence he refers to the notion of habitus, which he sees as something of an illusive concept since it exists only 'inside the head'. He refers to it in terms of a set of socially grounded dispositions to life that have their origins in the individual's cultural background. This makes for a set of distinctive modes of interaction with others and so defines a collective 'taste'. In consequence he suggests that there is a subtlety within groups a 'taken for granted' as to the appropriateness of particular sets of actions and activities that social groups are socialized into thinking how things should be (Bourdieu, 1990). The significance of applying this particular model of theorising to education markets and social class has been explored by a number of commentators (Gewirtz et al, 1995; Reay, 2000; Ball, 2003). Like them I have developed the concepts that Bourdieu has theorized and I consider both institutional and family habituses in order to explore their significance in shaping HE choices. Later chapters in this book will discuss the ways in which social class influences the levels of engagement with the university market.

Similarly the work of Bernstein is helpful in allowing the data to be explored and the role of both the school and the home considered in respect of group norms and activities in making university choices. In his 1975 work, *Class, Codes and Control*, Bernstein has provided a seminal account of the way in which a two-dimensional strategy can be applied to the analysis of educational systems. This allows us to gain an understanding of the ways in which knowledge is controlled and organized and the impact that these strategies have on social class. Sociological research within the compulsory school context has documented across time that working class children tend to experience persistently lower rates of attainment and are less likely to engage with post-compulsory education (Jackson and Marsden, 1962; Willis, 1977; Bates and Riseborough, 1993). Bernstein uses the term 'classification' to describe the boundaries that exist within the educational system to separate areas of knowledge. Strong classification ensures that academic subjects are taught separately through specialist departmental strands, while weak classification is provided for in a more interdisciplinary setting, with the potential for wide ranging rather than focused transmission of knowledge. He also uses this oppositional notion of strong and weak in his term 'framing' which he uses to denote the levels of organisation and control that are exercised over the choice of the knowledge base for the curriculum, the method and pace of delivery and the modes of assessment. An educational system, which combines strong classification and strong framing, has what Bernstein refers to as a visible pedagogy in contrast to the invisible pedagogy of those schools with a weakly classified and framed curriculum and organization. These terms link into his theories of different forms of socialization within family groups, what he refers to as the personal and positional family (this is discussed more fully in Chapter 9). It can be seen that these factors will strongly impact on the nature and the quality of the educational experience of young people and clear links can be made between the work of Bernstein on the opposition between visible and invisible pedagogies and that of

Douglas (1982). She theorizes about organisational membership, suggesting that the nature and exclusivity of the organisation serve to regulate entry. The stronger the grouping the more rigorous the commitment demanded of its members. In relation to higher education markets and issues of access this is illustrated by reference to the elite institutions such as Oxford and Cambridge, who can and do set very high admissions criteria. Douglas uses the term 'grid' to identify the degree of social control or regulation that an organisation exerts over its membership. When there is a strong grid, she argues that behaviour is prescribed and there is a rigid adherence to schedules. Again applying this theorising to university access, we can look at the Universities and Colleges Admissions Service (UCAS) which is a strongly regulated body that places stringent temporal and procedural dimensions to the applications process, this is discussed in a later chapter (Chapter 3) in relation to social class and differential levels of access to information. Throughout the book I want to stress the significance of theorising concepts of social class in order to explore the ways in which university choices are facilitated, or not, by families and schools. The data will show how social capital produces and reproduces educational advantages. Bourdieu (1977) argues that inequality is shaped by the four different forms of capital namely the economic, social, cultural and symbolic, all of which serve to privilege (or otherwise) individuals and groups in their struggle for position within a specific social space. The differential levels of 'empowerment' that emerge as a result of these struggles provide us with a useful analogous relationship of class analysis. In this study it is argued that for some families, having the appropriate 'capital' provides them with the competencies required to interpret and engage with the market in ways that ensure maximum social, educational and financial benefits. These competencies enable them to access information and networks that ensure a full engagement with the market and the choice process (see Chapters 6 and 7).

Methods Explained

The methodological strategies that informed the study are rooted in the interpretative paradigm. I adopted a mixed method approach and this shaped both the questions that were asked and the interpretations that were made. The study was located in south east Wales and focused on collecting data from three different sources, schools families and universities. The sampling was purposive, since I wanted to collect data from each of the different school types in the locality. The use of a minimum number of A-level points per student is one way in which, at the institutional level, it is possible to standardize entry requirements, and so attract academic high fliers. For example, the usual offer for Oxbridge entry is set at 30 points, three grade A passes at A-level, or equivalent. Since it is these A-level grade points that commonly determine what university choices can be made, I selected schools where the average A-level points score per pupil was sufficient to enable a degree of institutional choice. I chose schools and sixth form colleges where the average A-level points score per pupil were within the ten to twenty one points range. These scores were based on a system where a grade A score was equivalent to ten points, a B eight points, a C six points, a D four points and an E grade two points. In total, eight Schools, one Sixth Form College and one College of Further Education took part in the study. Qualitative research places emphasis on the meanings that key players attach to various acts. This allows the experiences of the individual to be reported and valued. As this was a longitudinal; study which tracked pupils throughout the two years of their sixth form careers, data were collected at various key stages. A self-completed questionnaire was administered to pupils in the early spring of the Lower Sixth year (n=711). These data were used to generate an open ended interview schedule and this was used in the focus group interviews with the pupils a few months later A second questionnaire survey was conducted in the second year, when the application choices had been made. The use of social surveys as means of data collection is well document (de Vaus, 1994; Babbie, 1992; Cohen and Manion, 1994) and a number of ethnographic researchers have noted its strength as a strategy (Burnett, 1969; Lacey, 1976; Peshkin, 1986; Rist, 1978). Using focus groups as a tool for qualitative research allows for a very flexible approach and one which provides data that have a high face validity (Morgan, 1997; Denscombe, 1995; Kitzinger, 1994; Stewart and Shamdasani, 1990; Kreuger, 1988). It is also efficient for the researcher since the group approach allow a number of respondents to be interviewed together. Each of the focus group interviews were conducted in the schools and colleges, There were 16 interviews in total and with the exception of the two single sex school, all had a gender mix. All of the interviews in the study were tape recorded, with the interviewees' permissions and the tapes transcribed fully before the analysis. I also interviewed key members of the teaching staff at each school and sixth form college. I used semi-structured interviews in order to identify the systems that were in place in these various institutions to inform pupils and parents about the university applications procedures and to facilitate their choices.

Commentators have noted that as part of the socialisation process 'children come to share the assumptive worlds of their parents and friends' (Furlong et al, 1996:562). In order to consider family dynamics and the ways in which they are influential in the lived realities that serve to shape and influence the choices process, I conducted 20 semi-structured, home based, interviews (two families each as representatives from each school or college in the study). A considerable amount of research has been conducted on issues relating to the family and school choice (Hughes et al, 1994; David et al, 1994; Gewirtz et al, 1995; Reay, and Ball, 1998). However, in the main, these studies have been conducted with only one parent and then usually the mother. In much of this research choices have been based on affective, social criteria, such as the happiness and the security of the child (Coldron and Boulton, 1991; Hunter, 1991). In order to consider the roles adopted by universities as provider in the higher education market. I interviewed the Chief Executive of a local university during the week of its transition from a college to a Higher Education Institution and members of the marketing teams at two local universities, one a Civic, the other a 'New' institution. Content analysis of a range of 50 university prospectuses served to provide some insight into the various marketing strategies used by institutions in order to attract students, who have now become the client group in this highly competitive market.

Charting the Way

This book sets out to provide an account of the processes that inform young peoples university choices. This is done by offering commentary from the macro level of policy initiatives that have served to shape and drive the marketization of the sector through to the micro level politics of choice as reflected in and enacted through the family dynamic. In the chapters that follow the aim is to identify the ways in which class based competencies can enable successful engagements with the university choice process. In order to contextualize the study the chapters are arranged such that they allow the focus to move from a descriptive account of policy initiatives and institutional change to the empirically driven accounts of the ways in which market choices are facilitated (or not). Consideration is given to the fact that these choices are negotiated during a period of transition and the tensions and dynamics within families discussed. Whilst there is an underlying and unifying theme of university markets and choice running throughout the book, each chapter acts in a sense as a self contained unit exploring a specific issue or theme. The participants in this study, the young people and their families have allowed me access to the ways in which they experienced the lived realities of these choices. In consequence much of the text throughout the book is devoted to them and to their voices. I have used their own words in order to allow their stories to be told. Quotations from them are followed by pseudonyms and where appropriate an indication of strategy used to obtain the data is provided. The fieldwork for this study took two years. During that time I came to know many of the young people well. I shared the excitement of some and the frustrations and disappointments of others.

Chapter 2 identifies and charts the changes that have occurred in the structure and governance of higher education during the post war period. It provides a portrait of the policy shifts that have enabled the move from an elite to a mass system of higher education to occur. It uses the 'Cardiff Affair' as a case study to highlight the changes in funding mechanisms that led to a loss of institutional autonomy, and this increased state intervention is set against the creation of a quasi market in higher education. The second part of the chapter draws on empirical data from the study in order to explore ways in which the market has created a university hierarchy. It considers the marketing strategies employed by some institutions to attract 'clients' and discusses the student responses to these market practices.

Chapter 3 looks at the changes that have occurred in the youth labour market and the concomitant increased levels of participation in post compulsory education and training over recent decades. It also considers the nature of career guidance in schools and argues that it should be redesigned so that it focuses on developing good practices to ensure that young people from all social backgrounds are provided with information and guidance that facilitates access to university.

The mechanics of the application process and the complexities of the UCAS system are considered in the second part of this chapter in order to highlight the potential that exists for first time consumers of higher education to become confused by the temporal framework of the choice mechanism.

These chapters provide accounts at the macro level in order to explore and explain the institutional and structural factors that shape university applications and access. In Chapters 4, 5, 6, 7 the frame shifts to the micro level in order to look at the ways in which practice informs choice. These chapters are empirical, they provide accounts of the institutional and family habituses and the ways in which social capital impacts on and shapes the HE market engagements. In Chapter 4 the specificity of locale is considered and the chapter provides brief vignettes of each of the schools and sixth form colleges in the study, identifying the differences in levels of guidance and facilitation offered by each. It explores the way in which A level is still the gold standard in terms of university entrance and highlights the different levels of institutional support offered to middle and working class students. In the second part of this chapter the focus shifts to consider the families and the problems for sociological analysis in defining both 'family' and 'class' in order to theorize social actions.

In Chapter 5 the ways in which different schools and colleges prepare pupils for university is discussed. The chapter documents the ways in which the secondary sector is highly differentiated and the impact this has on the university application process. Using case studies of pupils and data from across the whole of the study Chapter 6 continues the debate about differential access to information and the consequences for successfully engaging with the market that began in the previous chapter. Chapter 7 looks at the micro politics of the family and the ways in which decision making is negotiated. It also looks at the strategies which are employed within families to ensure that their children are 'kept close', these findings are compared with data from earlier family studies in Wales and the north of England. The penultimate chapter also contains empirical data, it considers the various anxieties that pupils expressed during the study. These data are considered and discussed in light of literature on transition and status passage. In the final chapter, the key analytical themes are discussed and typologies of the schools and the families who took part in the study are considered. It provides commentary on the various aspects of the study and considers the implications of its findings in terms of policy initiatives, higher education access social justice and choice.

Chapter 2

Change and the Academy

The International Scene

International comparisons are helpful when considering the structure and organisation surrounding access to higher education in the United Kingdom. Teichler (1996:302) suggests that they serve as 'useful heuristic tools in understanding one's own situation and in identifying possible options'. There has been a commonality of debate across Western Europe over several decades in respect of higher education reforms. These debates have been informed both by the economic and the political changes that have occurred across the European Union and a consensus of opinion in respect of the expansion of the sector and a move towards the introduction of mass systems of higher education throughout the Community. The thinking behind such a move has been that an increase in student numbers would not only provide the means of stimulating economic growth but would also allow for social advancement. While access to higher education in the United Kingdom has increased and a more diverse student population now exists, European practice offers some interesting points of contrast and comparison. Within Germany, the Netherlands and Scandinavia all the higher education institutions are of a comparable standard, so students are allocated places. The United Kingdom and France have quality differences across the sector and, in consequence, there is fierce competition to gain access to the 'elite' institutions.

In Finland, for example, higher education is strongly concentrated in the university sector, which is totally governed by the state. Approximately 28,000 secondary level pupils a year (about 46 per cent of the age cohort) sit the matriculation examination and the number is increasing annually. There are about 80,000 applications for higher education per annum. Students apply directly to the university of their choice and each institution has its own selection criteria and entrance methods. Some 45,000 prospective students take part in entrance examinations, the results of which allow about one third of the age group (approximately 20 per cent of the age group) to be admitted. However, since there are far more applications than there are places, in all fields of study, the sector has a *numerus clauses* system. This results in a 'bottleneck' of students who have the necessary matriculation grades, but fail to gain places in higher education (Kivinen and Rinne, 1991).

Denmark has had a planned system of admission to higher education since 1977, which employs grade point averages as the primary admissions criterion. This has encouraged a special type of student choice, which, while it has been rational at the individual level, has had unintended consequences at national level.

As Laursen and Foersom (1993) note, this has been sufficient to force the Ministry of Education to change its admissions procedure. Now students have choices about the course of study they will select but they are placed in universities according to availability of places. In contrast, higher education in France remains à site of political conflict and confrontation to a far greater extent than it is in the UK. There are two factors that influence this level of struggle. First, street politics are still powerful and as Neave (1991:66) notes 'it acts as a reminder that consumer power is not simply a matter of party rhetoric'. Second, rapid expansion of the sector places it on the political agenda. Slightly over 30 per cent of the age cohort that sits for the Baccalaureate examination is successful and 84 per cent of these pupils, (25 per cent of the age cohort) apply to higher education institutions. The application is made directly to the institution selected but, in the main, students in France choose to apply to their local institution.

In Italy, the distribution of students between universities is a matter of individual choice, and so, indirectly, of market forces (Moscati, 1991). Students can make application directly to the university of their choice and, in consequence, 55 per cent of the total enrolment is concentrated in nine of the 63 universities, an average of 66,000 students per institution. Each of the other 54 institutions has an average student body of 11,000. With demand at such a premium an 'informal, although very effective, process of screening out those students not culturally equipped for an elite institution does occur' (Moscati, 1991:106). Access to higher education in the Netherlands is open to anyone with the appropriate type of secondary education diploma. There is a highly diversified secondary education sector that provides various levels of certification. It is arranged in three sectors, universities, schools for higher vocational educational, and distance learning through the Open University. While students here also apply directly to the institution of their choice, the variety of diploma levels provided by the diversified secondary sector is judged able 'to provide an adequate selection for entering the higher education system' (Van Vught, 1991:109).

In Germany, as with most other European countries, there is a system that allows open access to students with suitable qualifications. However since 1992, the country has operated a distribution system which allows for a right of place, but not of choice. Germany is one of the few industrial countries still to have a relatively homogeneous university sector. There are no elite universities, however, Gellert (1996) argues that prestige differentials do exist which may give rise to corresponding differences in income and occupational entry. The formalised distinction between the institutions is between universities and colleges (Fachhochschulen) the latter offering practical professional training (Pritchard, 1990). The introduction of the Fachhochschulen provides a cheaper and more efficient alternative to the university, albeit with a limited range of subject options and caters for previously disadvantaged groups (Berger et al, 1993). The case is similar to that of the Republic of Ireland, which, historically, has been something of a late starter, both in industrialisation and modernisation. The changes in access to and participation in higher education have also been slower than in other regions in Europe. Even so, by 1985 eighteen-year-olds participating in full time higher education were 41 per cent of the age cohort. The secondary education sector in the

Republic is highly differentiated, but two thirds of all the pupils in each of the four types of schools sit the Leaving Examination Certificate. They can apply for admission directly to the universities but places are allocated on their performance levels in this examination. In consequence, this leaves the republic with a much higher level of potential students without higher education places than that found in most other European countries (Clancy, 1997).

In the United States of America there is a dual system of public and private universities and colleges. However, in the mid 1980s while over 50 per cent of the 3,250 colleges and universities were private, they enrolled only 20 per cent of the age cohort. While State governments have professed commitment to a policy of open admission to all high school graduates, only six have ever legislated for this. In reality, therefore, as Berdahl and Millet (1991) have shown, while students may apply to any number of institutions, there is a structured access based on their status, reputation and location. Access to higher education in Israel, as in France, is a highly contested and politicised issue. Here, however, there are strict selection procedures and entry is based on a composite mark from a psychometric entrance test and the Bagrut, the Israeli High School, Matriculation Examination. The higher education sector in Israel, in line with other developed countries, has expanded dramatically over the past 15 years. There were a little over 57,000 students 1981 and, by 1995, this number had almost doubled. However, there has been a dialectic force at work with tension between government controls and expansion of the sector. Higher education is highly differentiated and every university and each school or department within it can define their own quotas and entry requirements. Some disciplines may use additional screening mechanisms, such as interviews and proficiency tests, to select students. Students apply directly to the university of their choice and are considered on these various criteria (Guri-Rosenblit, 1996).

The expansion of higher education across these nine nations exemplifies the relationship between education and the economy. Issues of choice of university have changed and there has been a general move from a sellers to a buyers market Policy initiatives paralleled across these countries will see this buyer dominated market further emphasized. However, Neave and Van Vught (1991:3) have argued, that 'even with a dramatic expansion in the sector, higher education is still producer led'. This is certainly the British case since the Universities and the Funding Councils (UFCs) control the admissions policy by monitoring student numbers via per capita funding and quotas.

The British System

The concept of university education in post war Britain has changed dramatically. This has been brought about as a consequence of policy initiatives that have served to radically alter both the structure and governance of the academy. These changes have served to unify the system and allow a shift from an elitist to a mass model of participation. A detailed historical overview of the sector (Kogan and Kogan, 1983) concluded that by the start of the 1980s universities were considered to be too far removed from the needs of the economy and over complacent in their dependency on state funding. Following the publication of the Jarratt Report in 1985 there was a dramatic cultural shift with the new discourses for higher education shaped by managerial concepts. Pressure was placed on universities to reconsider their roles within a new centralised system (Halsey, 1992; Salter and Tapper, 1992).

Commissioned in 1963 the brief of the Robbins Committee was to review the pattern of participation in full time education in the United Kingdom and to advise on its long-term development. In common with earlier reports (Crowther, 1959; Newsom, 1963) the Committee found a high correlation between social class and educational achievement. Although absolute number had increased steadily since the 1920s, the proportions of children from each class group entering higher education remained much as they had (Statham et al, 1989). The Committee identified several objectives for higher education in relation to advancing and developing learning and transmitting a common culture. It also stressed the need for universities to play a role in training students to develop skills necessary required by the labour market. The espoused political intention was that university education should be available to everyone with the necessary entry qualifications and in order to meet this aim a massive expansion of the sector was recommended. Post Robbins ten 'green field' universities were established and university status granted to ten colleges of advanced technology.

The growth in the number of universities continued at varying rates and with varying degrees of success over successive decades. In quantitative terms a system of mass higher education has been defined as one which sees the enrolment of between 15 and 40 per cent of the age group (Trow, 1973). In 1999 over one third of all young people were participating in higher education and this proportion is set to rise to 50 per cent. However whilst student numbers have increased dramatically across time for both the middle and the working classes, Halsey (1992) notes that the incremental growth in student numbers has been greatest for the middle classes. In spite of the expansionist agenda patterns of participation remain relatively unchanged and universities have consistently recruited from a predominantly middle class population. The Further and Higher Education Act (1992) abolished the binary line between universities and polytechnics that had existed since 1966 and had allowed these institutions to run on parallel but separate lines. However there was considerable cross party concern as to how this newly expanded sector should be funded since the expansionist policies of the previous three decades had not been matched with concomitant increases in levels of funding.

Paying the Piper

The Universities Grants Committee was established in 1919 and its function was to distribute grants directly to universities. It acted as something of a buffer between the universities and government; administering block grants to the universities on a quinquennial basis. This allowed the university sector to maintain a considerable degree of autonomy since it enabled individual institutions to plan their financial expenditure free from state intervention. However Shattock (1994) notes that this buffer role was systematically eroded during the 1980s and by the beginning of the 1990s had totally disappeared. At its inception the University Grants Committee (UGC) had been placed under the control of the Treasury rather than the Board of Education whose responsibilities were confined to England and Wales. This decision was largely pragmatic. The Committee had jurisdiction across the whole of the United Kingdom and so needed to be contained within a department with a comparable remit. The key threat to university autonomy was any financial dependency on the State. In order to alleviate this fear the annual grant awards were calculated on a principle of shortfall. In effect the UGC provided a mechanism for allocating government subsidies to those universities which found themselves with a financial deficit. Grant funding was provided to meet all the essential costs of the university that could not be met from their other sources of income. However the links between the UGC and the universities were very informal and government subsides never constituted more than 30 per cent of any institutions current income. The remaining amount coming jointly from student fees and endowments. This formula allowed the sector to maintain considerable autonomy over its financial management.

However post-Robbins and partly in response to its recommendations, significant changes were made to the ways in which the UGC operated. Kogan (1987) notes that the status of the UGC was somewhat diminished after 1964 when government increased centralisation of public expenditure and education policy and control of the UGC was transferred from the Treasury to the newly created Department of education and Science. Under these new arrangements the Committee no longer provided the financial buffer which had been its remit when it was established in 1919. Rather by the early 1970s it had adopted a much more advisory role with the Committee involved in planning the scale and direction of higher education (Moodie, 1983). The machinery of the UGC expanded in response to its enhanced function, increasingly becoming an executive agency responsible to ministers. This shift in role brought with it a reduction in its ability to insulate universities from state interventions. The fiscal crisis faced by Britain in the 1970s placed constraints on all aspects of government planning and funding and the university sector was no exception The cut backs continued throughout the 1970s and 1980s in spite of the rapid expansions in student numbers. By 1979 the UGC faced with the loss of the quinquennial planning system was unable to do more than react to counter- inflationary policies as they were introduced. Although its principle function remained the distribution of discretionary grants the UGC had no statutory powers over universities or the ways in which they managed their financial affairs. Shattock (1994) attests that the final demise of the University Grants Committee can be described by specific reference to the 'Cardiff Affair'. University College Cardiff had enjoyed a period of rapid expansion post Robbins. As the largest and most prestigious of the constituent colleges of the federal University of Wales student numbers had increased. However, in common with other institutions in the sector, Cardiff had experienced a seven per cent reduction in its recurrent grant and in the 1984-1985 financial returns the College treasurer reported its financial difficulties to the College Council. In 1986 public attention focused on Cardiff, which was set to become bankrupt. Accountants Price Waterhouse were commissioned by the Permanent Secretary to the Department of Education to investigate and report on the Colleges' financial situation. Until then university autonomy had ensured privacy, now the academy and its finances were subject to public scrutiny. In order to preserve the 'notion' of institutional autonomy this financial mismanagement did not incur any formal sanction, other than that the College was asked to present the UGC with monthly financial reports. However the disclosures about Cardiff proved to have wider political implications regarding university funding.

In 1987 the Croham Report reviewed the role of the UGC and was followed immediately by a White Paper on Higher Education, 'Meeting the Challenge'. While Croham saw the UGC as being in need of some updating it still was still considered to be serving a useful function. In contrast the White Paper made clear the government intention to create a University Funding Council and a parallel body, the Polytechnics and Colleges Funding Council, to fund the polytechnics. However the most significant changes which resulted from the debate about financial mismanagement in higher education came about with the introduction of formula funding. Mace (1996) has indicated that the underlying aims behind this were threefold, namely to increase university accountability, to make the institutions more cost effective and concentrate the focus on research and teaching. In the late 1980s government abolished the grant allocation substituting a new system of contracts between the funding agencies and individual institutions. However following the 1992 Further and Higher Education Act and only four years after they were established four separate Higher Education Funding Councils replaced the two funding bodies across the United Kingdom. These newly created Funding Councils assumed responsibility for the funding of higher education in their regions in April 1992. Their principal task being the distribution of money to higher education institutions for teaching and research purposes. In line with the free market philosophy underpinning policy initiatives, they are also responsible for assessing the quality of provision. Some of these tasks, for example the Research Assessment Exercise are undertaken as joint initiatives. The changed mechanisms aimed to encourage expansion of the sector at marginal cost. As Williams (1997) has noted while student enrolment rose by more than 50 per cent between 1989 and 1994, per capita expenditure fell by 30 per cent during this same period. At the same time there was a shift in the balance of financial power from the provider to the consumer.

The University Goes to Market

Since 1979 and the first Thatcher government, Britain has witnessed a considerable and consistent shift in policy making. Successive governments across both parties have been committed to free market principles and minimal levels of state intervention. Swinnerton-Dyer notes that the main purpose behind the introduction of Funding Councils was to 'expose the universities to market forces' (1991:205). Commentators have noted that the initiatives served to make the universities more accountable and responsive to their client group and prompted them to look beyond the public sector for their sponsorship. However it can be argued that with the introduction of a free market ideology the function and value of higher education has been reduced to a 'saleable commodity' (Pritchard, 1994b:253). There has been an increasing emphasis in public policy on devolved responsibility and individual choice. Since the mid-1980s the notion of 'public service' has been replaced by contractual provider-client relations. Increasingly consumer pressures determine the provision of services from public enterprises. Le Grand and Bartlett (1993) have noted that within the restructuring there was clear evidence of the political creation and regulation of competition. In consequence a 'quasi market' rather than a pure market discipline now operates across the sector. This term has been adopted in relation to social policy because provision through a state monopoly has been replaced by provision from competitive independent sources. These created markets differ from the more conventional markets on both the supply and demand sides.

However, the introduction of the market effectively allowed the government to cease to function as the direct provider of higher education (Dill, 1997:182). Rather its role has become 'that of a purchaser of services from independent providers who compete with each other in an internal quasi market'. Universities now are more accountable and constrained, less able to make their own decisions. There has been a move away from individual and internal concerns, the focus now is on institutional positioning (Warner and Palfryman, 1996:42). This is particularly the case for the 'new' (post 1992) institutions who struggle to locate and maintain themselves within the market. Current political debate around the government proposals to increase the level of tuition fees and to allow universities to set different rates highlight the extent to which the sector is now highly differentiated. At the time of writing these proposed differential charges are being contested by a group of Vice Chancellors representing the 'Real New' universities who fear that these funding mechanisms will discriminate against them still further in terms of variable resource allocations. Parents and students are now consumers and universities need to be responsive to client demands. Gewirtz et al (1995:127) found that schools rely on a 'glossification' of image that is focused around certain core activities' in order to attract pupils. Similarly the highly competitive higher education market place requires universities to engage with varying degrees of 'face management' (Goffman, 1969). However there are clear oppositional tensions between the philosophies of commercialism and liberal education.

Between the 1960s and early 1980s few changes had been made to the ways in which financial support was provided for students. (Callender, 2001). Tuition fees were paid by the state and living expenses met by means tested maintenance grants and social security benefits, where necessary. However changes in benefit entitlements in the 1980s meant that from 1986 onward students were no longer eligible for unemployment benefits during the shorter Christmas and Easter vacations and after 1991 support for the long summer vacation also ended. In 1990 a system of mixed grants and top up loans was introduced as a means of providing financial support for student. Having 'frozen' the level of maintenance grants in 1990 a loan system was introduced, with a gradual increase in the ratio of loan to grant between 1990 and 1998. Repayments started once the graduate salary reached 85 per cent of the national average. The Dearing Report (1997) provided a wide ranging review of higher education and highlighted the potential crisis facing universities if the expansion of student numbers continued without a matched increase in funding. It recommended charging tuition fees on a flat rate, while retaining a system of means-tested maintenance grants. However the Labour government rejected these recommendations and announced alternative plans which were incorporated within the 1998 Teaching and Higher Education Act. While tuition fees were introduced, as Dearing had suggested, the level of contribution was means tested and maintenance grants were replaced entirely by loans. From the autumn of 1998 those entering higher education have been required to contribute towards their tuition fees, and this has further impacted on social inclusion and access for certain sections of the population, particularly working class, ethnic minority and mature students.

Clearly going to university is expensive and increasingly the burden for financing a degree is being shifted from the public to the personal level. There is increasing concern about the levels of student debt that have risen sharply since the introduction of the loan scheme (Hesketh, 1996; Forsyth and Furlong, 2000; Callender, 2001). The MORI survey reveals that in 2001 the average debt for a third year student was around £7,000 and that those from lower social class backgrounds had larger debts (THES, 2002). The shift from an elite to a mass system of higher education occurred within a political discourse of equality. However funding changes that paralleled the expansionist agenda clearly served to counter such claims. Policy changes have been convoluted and many of the underlying initiatives appear fuzzy and muddled.

Selling the Sector

Marketing is now a major part of the organisational strategy of any university. Institutions operate within a much greater competitive context and face an uncertain future in which they need to become 'more market responsive' (Conway and York, 1991:23). Universities offer broadly the same product, but the sector is highly differentiated in terms of status, and graduate pathways (Ainley, 1994; Paterson, 1997). This presents a real marketing challenge for the new institutions if they are to secure a niche in the market, as well as for the traditional institutions if they are to retain their client group in what is now a highly stratified and competitive sector. Their traditional roots can readily identify the 'Old' universities, but for the 'New', post Robbins and the 'Real New', post 1992 institutions, there is a need to position themselves in the marketplace. In order to survive, they have been obliged to direct their attentions away from the internal concerns of academia and focus instead on external issues such as institutional positioning (Warner and Palfreyman, 1996). A key feature of modernity has been the emphasis on identity (Giddens, 1991) and the removal of the binary divide, in

1992, resulted in the loss of identity for the former polytechnics and a need for their re-invention and positioning within an expanded university market place.

In the drive to ensure that each institution can compete for 'clients' marketing departments and marketing strategies now play a major part in the institutional structure and organisation across the sector. Each university is geared towards producing a range of materials designed to 'sell' themselves to various client groups. Student fairs are organized regionally throughout the UK, in order to provide information about university courses and as a means of attracting potential students. Many universities appoint a 'Schools Liaison Officer' whose responsibility it is to provide information and advertising materials to schools, Sixth Form Colleges and Further Education Colleges. Setting minimum entry requirements ensures recruitment to the traditional institutions from more academically able students. In consequence, 'Real New' universities recognize and acknowledge their need to form compact agreements with local schools and colleges in order to maintain a student flow into their standard degree courses. The strength of the 'New' institutions lie in their willingness to offer a greater variety of hybrid and applied degree options, unlike the more established institutions which aim to provide traditional degree courses and subject options. However these institutions are still able to be highly selective in respect of particular courses in which they have a solid reputation and where consequently applications for places are oversubscribed. The strategies for promoting the institution are largely the same in both 'Old' and 'New' institutions. Publicity materials are produced to 'sell' the product. In some instances aggressive marketing strategies are used in order to attract students, but the use of commission salesmen is not generally held to be the way forward. High-pressured marketing could have implications for student drop out rates that are costly in financial and human terms both to the institution and the individual. The survey on drop out rates conducted by UCAS (1996) reported that the prime reason given by students for not taking up a place was their having been badly advised about course, or subject, options. Over-promotion of an institution by high pressured salesmen would prove counter productive for students attempting to decode the multiplicity of factors associated with higher education choices.

In some instances, schools and universities may see marketing as an exercise in crisis management (James and Phillips, 1995). It can be argued that, with competition a key word in education policy it may well be that the marketing material is regarded as an essential weapon in the survival battle. While the courses available within any institution are the primary services offered, the other facilities, such as accommodation, social clubs and sporting provision are important factors in choice (Gray, 1991) and it is these other elements which higher education institutions are increasingly making use of in their marketing promotions. Not only is imagery becoming more important [to schools] 'but the focus and content of imagery is being transformed in the process creating new semiologies' (Gewirtz et al, 1995:126). The process of 'fronting up', of creating an image and presenting the world with an acceptable social face, is a well-chronicled phenomenon. Goffman (1969) relies heavily on the use of dramaturgical metaphor to explain the ways in which individuals and organisations engage in 'impression management'.

A contemporary example of the manipulative processes which organisations engage with in order to exhibit their 'best face' can be found in the marketing of the higher education sector. The institutions rely on extremely sophisticated strategies in order to sell themselves. Consequently, prospectuses and other materials are high quality, glossy marketing tools that are used to promote the 'product' in this highly competitive expanded sector.

Using promotional materials for the purposes of image management, or 'glossification', has been discussed by a number of commentators (Gewirtz et al, 1995; Headington and Howson, 1995; Smedley, 1995). In their study of the changing role of school governors, Deem et al (1994) suggest that the introduction of a market in education has made schools 'examine their image'. Since the mid-1980s, policies have aimed to introduce differentiation into the education sector in order to promote competition. However, rather than trying to be 'different', schools are adopting strategies which are bringing them together and, as Hesketh and Knight (1998:21) argue, they are 'busily managing their images in the same ways'. As Maguire et al (1996:3) note for the FE sector, education can be interpreted as become merely 'one more commodity to be sold to the consumer'.

At the level of higher education, commodification becomes even more apparent in a situation where the standard of sophistication of the language of engagement increases. Class based value systems and access to codified specialist knowledge is magnified and exacerbated within a political framework that preferences a market base. As Ball et al (1996:110) note 'choice is very directly and powerfully related to social class differences'. Fiscal concerns drive recruitment policies and in consequence the ways in which universities feel the need for 'glossification' in order to enhance their market position. In a survey of 4,300 sixth form students, Block and Hesketh (1997) noted that the university prospectus failed to carry conviction in areas where it was clearly designed to persuade the user. These young people, like those in my study are in all respects 'Thatcher's children' (Pilcher and Wagg, 1996). Born between 1979 and 1980, until the spring of 1997, their entire lives were lived under successive Conservative governments and a philosophy of the free market and choice. Post-1997 New Labour has maintained a commitment to the policies of choice (Power and Whitty, 1999; McCaig, 2001) and these young people and their families have experienced at first hand, the vagaries of the market when it is applied to education. We now have a consumerist generation, the cultures of consumption ensure an awareness of branding and the ways in which choices can be shaped and influenced by marketing strategies. The expansion of the sector has ensured that universities and university education is no longer an elite provision and in consequence there is a need to culturize and commodify the sector. Differential branding and promotional advertising has become a standard market practice. Glossified imagery is a familiar concept and young people are well aware that universities use this as a marketing tool in the design of the prospectus. During school based focus group interviews they told me:

The ones [prospectuses] that I've looked at are a bit like travel brochures. You
know the sun is shining and the grass is green. But they want you to go there
and so they are not going to say anything else, anything bad.
(Sarah, pupil at Brangwyn Hall)

No, the glossy brochures did not impress me. I don't look at the pretty pictures
and think oh I want to go there.
(Richard, pupil at Regency House)

Commentators have noted the significance of social and cultural capital in
relation to markets and choice. (Gewirtz et al, 1995; Reay and Ball, 1997; Ball,
2003). Market awareness and a set of social networks that can enable access to
information was a key asset for the middle class families in this, as in other studies.
The value of engaging with university choices and the need to research their
options was very much a middle class concept. Although a large number of pupils
identified the importance of attending Open Days in the questionnaire, the realities
of choice were somewhat different as I learned in the qualitative interviews with
the pupils and their families.

I think it's important to go [to Open Days] to look at the people who are
running the course. One I went to, the admissions tutor for psychology gave
us a talk and they put us in a really small room and they were having to turn
people away because there wasn't enough room and it just struck me that it
wasn't well organized. I suppose much of it depends on how you interpret it,
but it struck me as poorly run and I won't be applying there.
(Joanne, Brangwyn Hall)

I'm doing things in reverse. I mean, I am going to the Open Days and looking
at the universities first really. I mean, well basically I know what I want to do
and so I didn't just take six universities, I took a selection of the *best* ones
with my subject choice and then went to see what they could offer me.
(Claudia, Redcoats School)

For both these young people, their middle class identities have allowed
them to engage with Open Days to their own advantages. However, the need to
remain within a bounded social structure, to make 'class-attributive judgements'
(Bourdieu, 1986:473) can serve to limit choice, as Trudy revealed:

Like when I went to the Open Day to look, a lot of the students were from
private schools and that really put me off. I mean wouldn't feel comfortable.
(Trudy, Cardinal Gwyn College)

In an attempt to draw some conclusions from the texts themselves I
undertook a content analysis (Scott, 1990; Carley, 1994, Slater, 1998), of
prospectuses from a range of 40 different universities. This analysis enabled me to
draw various conclusions from the texts themselves. These were considered in
conjunction with evidence of the ways in which young people actually consume
these texts generated by an analysis of data from focus group interviews with sixth

form pupils. Apart from looking attractive, much of the layout and content of each of the university prospectuses was constructed such that it successfully discriminated between those who possess the necessary cultural competencies to engage with and decode them and those who do not. An analysis of school brochures (Hesketh and Knight, 1998) found a remarkable degree of similarity and consistency in the presentational format and style and content of each. This was also the case for the university prospectuses. However where they did differ was in relation to the different stylistic devices which different institutions adopted to correlate with their market niche and institutional 'type'. The prospectus serves to promote a corporate image and corporate identity for the institution. It is an effective marker that clearly underlines an individual institutional positioning within a highly differentiated and hierarchical sector. The imagery adopted in the design of the front cover of the prospectus may be allied to and closely mirrors the university clusters that were identified and defined in the HEFCE (1996) report on higher education access and participation. This suggested that universities could be classified in four groups, namely the traditional 'elite' universities, (for example Oxbridge) the 'quasi-old' universities (Redbrick), the 'quasi-new' universities (post Robbins) and the 'real new' universities (post 1992). Where the university has status and a sense of history, as in the case of the 'traditional elite' institutions, the cover of the prospectus will focus mainly on the grand architecture of the university buildings, the Chapel, the Senate House, an ornamental arch or gateway. The 'quasi-old' universities, in the main, post Robbins campus institutions, are primarily located near historic cities such as York and Canterbury. These institutions opt for green-field campus scenes, or views of the castles and cathedrals that form the more historic identity of the surrounding areas. The 'quasi-new' universities, often located in industrial areas, seem keen to promote their student centred approach. In consequence the cover of these prospectuses often comprises a student group, carefully balanced such that they are representative of gender, ethnicity and age, to underscore their access and equality policies. The real new' institutions rely on a corporate image, often achieved through the representation of a corporate logo or with an abstract geometric design. A typology of the imagery on the cover of the different university prospectuses can be summarized with reference to Table 2.1.

Table 2.1 University Imagery and the Prospectus

'Traditional Elite' ARCHITECTURE	'Quasi-Old' AERIAL VIEWS	'Quasi-New' PEOPLE	'Real New' ABSTRACTS
Senate House University	Campus Nature Area	Student Groups Mountains	Abstract Natural History
Library Castle	Cathedral Historic Building	Skyline Shots Coastline	Geometric

Despite the obvious attempts to make these prospectuses easily accessible and 'user friendly', a number of the pupils interviewed during this research said that they found them difficult to navigate and understand. The lingua franca of academia is highly specialized and needs to be carefully deconstructed if it is to be understood. At present this inaccessibility has implications in terms of class based competencies and access to information. This theme is continued in later chapters (see Chapter 6 and Chapter 7). As potential consumers, a number of the young people in this study recognized that they needed to look behind the gloss and determine exactly what it is that each institution has to offer. However in this as in many other aspects of the choice process, many of those from working class backgrounds have not acquired the necessary competencies to engage with the decoding process. This is particularly the case for those young people whose families have little or no prior experience of higher education. Power and privilege is still embedded within a class structure. Writing three decades ago Giddens commented that 'ownership of wealth and property continues to play a fundamental part in facilitating access to the sort of educational process which influences entry to elite positions' (Giddens, 1973:264). The university system continues to ensure the reproduction of class privileges, universities control their recruitment and their teaching through 'misunderstanding and the fiction that there is no misunderstanding' Bourdieu et al. (1994:41). In an effort to unravel some of these 'misunderstandings' and dig beneath the political rhetoric of widening participation and equality of access, I conducted a questionnaire survey of 711 lower sixth pupils. This enabled me to gain some awareness of the realities of choice for the young people in this study. Table 2.2 illustrates the extent to which choices were shaped in response to the different marketing strategies and levels of information provided across the sector.

Table 2.2 University Marketing Strategies Implications for Choice

Marketing Strategy	Very Important %	Important %	Not Important %
Guaranteed Accommodation	64.0	25.8	3.1
Open Day Visits	63.0	29.2	1.0
Departmental Visit	58.0	33.4	1.6
Prospectus	56.6	35.1	1.6
Cash Incentives	37.1	38.8	16.8
Personal Recommendation	27.6	59.5	5.8
University Faculty Talk at School	17.2	54.7	20.7
Promotional Videos	8.3	57.1	27.6

As Table 2.2 indicates, those surveyed felt that attending open days was equally as important as having an offer of guaranteed accommodation for the first year of study. Visits to specific departments and using prospectuses were also considered as effective ways of choosing a university. With the exception of the guarantee of accommodation the other three responses require pupils to be somewhat proactive in their approach to the market. In response to the question on the significance of particular attributes of an institution, as might be anticipated, the suitability of the course and the entry grade requirements were the two most important factors for choice, with recreational and library facilities scoring almost identically followed by the type of accommodation available. As a marketing strategy then, prospective students are more concerned to be offered a guarantee of accommodation, than they are with the quality of the leisure and study facilities. The reputation of the university featured as having more importance than either the course structure or the methods of assessment. The perceptions of important factors related to choice are shown in Table 2.3.

Table 2.3 University Facilities and Choice

SPECIFIC FACTOR	Very Important %	Important %	Not Important %
The Course	85.7	6.6	1.0
Entrance Grades	73.8	17.5	2.0
Recreational Facilities	59.7	30.2	3.1
Library Facilities	59.5	30.1	3.5
Accommodation	52.4	35.0	5.8
The Reputation	47.9	41.8	3.7
The Course Structure	44.0	41.2	7.3
Methods of Assessment	42.9	43.6	6.1
Recommendation	32.8	53.5	6.9
Sports Facilities	31.3	38.4	23.3
League Positions	23.6	59.7	9.9
Pastoral Support	20.0	56.0	16.2

The responses to the questionnaire, administered in the lower sixth, suggested that pupils considered that attending university Open Days is highly significant as a factor of influence in the choice process. In total, 63 per cent of the pupils in the first questionnaire survey said they felt such visits were 'very important'. However qualitative data collected from pupils and their families, a year later revealed a significant number of young people who had not attended any Open Days, prior to applying. If Open Day visits were organized by the Schools or

Colleges, then pupils generally took advantage of the opportunity to join the trip. However for some working class pupils, the travel costs were prohibitive:

> I think I will limit the visits to ones I am really serious about applying to, because it's expensive to travel all around.
> (Megan, Ysgol Bryn Alun)

> The thing is that places like Edinburgh, Durham, York where you might fancy going, well they are miles away and you can't afford to go up there to look.
> (Darren, Regent High)

Many working class families were unfamiliar with the university applications process and so failed to appreciate the significance of these early Open Day visits, as I found in the family interviews:

> I know that I have missed everything now, most places seemed to have had Open Days months ago. Nobody seems to be open now, so I can't do much can I?
> (David Jones, Ysgol Bryn Alun)

> Well we didn't know nothing [sic] about these Open Day trips did we? How are you supposed to? How do you find out about them?
> (Mr Jones, Father)

These attitudes towards attending Open Days are in strong contrast with those of middle class pupils and their families. The schools with middle class pupils organized at least one Open Day visit annually. This was held on a school day and pupils taken by coach. Additionally visits to other universities were made, organized by individual families or groups of friends.

> Well during the summer several of my friends were going to look at different universities and so I just cadged a lift with them and we went all over. I have been up to Durham, and to Nottingham, Sheffield, Warwick, Exeter, its been great. You need to see them to get some idea of where you don't want to go as much as where you do.
> (Nigel, Regent High School)

Interviews with middle class families also provided evidence of this proactive approach to choosing a university. It illustrates the extent to which middle class families are prepared to go to considerable lengths to enable choices to be made in the market place. Rather as Ball (2003:53) has suggested 'families must work on, in and with public and private institutions to achieve their particular ends and interests'. He stresses the need to take account of the ways in which families utilise their social and cultural capital in order to maximize their opportunities and maintain their educational advantages. I heard clear examples of the ways in which the middle class families used their advantages and 'worked at' the choice process. In one family interview I was told:

Well I actually sat down with my friends and we decided on the ones that we wanted to go to before hand. Well for example, we went to Warwick, some friends and me, we all went up as a carload, didn't we mum? We spent the whole day just walking around and going from lecture to lecture didn't we?

Well I was really just the taxi driver. But I went nosing around on my own in order to see what was what everywhere.

Yes and then we compared notes afterwards didn't we?
(Mrs Hubert-Jenkins and Amy, pupil at Brangwyn Hall)

An education market presupposes that the consumer possess the requisite cultural codes and competencies to enable them to engage fully with the choice process. However research into marketing both health and education has found considerable differences in the levels of information and awareness among different socio economic groups (Sidgewick et al, 1994). These data begin to indicate then some of the different ways in which social class determines how families and young people approach the business of accessing universities. I return to this issue in the following chapters drawing increasingly on the qualitative data from the study to illuminate the ways in which an education market demands sophisticated and complex levels of engagement. I shall identify the ways in which these competencies are embedded within class structures and examine the ways in which differential levels of access to information, guidance and support have wider implications in terms of patterns of participation in both higher education and the graduate labour market.

Chapter 3

Patterns of Participation

As early as 1954, concerns were expressed about the relationship between social class and participation in post compulsory education. In consequence, the Gurney-Dixon committee was set up to consider the school leaving rates and attainment levels among grammar school pupils in England and Wales. It concluded that pupil performance was related to the occupational status of the father. In addition, it found that the higher this status, not only was the pupil's performance better, but there was a greater tendency for the pupil to engage with post compulsory education. Participation rates have risen steadily over time and research has shown that the expanded sector has increasingly included higher proportions of pupils from working class backgrounds. This is the section of the population which the Gurney-Dixon committee had noted traditionally left school as soon as was legally possible (Raffe and Willms, 1989; Furlong, 1992). Gaining educational qualifications has traditionally been held to be the mechanism by which the middle classes have been able both to legitimise and strengthen their advantaged position within the labour market (Bowles and Gintis, 1976). As the demand for an educated workforce has increased, it may well have been anticipated that this might have correlated with a move towards a more meritocratic society.

However, somewhat contrary to such expectations, the extension of both the school career and the increased certification that accompanies it, has failed to produce such a meritocracy. Rather, we have seen a shift towards credential inflation (Fevre et al, 1997; Brown and Scase, 1994). The expansion of higher education has forced employers to raise their entry requirements, which in turn, requires students to gain even more advanced qualifications (Brown and Scase, 1994; Ainley, 1994). School leavers in the 1970s and early 1980s could be confident of gaining employment that would offer them both 'on the job' experience and qualifications. Now however credentialism privileges academic qualifications (Dore, 1976). As the previous chapter has illustrated, policy changes in the United Kingdom have led to a considerable increase in participation in higher education over time and there has been a 'sea change since the end of the 1960s when the majority left school as soon as they were legally able to do so' (Roberts, 1997:56). Policy changes regarding access to and participation in higher education were paralleled with policy changes in relation to welfare benefits and the youth labour market. These changes merit discussion since they relate directly to the changes in the post-compulsory education trajectories of young people over the past half-century and these are discussed in relation to their impact on post-18 participation rates. A major part of the chapter is also devoted to a discussion on the ways in which Career Guidance and Counselling provisions have been developed in schools and sixth form colleges over recent years. Focusing on the philosophical rationale that has underpinned such provision lends support to the argument that there has been a radical shift in both the function and nature of Career Guidance activities since the 1988 Education Reform Act. In order to accommodate the changed shape of the youth labour market and the shifting patterns of post compulsory education, it is increasingly unlikely that young people will receive employment advice. Rather the focus is much more likely to be aimed at university access.

The Youth Labour Market in the UK

The shift in the patterns of participation in post compulsory education in Britain over the past decade can be conceptualized in relation to structural changes that have occurred in the youth labour market and in welfare provision for 16 to 18 year olds. In his study of 'ordinary kids' Brown (1987) found that increasingly staying on in school was regarded as a natural progression. One consequence of such increased participation in post compulsory education has been a steady shift in credential inflation (Roberts, 1993). Increased acknowledgement of the need for qualifications among 16 year olds, coupled with demographic changes have led to a move away from an era of 'youth labour into that of middle aged labour' (Killeen, 1996:9). A number of policy initiatives that have been introduced since the mid seventies such as the Youth Training Schemes (YTS) and Vocational Educational Training (VET) were aimed at addressing issues of youth employment and training (Roberts, 1995; Lowe, 1993). However commentators have suggested that these policies were largely ineffectual in achieving their aims and that they merely served to lead the working class youth towards a 'mirage' of wider opportunities (Roberts, 1993; Hodkinson and Mattinson, 1994; Holland, 1990). As the higher education sector has moved towards a mass model there have been changes in school leaving patterns which have similarly shifted to accommodate a greater proportion of students opting for post-compulsory education. In the 1970s, 27 per cent of 16 to 18 year olds were in full time education and the rest were in the labour market (65 per cent employed and eight per cent unemployed). By 1990, the numbers of young people in the age cohort who were in full time education had risen to 36 per cent, 15 per cent were on youth training schemes and less that half (49 per cent) were in the labour force. In early 1993, of those who had reached the school leaving age, only about eight per cent of 16 year olds and 33 per cent of 17 year olds were in full time employment (Killeen, 1996). This increased rise in the number of young people in post compulsory education was in line with policies that aimed to have more than one third of the age cohort in higher education by the end of the century. However policy changes had done little or nothing to impact on social mobility and the different class based career trajectories (Roberts, 1993).

Throughout the 1980s there were significant changes in both the nature and patterns of employment. An increased demand for a flexible, highly skilled workforce occurred in tandem with a cut back in jobs for casual, unskilled labour (Ashton et al, 1990). In the 1990s, unqualified school leavers found that they faced exclusion from the workplace. Patterns of participation in post-compulsory education in the United Kingdom and Europe suggest that by the mid 1990s the majority of young people had concluded that this was the only successful route into employment. However, as Hammer and Furlong (1996) have indicated there is a lack of evidence to support any suggestion of an association between sixth form education and successful integration into the labour market. Research showed that for young people who were not intending to go on to higher education, remaining in school after the fifth form could actually 'reduce, rather than enhance their chance of being in a job in two or three years time' (Halpin, 1992:51).

Although there has been an increase in the numbers of pupils remaining in post compulsory education in the levels of participation in higher education is still inequitable between social groups (Egerton and Halsey, 1993; Robertson and Hillman, 1997). The incremental growth in student numbers remained greatest for those in the middle classes. In terms of expectations, as the empirical data in Chapter 6 will show, while higher education is now considered to be the normal rite of passage for middle class young people, it remains a 'privilege' for many in the lower social groupings. Also as a report by the advisory group on access and participation (HECFE 1996) found, in spite of the removal of the binary divide, an internal stratification within the system has remained. This differentiation within the sector has very real implications for prospective students The newer universities, those created post 1992, have a higher proportion of mature students and working class non 'traditional' entrants. Although statistics indicate that there is now an almost equal gender divide in relation to participation rates (HESA, 1997; 2000), those figures should not be taken at face value. Gender differences remain in relation to subject choices, for example science and engineering are male dominated, while others such as pharmacy and education are over represented by women. The differences in patterns of participation extend to include degree classifications, and graduate employment prospects (Thomas, 1991; Kelly and Slaughter, 1991; Crompton and Sanderson, 1990; Brown and Scase, 1994; Evetts, 1995). Most significantly though social class continues to impact on the participation rates and UCAS statistics (Table 3.1) reveal the socio-economic spread of university students enrolled in higher education at different ages.

Table 3.1 Higher Education Participation Rates by Social Class and Age

Social Class	Professional	Intermediate	Skilled non manual	Skilled manual	Semi skilled	Unskilled
<18	3.7	2.9	2.3	2.7	2.4	1.9
18	60.1	54.1	43.9	49.8	42.2	43.0
19	24.5	23.8	20.9	24.9	21.9	26.0
20	6.6	7.2	7.2	8.7	8.4	11.3
21	1.0	2.5	4.7	3.1	4.6	4.6
22	0.5	1.0	3.4	1.4	3.1	1.8
23	0.3	0.7	2.3	0.9	2.0	1.7
24	0.2	0.6	1.7	0.7	1.7	1.3
25-29	0.7	2.4	5.5	2.9	5.4	3.5
30-39	0.9	3.2	5.9	3.6	6.2	3.6
40+	0.6	1.7	2.1	1.3	2.2	1.4
Total	100	100	100	100	100	100
N (000s)	42.1	122.3	40.3	45.1	30.5	5.5

A number of explanations have been put forward in an attempt to explain this under representation of students from working class backgrounds in the higher education sector. One theory is that of identity and class solidarity. Over time a number of sociologists have theorized about the working classes leaving school at the earliest opportunity in terms of resistance to the middle class educational culture (Jackson and Marsden, 1962; Hargreaves, 1967; Lacey, 1970; Sharp, 1976; Willis, 1977; Hall and Jefferson, 1976; McRobbie, 1978; Ball, 1981; Anyon, 1983; Coffield et al, 1986; Brown, 1987). Similarly, this resistance treatise has been applied to discussions of 'race', since participation in post-compulsory education has also been significantly lower among different ethnic minority groups (Fuller, 1984; Youth Cohort Study, 1989; Mac an Ghaill, 1988; Gilborn, 1990; Eggleston, 1993). Identities are rooted in social and cultural norms and value systems, and crucially, as Ball et al (2000:24) have noted 'post-16 "choices" are bound up with the expressions and suppressions of identities'.

Structural changes have served to shape the perceptions of some working class young people, who now, in common with other groups, recognize the need to remain 'in' the education system for longer periods of time. Nevertheless, as Bates (1993:14) has noted, there has been no evidence to support any 'anticipated dislocation in processes of class and gender reproduction which a post-Fordist society would allow'. There were claims from some commentators in the eighties which suggested that Britain had become a 'classless' society, however these are now met by counterclaims of its having an even more highly stratified society. The emergence of a 'thriving underclass' (Field, 1989; Adonis and Pollard, 1997) can now be interpreted as policy driven social exclusion. Staying on in education after the age of 16 can require young people and their families to make decisions and choice from a complex menu of educational options and pathways. In England and Wales, post compulsory education may be provided through a number of different routes. Many schools have a sixth form that caters for pupils in the 16 to 18 age bracket and offers A level and possibly GNVQ subject options. There are tertiary colleges and FE colleges which young people may choose to attend. In their study of the post 16-education market and choice, in one area of London Macrae et al (1996) found that a range of educational options was available to parents and young people. In consequence it was possible to identify families who engaged fully with the further education market and could be classified as 'active choosers'. By way of contrast, in south east Wales, where this study was conducted, there is little evidence of any real engagement with a post-16 market place. Here, movement between schools and sixth form or tertiary colleges is very limited. For the majority of pupils in this locale, progression on and in to the sixth form of their school is 'what happens' and this theme will be discussed with reference to the empirical data in later chapters. One attempt to explain the differential levels of participation in higher education focuses on the differential access to information experienced across social class. As Thomas (2001:135) has noted 'certain groups in society lack information about the opportunities that are available'. Crucially too, different social classes possess different competencies which can inhibit the degree to which they can engage with and decode any information that they do access. The empirical data discussed in later chapters (see Chapters 6 and 7) indicate how the middle class families that have experience of and are familiar with the higher education system are well placed to negotiate the application process. In contrast, working class families, for whom there is first generation engagement with the sector, lack the skills and competencies and crucially the support networks to enable them to make considered choices.

The pastoral curriculum has been an integral, if informal, aspect in the UK education system throughout this century but Daws (1972) notes that 'careers' education was not taught in schools until the 1920s. Then until the late 1960s, the services that were offered were seen simply as a means of providing supplementary advice. It was not until the early 1970s that any attempt was made to deal specifically with choices and lifestyle options (Bates and Riseborough, 1993). While careers education remained an optional part of the formal teaching programme in schools, the model which had emerged was focused on career decisions and self awareness, but no consensus was reached as to what careers education was or what it was for (Harris, 1997). The 1988 Education Reform Act saw career guidance in schools in England and Wales confirmed as a statutory part of the curriculum, however structural changes in the labour market and policy changes in relation to education and welfare saw a difference in the approach to career guidance. In the 1990s its role was substantially curtailed, and the focus shifted from discussions around job opportunities and career pathways, to the provision of information about accessing post compulsory education. This led commentators to suggest that the competency of guidance teachers should no longer be assessed in relation to the number of 16 year olds with jobs but, rather, should focus on the number still in school (Law, 1996). The Careers Service itself experienced considerable difficulties as a consequence of 'New Right' policy. A defining characteristic of Thatcherism and Majorism has been the weakening of professionalism and the Thatcher influence could be identified within career guidance as a means of 'making markets work', indeed Watts (1991) identified the introduction of training credits as one such mechanism. As a consequence of such policy initiatives, Lawrence (1992) suggested that there was a danger that Careers Officers might find that they were 'legislated out of existence' and in 1992-1993, the Career Service, which had previously been funded by the local authorities, became privatised. As part of their internal budgetary control mechanisms, schools are now required to 'buy in' guidance or rely on what they can provide 'in house' (Morris et al, 1995; Watson et al, 1995). The subject specific hierarchy that the introduction of a National Curriculum created has resulted in a loss of status for Personal and Social education teaching (traditionally where career guidance was taught) and in consequence, there are few, formally qualified careers advisors on the teaching staff of most state schools (Harris, 1992). Also in a survey of career education in British schools, Cleaton (1993:74) found that, in the main, careers education teachers had 'no training, not enough time and not enough money'.

Although schools are required to have a written policy for career guidance, in practical terms, in many instances, the quality of the provision was found to be poor, with less than one fifth of schools having a 'specialist' teacher. In his study Cleaton (1993) concluded that while more than 90 per cent of schools had a nominated career co-ordinator and more than half had between two and ten teachers timetabled for career work, the number of teachers formally involved with careers work had fallen dramatically since the 1980s. My study in the schools and colleges in south east Wales Sixth Form confirms other commentators accounts of the ways in which the emphasis on career guidance had become marginalized (Law, 1996; Bates and Riseborough, 1993). The introduction of market concepts into education has allowed for interest groups, such as the Confederation for British Industry, to reinforce their support for further and higher education. In consequence, Law (1996:95) suggests that the model of a 'career as episodes linked by transitions' is increasingly being applied to career guidance within the 16 to 19 year old age group. Young people in post compulsory education in schools and further education colleges have reported high levels of dissatisfaction with the careers education they receive. The focus for guidance is concerned in the main with the mechanics of the higher education application process (Westegaard and Barnes, 1994). A survey of careers education in 105 secondary schools in Wales (OHMCI, 1997) found that only two schools had any formal timetable provision for Career Education and Guidance (CEG). In the rest, provision was ad hoc depending on the commitment of individual tutors and was, in consequence both difficult to monitor and evaluate. The survey found that the quality of provision overall varied considerably both within and between schools and noted (p.8) that 'teaching in most schools was almost totally confined to preparing pupils for higher education'. Of the schools surveyed only two had a head of department with responsibility for careers. In the remaining schools this was part of the responsibility of the head of sixth form and the survey concluded 'many lack the expertise to deliver a broad based careers education and guidance programme (CEG) and consequently the teaching rarely refers to the world of work' (OHMCI, 1997:5). The survey notes that there is very strong competition among schools to ensure that they have a viable number of pupils in their sixth forms. In consequence this 'reduces the effectiveness and the impartiality of advice offered to many year 11 pupils as to the most appropriate post-16 route' (1997:10).

Funding methodologies for schools can skew information to families and the majority of pupils will receive information and advice which leads them to believe that their career interests will best served by returning to the sixth form to continue their studies. The consequences of such advice without a comprehensive infrastructure of support and guidance can have serious consequences in terms of career pathways and choices. This dissatisfaction with the teaching and provision of guidance materials is exemplified in my research and will be discussed in the later empirical chapters (see Chapter 5). Here the suggestion will be that the variation in quality of provision is often determined by the perceptions that the individual schools and sixth form colleges hold about themselves in relation to a market position and the perceived 'needs' of their 'client group'. The hypothesis will argue that there is a definite advantage to be gained by pupils who are rigorously tutored through the application process. It demonstrates how career guidance has been absorbed into the general pastoral curriculum and how the responsibilities for delivering higher education guidance is increasingly devolved to the form tutors in the state sector. In contrast, it identifies the infrastructures that are in place within the private sector to allow the schools to draw on a range of expertise to facilitate university applications for their pupils.

A market-based philosophy for education policy is founded on the premise that consumers will make rational choices, in order to maximize their long-term economic benefits. However research has shown that decision-making is not a clear-cut process. For the middle classes there is an 'expectation', a taken for granted route into higher education for 'people like us' (Allatt, 1996, Roker, 1993). While for many young people from a working class background, the changes in the youth labour market and welfare benefit systems have led to their 'drifting' into university (Hodkinson et al, 1996). Early work relating to the theories of occupational choice suggested that career guidance linked personal attributes to vocational choices (Ginzberg et al, 1951; Super, 1957). However Roberts (1977) has argued that such an approach to career guidance was unrealistic, suggesting rather that school-leavers had adopted a more pragmatic approach to higher education and employment based on the opportunity structure of the workplace. Hodkinson et al (1996) have taken the model of pragmatically rational decision making to contextualize the career decisions of young people. They argue that social groups share the same self-generalising grammar and thus the same, sheer 'routine knowledge' of where they are going and how they will get there. This in effect limits choices for some young people, usually those from the working class backgrounds. There is clearly the potential for a collision to occur between the quantity of information available and the competencies needed to interpret and act upon it. Since information is never neutral, young people can receive information about higher education, but this is interpreted and acted upon within their own cultural spheres and in light of their own and range of norms, values and experiences.

Although there is a plethora of information produced by a number of different agencies and by the universities themselves, much of it is complex and difficult to navigate, particularly for those in working class groups where application to university will be a first time experience. Schools and sixth form colleges also make use of a number of computer assisted guidance programmes to assist their pupils to make choices about which universities to make application to and which courses they might consider choosing. The more commonly used are the Educational Counselling and Credit Transfer System (ECCTIS), and the CENTIGRADE package. These databases contain details on courses, institutions and potential career pathways and occupational choices. These programmes can be highly effective in assisting pupils in their decision making. However their level of effectiveness is dependent on the expertise of teaching staff, who need to use them actively in order to inform discussions and so enhance the guidance process. Also as Crowley (1992) has stressed, if they are to be of any practical help to young people these packages need to be easy to access. Crucially, the research has stressed that computer software should not be seen as a substitute for formal guidance but rather as a means of enhancing this area of the curriculum (Watts, 1988; Crowley, 1992).

For prospective students, reaching a decision as to courses of study and choice of institution is only the beginning of a long and highly formalized application process. Every applicant is required to apply through the Universities and Colleges Admissions Service (UCAS) which serves as a central handling unit. A number of commentators have noted that many young people, especially those from working class backgrounds, feel that they lack information about higher education (Connor and Dewson, 2001, Howieson and Semple, 1996). The empirical data from focus groups and interviews with young people and their families that underpins this analysis supports this line of argument. It suggests that the structures and processes for applying to university are prohibitive to working class engagement. Working class families lack the cultural capital to engage with the choice process, they have fewer family members or friends who have been in higher education and so are at a loss to understand and negotiate the university applications system, its codes and practices. This lack of access to key informants in their social settings is further compounded by the lack of appropriate information that schools and sixth form colleges provide for pupils from working class backgrounds, as a later chapter will illustrate. The role of the Universities Central Admissions System (UCAS) and the application procedure by which access to higher education in the United Kingdom is mediated is quite unique. The framework within which UCAS operates is considered below and it can be argued that this process itself is in part instrumental in restricting access to university. The UCAS system can be perceived as complex. It requires applicants to comply with specific timeframes and can ensure a successful engagement with the choice process at university level.

The UCAS Model: Monitoring and Moderating Access

Currently, there are more than 277 universities and higher education institutes that admit students through the UCAS system. They offer in excess of 33,000 courses. While in theory students can 'choose' to apply for any course at any institution, in practice it is the universities themselves who do the choosing. They can set entry criteria, and then select their student intake from the applications made via UCAS. Recruitment is done in response to the external pressures of a quota system of per capita funding, which is imposed on the institutions by the Funding Councils, and which carry with them heavy financial sanctions, if not strictly adhered to. UCAS acts as an intermediary on behalf of the universities and prospective students and provides a structural framework for the application process, handling all applications for first degrees.

While it can in no way affect or influence the offers made to students by the various institutions, it can and does set strict criteria for processing applications. Competencies in decoding the forms and engaging with the application process as a whole has very significant consequences in terms of outcomes for young people. For middle class young people 'choice is presented as natural, orderly, clearcut almost beyond question, very unlike the chancy, uncertain process many working class students are caught up in' (Maguire et al, 2000:5). The UCAS process presents yet another 'risk' for young people caught up in the choice process. It enforces a strict temporal order to the procedure. Complex form filling and submission processes ensure that choices are made and applications are received by the institutions early enough to allow them to reach their decisions, advise applicants, through UCAS, and receive responses to any offers which they make, prior to the start of the university academic year in late September. However as Adam (1995:42) has argued, it is vital to acknowledge and get to know the 'unreflected back cloth of "own" time on which "other" time is constructed'. In terms of decisions and choices about whether or not to apply to university the timing is crucial and is externally imposed. Part of the complexity of the choice process is bounded within this artificially constructed applications timeframe and the familiarity, or lack of familiarity, with the complexities of the application process and access to information about it.

Within each university there are departmental admissions tutors and it is their job to 'play the numbers game'. They need to ensure that they accept exactly the right number of candidates with appropriate qualifications for any particular course, to correspond with their funding quota. The UCAS application form requires candidates to supply demographic information and to nominate up to six institutions and courses, or to nominate several different courses at the same institution, to complete the criterion of six choices. The applicants may indicate no order of preference on the form and the form, together with a confidential reference, usually supplied by the school or college, is sent to UCAS. Applicants may elect to apply for entry in the academic year immediately following their entry examinations, or they may apply for deferred entry, opting to take a year out for further study, to travel, or to work in order to save money in preparation for their time at university. Each of the institutions, or departments named on the form are sent a copy of the application for their consideration and the candidates are considered by each institution and offers are made. The location of UCAS within the university applications framework is best conceptualized by reference to Figure 3.1.

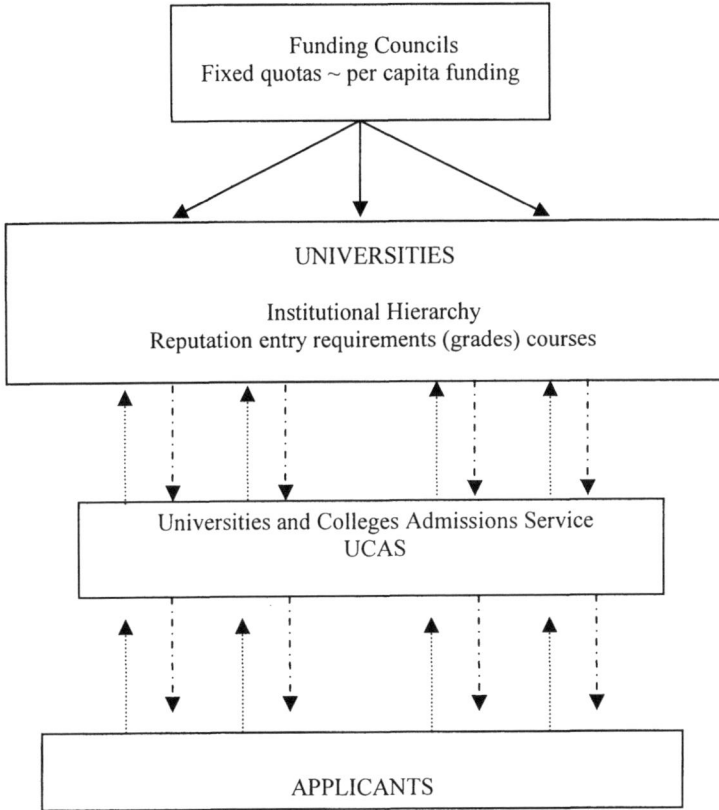

Figure 3.1 UCAS and the Application Framework

In England and Wales, the A-level examination is the gold standard for university applicants (Ainley, 1994). This remains the case in spite of policy initiatives that aimed at a parity of esteem between this traditional educational route and the more vocational courses that have been introduced into schools (Hesketh, 1997; Hodkinson and Mattinson, 1994). National Vocational Qualifications (NVQs) were introduced in 1985, primarily as work based qualifications. In 1992 General National Vocational Qualifications (GNVQs) were introduced as part of a three track qualification framework alongside A-levels and NVQs. However they have not been universally accepted and as Davies et al, (1997) have noted there is still a perceived difference in status between academic and the vocational awards. This has an implication in terms of institutional choice, since many of the more elite, pre 1992 universities, will not accept applications from students with these vocational qualifications. In 1999 UCAS data show that the profile for applicants could be differentiated not only by class but by qualifications, with a majority of applications in the traditional age group coming from young people with A-level qualifications from social classes 1, 11 and 111a. The academic curriculum in schools has resisted the temptation to reform and A-levels continue to dominate and drive the post-16 system.

Scotland has a separate system of education and, in recent times, the country has had higher rates of entry into higher education that other parts of the British Isles (McPherson, 1973). Pupils are entered for Scottish Higher Examinations but may apply through UCAS for places in institutions in other parts of the United Kingdom. However, as Paterson (1997:36) notes, 'the tendency for students to leave Scotland on entering higher education is weak'. Since the majority of candidates, in the traditional age cohort, apply for university places prior to sitting their examinations, offers are usually made on a conditional basis. This is dependent upon the outcome of the national examinations held in the summer term of the upper sixth (or its equivalent). This necessitates admissions tutors making decisions on offering a place to candidates based on the referees' ability to forecast the results. But as Murphy (1981) argues the predictions by referees are not absolute and in many cases the variance between is quite wide. Nevertheless this application process allows examination marks to take the role of 'price' in clearing the market (Molinero, 1990). UCAS collates all the offers and rejections which it receives for each applicant from the institutions. These decisions are forwarded to the candidates who are then required to make a first choice and an optional insurance offer. Following publication of examination results in mid August, the final decisions for each applicant are made by the institutions concerned. If the applicants have met or bettered their offer grades, then a place must be made available. The institution can also exercise discretion if the applicant fails to meet the grade requirements and still allow them access. Firm offers are binding contracts on both sides. Those students who meet the entry requirements of their first choice institution, must accept a place there, or, must ask to be released by the university. If the institution in question is not willing to agree to a release from contract, the candidate is required to withdraw from the entire process, until the following year. Candidates who fail to meet the conditions of the first choice offer are guaranteed a place on the course that they accepted as second (insurance) choice, providing that the entry conditions of that offer are met. This means that it will be in the candidates' interest to accept an insurance offer that is lower than that of their first choice offer. Those applicants who are unsuccessful in securing a place by this stage go into a 'clearing' process. Here applicants are notified about the institutional vacancies that exist for the courses that they wish to study. They are then free to negotiate directly with admissions tutors in order to try to secure a place.

The potential for uninformed groups or individuals to make ill-advised choices at these various stages of the applications process are clearly vast. For young people from middle class families, their social and cultural capital can ensure that they possess a high level of competency to enable them to engage with their university choices and successfully negotiate the complexities of the application process into higher education. The UCAS forms can prove a useful data source of marketing information for universities. The individual institutions can determine how prospective students' view the courses offered. They can identify where the main competition is for each course together with the admissions policies of each of these institutions. This allows universities and individual departments to tailor their admissions policies and marketing strategies, to take account of the competitors (Molinero, 1990). The shift from grants to fees and loans which was implemented in 1998 has seen the admissions system fully subjected to market forces and in consequence, universities are now making even greater use of the UCAS databases. Since the system is geared to process 'traditional' 18 year old applicants, the temporal framework imposed by UCAS takes effect in the second year sixth, year 13, or its equivalent in colleges of further education. For those prospective students who intend to enter university in the academic year immediately following their examinations, the application process through UCAS can be represented by Table 3.2. The deadlines that the system imposes in relation to receiving applications must be strictly adhered to. These contingencies make it imperative that parents, pupils and schools are fully alerted to the mechanical complexities of the application process.

Table 3.2 UCAS Timeframes and Choice

TIME PERIOD September - September	ACTIVITY Regulated by UCAS
September - December	Application forms submitted to UCAS
Mid October	Deadline for Oxbridge applications
Mid May	Candidates notified of all offers / rejections
Mid August	Examination Results announced
Late August	Clearing Process Begins
Late September	University Academic Year Begins

There are a number of difficulties associated with this application format. As Higgins (1994) has indicated, not only are prospective students asked to make important decisions about universities more than a year and a half prior to entry, but these decisions are required at a time when they are at the most developmental stage of their lives. Furthermore, as Keen and Higgins (1990) found, 31 per cent of students in the second year of their A-level course of study felt they had insufficient information about higher education, to allow them to make wise choices of courses. As Ball (2003:101) has noted in relation to school choice, there can be a 'slippage between information and promotion in the education market'. This blurring of the boundaries between the market and 'civic institutions' can serve to add a layer of complexity to the choice process that can be confusing for middle classes and may prove totally impenetrable for working class groups. Marketing strategies allow organisations to introduce an element of 'spin' to their presentation of self. For examples, universities may adopt a number of strategies in order to market an unpopular course. The admissions tutor may make low offers to ensure that a number of applicants choose the course as an insurance place. This will mean that some candidates who miss a first choice offer, will be faced with the dilemma of accepting this unpopular insurance offer, or postponing university for a year. If on the other hand there is a high demand for a course, then the dilemma facing the particular department is whether to ask for high grades and perhaps deter some good candidates from applying or alternately, to make lower offers to some and reject the rest. These are calculated, rational choices that are made by the universities at the institutional level. However, at the micro level, young people and their families are required to take responsibility for making university choices often with little or no information or guidance.

The ways in which information may be transmitted via oral sub cultures is well documented. There has been considerable research into the ways in which myths and legends are used and passed down through groups (Brunvand, 1984; Cortazzi, 1992). These messages often serve as warnings, advising the uninitiated as to the best ways to proceed. They can inform and develop understandings of the ways in which children (and young adults retrospectively) make sense of major events and key points in their lives. Schools are a vibrant source of many such regulatory myths. Much of the focus of research into these narratives has been located in the status passage associated with the transfer from primary to secondary school (Bryan, 1980; Measor and Woods, 1984; Delamont and Galton, 1986; Delamont, 1989a; Pugsley et al, 1996). In common with many other aspects relating to the sociology of higher education little attention has focused on the myths and legends associated with transfer from secondary to university level. Higgins (1994) talks of the 'tactics' employed by students when deciding on application choices. However, in so doing, he makes only passing reference to the 'beliefs' that are held by some prospective students, which suggest to them, for instance, that some universities 'discriminate' either in favour of or against students who have also made application to Oxbridge. Also as researchers have shown, in relation to making choices about schools, families' rely on information and advice that they receive from a range of sources (Ball and Vincent, 1998). These sources provide 'hot' and 'cold' information, the 'hot' knowledge is acquired through the grapevine of social contacts and networks while 'cold' knowledge is that acquired via more formal 'official' routes. Ball and Vincent (1998) suggest that it is the 'hot' knowledge gained from accessing social networks that is more highly valued, than other forms of information. There are clearly intra group differences that will advantage or not this privileging of shared knowledge exchanges about choice.

Clouding or Clarifying

Whilst the application and choice process for university may appear ordered and rational at first glance, in practice the process is largely serendipitous, and serves to reinforce class based competencies and differences. In the main, universities make their offers to applicants on the basis of the predicted outcomes of examinations. But teachers make these predictions and the references are supplied by the schools, to institutions for whom requirement is quota driven. In consequence it can be suggested that there is a high degree of subjectivity in both the construction and the reading of these application forms. Also as Higgins (1994:17) suggests there is an even greater element of chance in the process since 'in reality, many Tutors anxious to fill their student quota, will choose to accept the first applications that are received'. This predictive selection process is followed throughout the sector, despite research evidence which has shown that A-level examination performance is a poor predictor of the level of performance at the degree stage (Bourner and Mahmoud, 1987).

There is a dichotomous relationship between the marginalisation of the guidance curriculum in school and the expansion of the post compulsory education sector. The higher education market needs to be considered in relation to the increasingly onerous financial implications that are likely to felt by the individual students and the changing nature of the graduate labour market. The combination of these factors makes the choosing process crucial. The 1995 UCAS statistics revealed that almost 33,000 of the 205,000 A-level and GNVQ applicants who had achieved the minimum qualifications to enrol on a higher education course had not taken up a place by the following autumn. In order to determine the reasons behind this failure to take up places, UCAS conducted a survey of all applicants for 1995 entry who were under 21 years of age, with at least two A-level, or equivalent passes. Respondents were asked to rate the career advice they had been given at various stages of the UCAS application cycle both from their school or sixth form college and the local careers office. This was done using a five point rating scale in which a four rated as 'excellent' and a zero indicated 'no advice' had been given. The table below shows a comparison between mean scores as to the levels of advice offered at each of five key stages in the applications process.

Table 3.3 Schools and Higher Education Guidance: Ranking the Advice

Key stage in the choice process	School/College	Careers Office	Total
A level / GNVQ subject selection	2.32	1.68	2.03
Course / Institution selection	2.27	1.65	1.99
Application to UCAS	2.62	1.45	2.11
Receipt of Offers	1.99	1.15	1.63
Examination Results	1.75	1.53	1.65
Total	2.19	1.49	1.89

(Source: UCAS Statistical Survey, 1996)

The most frequently cited reason for applicants declining an unconditional offer of a university place was that they 'needed to rethink their career path' (UCAS Report, 1996:11). Advice from schools and colleges was, in most cases, seen as more useful to the respondents than that received from the local career office. Schools and colleges provided the respondents with better advice during their application to UCAS than at any other stage. It is clear from Table 3.3 that all the mean scores are relatively low and most are rated poor to fair. The UCAS Report (1996:22) concluded that 'further inquiry needs to be made into the quality of careers advice that people receive...and additional exploration is required into whether people have been forced into making early and rushed decisions during the application process'. The significance of career education has been noted in relation to the career aspirations of school girls in south Wales. Here, low aspirations, coupled with a lack of effective guidance resulted in constrained 'choices' (Pilcher et al, 1989; Southall, 1990; Rees, 1992). The 'ordinary kids' in Brown's (1987) study recognized the significance of gaining qualifications but in common with others, sometimes lacked the guidance to do what was 'best' for them (Law and Storey, 1987; Whitty et al, 1994). Government policy is committed to increasing participation rates in higher education to 50 per cent. Their stated aim is to enhance access by widening participation by specifically targeting students from poorer working class families. This commitment to increased access and participation among disadvantaged groups, sits oddly along side the recent debates regarding university funding and 'top up' tuition fees. The current data on participation indicates how, despite the increased provision and access to post-compulsory education, the middle classes are still managing to maintain their advantaged position (HESA, 2000; UCAS, 2000). Commentating on the expansionist agenda Paterson and Raffe (1995:21) suggested that 'any increase in opportunities will be monopolized by the middle classes, with any residue filtering down to the working class'. There is now clear evidence to support this contention (Gilchrist et al, 2003) have demonstrated the under representation of working class groups in higher education and identified a lack of information as one key factor in restricting their access opportunities. As this chapter has indicated, accessing information about universities and crucially about the applications and entry processes as they are brokered by UCAS demands a level of sophistication of engagement with the higher education system.

Chapter 4

Choice and Class

The following chapter moves the discussion away from the macro level of policy formulation to the micro level of social practices. In order to set the scene, I have written this chapter in two sections. The first part focuses on the schools and Sixth Form Colleges in the study, while the second section provides an overview of the young people and their families. The key informants in this study *are the study* and this section of the book comprises *their* experiences and it is *their* voices that are given prominence in the account. As Wilcox (1982:458) notes 'ethnography is first and foremost a descriptive endeavour in which the researcher attempts accurately to describe and interpret the nature of social discourse among a group of people'. Providing vignettes of each of the research settings in this study serves to contextualize the various discourses that are then reported and will provide an opportunity to consider the ways in which family, school choice and ·class all impact on higher education market engagements.

The specificity of locality in relation to issues of choice has been stressed in relation to the research on school choice and markets (Gerwirtz et al, 1995; Gorard, 1996a; Ball, 2003). Some parents make decisions about preferred school catchment areas and then buy houses accordingly. Having this flexibility in their mortgage capacity gives them a market 'edge' and enables them to adopt a strategic approach to the education market and the choice process. Not only do the 'better schools' have better A-level results, they also prepare their pupils more fully to enable them to engage with the university application process. Since the data were collected in Wales it is important to highlight the various ways in which the school system here differs from that of England. Most significant differences are to be found in the structure and governance of education in Wales. The system is administered Nationally by the Welsh Assembly Government and Wales has no City Technology Colleges and only a small proportion of Grant Maintained schools. The National Curriculum for Wales, differs slightly from that taught in the English system and the provision of Ysgolion Cymraeg (Welsh schools) enables pupils at both primary and secondary levels to be educated through the medium of Welsh. However in Wales, as in England, the market at school level is highly developed allowing parents to chose from a range of options and school types.

The sample population used for this study was drawn from pupils in ten different schools and Sixth Form Colleges. These were representative of the range of post 16 provision available across south east Wales. In any ethnographic study providing an account of the sites and impressions taken in the field enables the writer to embed the characters and characteristics of the study and allows the reader to engage more with their stories (Atkinson, 1990; Delamont, 2002).

However, the facts about places, people and organizations do more than give readers a general familiarity. 'Preliminary descriptive materials set down some of the basic premises on which the argument rests' (Becker, 1986:62). Highlighting the characteristics and histories of each case study adds to the richness and the authenticity of the accounting. It will illustrate the ways in which the class based composition of the pupils and the type and ethos of a school can shape the patterns of engagement and influence university choices. In consequence brief vignettes of each of the ten sites are provided below. As I identified in Chapter 1 a minimum number of A-level points per student is a convenient way for universities to standardize entry requirements and screen applicants. Making use of the Welsh Office figures at the time of the study allows the average A-level points score per pupil to be listed for each of the schools. Social class compositions were determined with reference to the pupil data bank at each of the study sites. A brief vignette of each of the Schools and Sixth Form Colleges in the study is given below.

Argoed College
This is the largest College of Further Education in the region of the study. There are more than 4,000 full time students registered with the College and they study a wide range of academic and vocational courses. The college occupies three sites, two of which are fairly centrally located. However the main college campus occupies a sprawling site situated in one of the more deprived working class areas of the city. Neither of the two local comprehensive schools in this area has sufficient number of pupils wanting to remain in post compulsory education to justify their having a sixth form. In consequence they act as feeder sites for Argoed College. This means that the 'traditional' age cohort studying for A-level at Argoed College is predominantly working class in composition. The College has a 'Compact' arrangement with the two 'Real New' local universities and this guarantees places to students on a number of pre selected courses, even if they do not achieve the usual requisite A-level entry grades. The average A-level points score per student at Argoed College is ten; this is the lowest achieving of all the institutions in the study (Welsh Office, 1997).

Llanover High School
In terms of social composition, this is the most working class school in the study. It is a Locally Managed inner city co-educational comprehensive school and has an average A-level points score per pupil of 11. The school was purpose built in the early 1970s, but is overcrowded and needs some renovation. The study group consisted of 105 pupils, 36 were taking A level subjects and the remainder was either studying vocational course (GNVQ levels two and three) or re-taking GCSE examinations. Like Argoed College, Llanover High also has a 'Compact' agreement with the two local 'Real New' universities. The impact of this agreement is discussed in later chapters in relation to limiting access to information and restricted choice.

Cardinal Gwyn College

The policy for Roman Catholic secondary schools across Wales is that they act as 'feeder schools' for centrally located and voluntarily aided Catholic Tertiary Colleges. In consequence, the College has a wide social mix of students from Catholic schools across the region. Students are also accepted from non-Catholic backgrounds and this provides an eclectic mix of students. Middle class families choose the Sixth Form College because of its location, a leafy middle class suburb, and its pastoral care ethos and philosophy. The average A-level points score per pupil is 15 and during the study there were 200 pupils enrolled for A-level and GNVQ level 3 options.

Briarwood High School

This too is a Locally Managed co-educational comprehensive school. It is in an area, which is socially mixed, but undergoing a rapid gentrification. The school is bordered on one side by a large housing estate and on two sides by newly built commuter homes. The average A-level points score per pupil at Briarwood High School is 15 points. The sixth form had 145 pupils of whom 120 were studying for A-level examinations.

Ysgol Bryn Alun

This school is one of three Welsh medium secondary school in this region. It is Locally Managed, comprehensive and co-educational and was purpose built to meet the growing demand for Welsh language education in south east Wales. Welsh medium schools enjoy a high level of academic success with more than 50 per cent of pupils gaining grades A to C at GCSE compared with a 33 per cent average in other schools in Wales (Welsh Office, 1996). In consequence these schools are supported by families for whom Welsh is their first language and who want to maintain a strong cultural identity. However, they are also popular among aspirant middle class English speaking families for whom these schools offer an optional market choice. At Ysgol Bryn Alun, the average A-level points score per pupil is 18. The study included the 147 pupils in the sixth form all of whom studied A-level options.

St. Non's High School

This school is a Voluntary Aided Church in Wales co-educational comprehensive school. It was purpose built in the 1960s, in response to a schooling programme funded, in part, by the Church in Wales (the disestablished denomination of the Anglican community in Wales). In conjunction with the Local Education Authority. Like the Welsh medium school, it is also seen as having a 'value added' element and in consequence while there is a social class mix, the intake is predominantly middle class. It is worthy of commentary to note that some middle class parents are becoming members of the Church in order to maximize their opportunities for choices at 11. The combination of mortgage and religion as key determinants of choice is an interesting concept. The average A-level points score per pupil is 19 and during the study there were 112 sixth form pupils all of whom studied A-level subjects.

Regent High School

At the time that this study was undertaken, this school was one of only 12 secondary schools in Wales to have opted for Grant Maintained Status (Welsh Office, 1997). The co-educational school is located in a coastal setting and since becoming a grant maintained school has invested in several large scale building projects that have substantially developed the facilities at the school. It recruits from a wide catchment area that includes working and middle class families, however the reputation of the school is high and competition for places is keen. The average points score per pupil at A-level is 20. There were 88 pupils in this cohort all of whom were studying for A-level examinations.

Jenkin High School

The third Locally Managed comprehensive co-educational school in the study, Jenkin High School is located in one of the more prestigious middle class residential areas of the study. Recognized as a 'good' school, it enjoys a solid reputation and is annually oversubscribed in pupil applications for places. The school has an extensive building programme under the 'Popular Schools' Initiative'. This is a Wales-specific programme, devised to enable popular schools to expand beyond their standard number. This will provide a multi-purpose, all weather floodlit sports pitch and a new 'Technology Block'. Pupils at the school gain on average 19 points at A-level. There was a total of 77 pupils in the study cohort, all of whom were studying A-level options.

Brangwyn Hall

This is a single sex Independent School. Established almost a century ago, it enjoys a rural riverside location. The school buildings are a mix of traditional and new purpose built, to include a swimming pool, sports hall and residential blocks. It has a non-selective policy, taking girls as both day and boarding pupils. It enjoys a solid middle class image and a strong reputation for academic and sporting excellence. The year cohort who took part in the study was comprised of a total of 82 girls. In 1995 the school introduced GNVQ Level 3 Business Studies as an alternative option to the traditional A-level subjects. Six girls in the group were taking this option in addition to studying two traditional A-level subjects.

Redcoats School

Redcoats School is an Independent single sex day school for girls. Like Brangwyn Hall, the school dates back almost 100 years, however it does have a selection policy and pupils are required to sit an entrance examination at age 11. At the time of the study the average A-level points score per pupil was 21 points. A total of eighty pupils comprised the research cohort all of whom were studying for A-level examinations.

Table 4.1 below summarizes the different categories and characteristics of the schools in the study. Chapter 1 has identified the significance of the points averages at A-level in terms of university choices and access and this table illustrates the wide range differential which exists across each of the research sites.

Table 4.1 The School Sites

Name	Type	Average A level points per pupil
Argoed College	Further Education College	10
Llanover High School	LMS Comprehensive	11
Cardinal Gwyn College	Catholic Tertiary College	12
Briarwood High School	LMS Comprehensive	15
Ysgol Bryn Alun	Welsh Medium	18
St Non's High School	Church Vol. Aided	19
Regent High School	Grant Maintained	19
Jenkin High School	LMS Comprehensive	19
Brangwyn Hall	Girls Independent Boarding School	21
Redcoats School	Girls Independent Day School	21

[Some] Schools Rule OK

There was a wide range of difference in the extent to which pupils were offered guidance and support to prepare them to make their university choices. The previous chapter has identified the ways in which policy initiatives over recent years have successfully reduced the role of career guidance in schools. It has illustrated how the focus is firmly on providing information about higher education. However this chapter will consider the extent to which some schools are very successful in maximising pupils opportunities to engage with a full range of choices. It will illustrate the ways in which social reproduction is maintained in the higher education market. For some pupils, those in the middle class schools, staff made use of their social capital through social networks in the higher education sector to ensure that they and their families had access to high quality information and advice. In contrast other schools were less proactive in offering guidance. Some were content to rely on the parents to engage with the market themselves. There was an unspoken assumption, that parents could or should be able to facilitate the choice process on behalf of their children, that their social and cultural resources would enable them to navigate the complex pathways of university choices. However the schools and Sixth Form Colleges with high numbers of working class families, many of whom were first generation university applicants information provided little or no guidance or support. Rather these institutions were over reliant on Compact agreements that they held with some of the 'new' universities. As the data will indicate, for these young people there was simply a single tracking through the system rather than any opportunity to consider their choices and explore options.

Each of the schools and colleges in the research provided a different level of support for the pupils during the two years of their sixth form careers. The guidance and higher education advice and the facilities available to pupils in each of the sites to access information and research their options are discussed more fully below. This is done with reference to a range of data. These were generated from observations and interviews with key members of staff at each school or college and a pupil questionnaire. The pupils were asked to rate the quality of the information and the level of help that they had received regarding subject choices for A-level prior to their entering the sixth form. They were also asked about the level of information and guidance they were currently receiving in school and the facilities that were available to support them to research their options and make decisions about appropriate applications. These attitudinal responses were scored on along a scale where, 1 = Poor, 2 = Fair, 3 = Good. I also conducted qualitative in depth interviews with those members of staff responsible for the university applications at each of the ten schools in the study.

'Counting In' the Sixth Form: Questionnaire Responses

Of the total number of pupils initially surveyed in Year 12 (N=711), in all but one of the sites, more than 85 per cent of these young people intended to go on to university. Llanover High School was the exception where this figure fell to 69 per cent. See Table 4.2.

Table 4.2 Per Pupil Applying to University: Percentage by School

SCHOOL/COLLEGE	Total number of pupils surveyed	Number applying through UCAS	%
Brangwyn Hall	63	63	100
Regent High School	70	68	97.1
Redcoats School	72	69	95.8
Jenkin High School	72	69	95.8
St Non's High School	44	39	92.9
Briarwood High School	84	77	91.7
Argoed College	54	49	90.7
Ysgol Bryn Alun	40	35	87.5
Cardinal Gwyn College	177	159	85.8
Llanover High School	33	23	69.7

Of the small number of those pupils surveyed who did not intend applying to university, only 13 pupils said they had no interest in higher education and only ten thought that they were 'not clever enough' to go to university. Interestingly, at the time of this survey (1996) only nine pupils said that they felt that a university education was 'too expensive' and so they felt they could not afford to go on to study. The Dearing Report (1997) argued that there would be substantial cost benefits for those with university degrees. However, the introduction of tuition fees and student loans and the high levels of student debt have led to growing debate about the actual costs of a degree (Hesketh 1998) and this has increasingly served as a deterrent for many young people (Hutchings, 2003a). At the time of writing there is renewed government pressure for changes in key elements of the Higher Education Bill that will significantly impact on university fees and so impact on access. This is discussed more fully in the final chapter (Chapter 9) in terms of social justice and equity.

The use of the questionnaire as an initial research strategy served several functions. It allowed me to meet the pupils that I would be tracking over these two years while they made decisions about applying to university. It also provided a means of recruiting people for the home based, family interviews, the results of which are discussed in Chapters 6 and 7. As has been noted previously in Chapter 3, in a number of studies commentators have noted that many young people, most particularly those from working class backgrounds, feel that they do not have sufficient information about higher education (Connor and Dewson, 2001; Keen and Higgins, 1990). Data from my study supported these findings and I noted wide differences in the range of facilities that were available to pupils to provide higher education guidance. Interviews with key member of staff revealed huge differences in the extent to which the schools acted as facilitators in the choice process. Levels of staff, the amount of teaching time devoted to higher education options in particular and guidance in general varied widely in these different settings. As Parry (1986:43) notes, ' the language of access, like that of quality, operates with a variety of vocabularies'. The discourses around the admissions process can be highly complex. There are a number of gatekeepers and gate keeping practices that underpin the application system. Many pupils, particularly those families engaging with university applications for the first time were not provided with any information about even the most basic aspects of university entry. Many working class families were unaware of the timeframes imposed on university application by the UCAS process or their need to be proactive in researching higher education options (see Chapter 6). Some of the schools failed to make even this basic information explicit to their pupils. However the university market demands a complex level of understanding about the rules of engagement in the choice process. Knowledge of the institutional hierarchy and the implications of institutional and subject choices in terms of future employment opportunities were, for many young people, not even presented for discussion. In many instances there was a rote element to the entire application process.

Guiding by Ro[u]te

In most instances any higher education guidance is provided as part of the Personal and Social Education (PSE) curriculum. This subject area frequently forms a part of the responsibilities of a senior member of staff, usually either a deputy head teacher, or the head of sixth form. As I noted during one interview:

> The problem is the money you see we are really short of cash. We had a very high overspend on our budget this year and so we have to cut back where we can. Clearly staff have to take on other, additional roles and this is one area of the curriculum that allows for a non-specialist to do the job.
> (Mr James, Head of Sixth Form Briarwood High School)

In only two of the schools and colleges surveyed Brangwyn Hall and Cardinal Gwyn Tertiary College, was there a teacher with full time specific responsibility for providing pupils with higher education information and guidance. There was a taken for granted assumption in the majority of the settings that staying on and staying in the system was now becoming the norm and that as a consequence little or no guidance was needed.

> Only a very, very few of our pupils leave the school after taking GCSE. In the main our lot looks to university as the next stage, so we don't have any one full time career teacher here. The advice that our students get offered is mainly from within the school, they get the UCAS forms and that sort of thing from us. Although we do occasionally bring in academics from universities to talk to them, the danger then is they are not impartial and they see this as a way of plugging their own institutions.
> (Mr Martin, Head of Sixth Form St Non's High)

At Argoed College, which caters for a very large and highly differentiated student cohort, each of the class tutors is responsible for providing students with information and advice about higher education. This results in a rather inconsistent and somewhat patchy level of guidance across the tutor groups as I was told:

> It depends on who does it as to how and what is provided really. Some of our staff are very keen, but well you can't expect that from everyone can you? For the A-level lot, well we do try to do all the higher education stuff nearer the time, give them the UCAS form and tell about filling it in. I do know that Mr Nolton tells them about the open day at the local ['new'] university.
> (Mr Rhoslyn, Argoed College)

This illustrates the way in which A level courses continue to be the recognized and preferred currency in a competitive market. The College offers a range of vocational subjects and its Compact agreement with the local 'new' university will accept students with non A level qualifications. However the formalized access to knowledge and university information was not the same for all these groups of students. While each of the schools and colleges in the study had an area that provided higher education and UCAS information, there were wide variations in the extent of these facilities. In some, there was only a limited amount of material available, and this was not always the most recent, while other sixth forms offered pupils access to an extensive range of highly sophisticated information and guidance. Of the ten sites, Brangwyn Hall, the Independent boarding and day school for girls had the best facilities to enable pupils to research their university options. The school has its own 'higher education centre' as a part of their sixth form block. The school also has a full time member of staff who is responsible for providing the girls with higher education information and career guidance. The centre is adjacent to the well-stocked sixth form library and comprises a very large resource room and an inner office that is used for individual consultations with Mrs Ellis, the teacher. The main resource room is light and airy with a bank of networked computers along one wall. These allow pupils access to the entire range of university web sites, the higher education and guidance materials, careers information and the UCAS web sites. The girls are encouraged to make free use of these facilities whenever they wish. In addition to the networked computers, others in the room are on the school Intranet and are loaded with a wide range of higher education guidance materials including career programmes and CD-ROM copies which can be signed out for home use.

The higher education guidance programme begins at the start of Year 12 (lower sixth), every Wednesday afternoon is devoted to General Studies, a substantial part of which covers the key elements of how to make considered and strategic university choices. Each girl has individual tuition using the various computer assisted guidance packages and they are all expected to produce a plan of action detailing their subject areas, preferred degree courses and universities. The school actively encourages its girls to consider doing a one-year voluntary placement abroad before going to university. These GAP year projects are seen as a key part of their personal development and arrangements for placements under this scheme is highly formalized. Each year the school has between 15 and 20 pupils who participate in the scheme and they travel as far afield as India, Japan, South America and Israel.

In the other schools and colleges there was a mixed approach to the use of computer packages. Redcoats School, St Non's High School and Ysgol Bryn Alun all provide their pupils with access to both the ECCTIS and CENTIGRADE career guidance packages. However, while no charge is made for their use, access is restricted and in some instances I found that pupils had not had opportunities to use these facilities because of timetable clashes. Although computer guidance packages are also available at Jenkin High, Llanover High School, and Regent High their use is optional and the schools charge pupils between £8 and £10 per session. In contrast, Argoed College, Briarwood High School and Cardinal Gwyn College do not provide access to computer aided programmes because of the costs involved, as I noted in an interview:

> Last year we did provide it and 50 per cent of the cost was met by a TEC fund and that was great. But that was a one off, unfortunately they are not repeating it this year.
> (Mrs Rorty, Tutor Cardinal Gwyn College)

Before the end of their first term in the sixth form all the girls at Brangwyn Hall had at least one, hour long, individual interview with Mrs Ellis (the higher education guidance teacher). In addition to which the school also makes

considerable use of specialist advisors from the Independent Schools Career Office
(ISCO). During my interview with her Mrs Ellis told me:

> Initially the girls are all required to sort out plans, with *some* help from me.
> That means they can arrange for work experience placements. I also get them
> to draw up what I call the '*Action Plan*' for their university applications.
> These **must** be completed and submitted to me for my approval as soon as is
> possible. It is vital they think their options through.
> (Mrs Ellis, Brangwyn Hall)

Brangwyn Hall adopts a very proactive and hands on approach to helping
its pupils engage with the higher education market and the whole application
process. The girls begin to consider their higher education options immediately
they start in the sixth form. This is in contrast to the majority of the other schools
in the study, where the applications process is not consider until at least the end of
the lower sixth year, or in some cases, left until shortly before the UCAS deadline.
As Mrs Ellis noted:

> I want them to get the Action plan sorted, you know. Of course the beauty of
> this school is they can't escape me. I can catch up with them on the stairs, or
> at lunch, or during prep and just nag at them until it's done.
> (Mrs Ellis, Brangwyn Hall)

Ball and Vincent (1998) use the concepts of 'hot' and 'cold' knowledge
and suggest that middle class parents will access both, relying on this mixture of
sources in order to help them make informed choices.

By way of contrast, it is interesting to consider the extent of the facilities
at Llanover School, one of the schools, which recruits pupils from predominantly
working class families. A 'spare' classroom, which has a few plastic topped tables
and upright chairs scattered around, doubles as the sixth form common room and
as the higher education resources room. When I went in there was a shelving unit
in one corner that held two copies of the current UCAS handbook and an out of
date edition of 'Which University'. There were several current prospectuses on a
shelf but they appeared rather worn. Copies of outdated prospectuses were stored
in a cardboard box in the corner of the common room. Although there was a notice
board with posters advertising university open days it was haphazardly arranged
and much of the information contained there was out of date. Mr Rears, the deputy
head, with special responsibility for university applications, told me:

> Well we don't do that much with Open Days no, but well we have the
> arrangements with the Unis [Compact agreement] and well to be honest that's
> what most of ours will go for, so we don't need to be too worried. I mean if
> they want to go on visits they can.
> (Mr Rears, Deputy Head Llanover School)

> However this could, and did, result in some breakdowns in communication
> among staff. I sometimes feel like I am the last one to know what is going on,
> I mean, I don't do anything about the open days or any visits. That's not seen

as my job, so I sometimes just get told that a group of students in 6L will be away on Thursday because they are 'on a visit'. And well yes, I *do resent* this to be honest with you. I think it should be much more of a team thing. Not this secretive approach where you didn't have a clue what was happening.
(Mr Rears, Deputy Head Llanover School)

What About Parity: The 'Thicko' Option?

Both Cardinal Gwyn (the Tertiary College) and Argoed College (the College of Further Education) offer a range of courses in addition to A level subjects. Each institution has a large number of young people studying GNVQ options. This was in sharp contrast to each of the eight schools in the study. Only a few schools offered this more vocational route and only a limited number of pupils opted for these courses. Only Llanover School, Regent High and Brangwyn Hall cater for pupils wanting to study GNVQ level 3 course. In the other five schools, there was a definite sense that the schools were distancing themselves from pursuing this route. In some instances this response was client driven, with schools aware of the wishes of the parent body, as I heard from one school,

> It's too expensive an option for us to take up at them moment and anyway we feel there would be little or no demand for it in any case. Certainly not here and not with our type of parents.
> (Mr Martin, Head of Sixth Form St Non's)

Elite status in higher education is grounded in traditional discourses. Middle class parents recognize that the positioning of an institution in the market place is still supported by the A-level points score demanded at entry. In consequence those schools wishing to attract middle class families recognize the credential value of this over other entry options.

> We don't provide GNVQ options nor is this provision anticipated in the near future since it relies on a lower ability take up and there is not the demand for it. Well certainly not in *this* school. We find that parents here *want* the A-level options.
> (Mrs Jason, Redcoats School)
>
> No we don't go in for GNVQs, if they want that then they have to go down the road to Cardinal Gwyn. Mostly our parents don't want it and we don't really see the need to get involved in that sort of option.
> (Mrs Blount, Jenkin High School)

It is interesting to note the way in which these schools are responding to the demands of the parents. It is very much an example of Brown's 'notion of parentocracy' where 'a child's education is increasingly dependent upon the wealth and wishes of the parents, rather than the ability and effort of pupils' (Brown, 1996:393). In the schools where GNVQ options are offered the discourses that surround the decisions to offer these courses is varied, but again are clearly market led. Regent High provides GNVQ level 3 in Business Studies and Travel and Tourism and had 40 pupils taking these options. As the only Grant Maintained school in the locality, Regent High caters for a mainly middle class clientel and for this school offering GNVQs provided these 'market alert' families to a greater variety of options from which to chose.

> Well we thought about it and what we want is to provide a menu of options really. To do the best to provide choices, you know cater for all the pupils across the academic range.
> (Mr Ray, Regent High)

In contrast, Llanover School, with its primarily working class intake is conscious of the funding that follows the size of the Sixth Form. The school offers four GNVQ level 3 courses and the school has a much more pragmatically market orientated approach to providing this route.

> Offering them [GNVQs] was great. Well they really bumped up the sixth form numbers. Two years ago we had a sixth form of 89 pupils in Year 13 (second year of sixth form) and now it's 126. What you have got to remember is that this is not your St Non's, or your Jenkin High, we don't get the high flyers here as the norm. So, for us, GNVQ is the way to go.
> (Mr Rears, Llanover School)

However the GNVQ courses were widely regarded as second rate options by both the staff and the pupils at these schools. This held true for both the A-level pupils and the GNVQ pupils themselves. One A-level pupil at Regent High told me:

> Oh, that [GNVQ], it's a course for the thickos.

This attitude was reinforced at Llanover High where a member of staff told me;

> The A level students are OK, the problems are with the others [GNVQ pupils] a lot of them are 'wasters', if they bother to turn up for school they will often just doss around.
> (Mrs Jones, teacher Llanover High)

In contrast, at Brangwyn Hall, GNVQ options had been introduced for the first time for the cohort of girls in my study. Only six pupils had opted for this route and each was taking a Level 3 GNVQ in conjunction with one or two A-level subjects. But the senior staff were all very enthusiastic about the breadth of the course and the skills, which they felt, were developed.

> It's a marvellous opportunity we think Of course some of the staff didn't welcome it, they saw it as a dilution of standards and all that, you know, but well, we have been keen to get it installed. We had to 'sell' it, mind you, but

since then there has been support from pupils and parents and we think we are
on to a winner.
(Mrs Ellis, Brangwyn Hall)

Who You Know In The Know: Networking

Some schools in the study made considerable use of social networks in order to
help prepare pupils to chose universities. The value of networks, a key aspect of
social capital, in maintaining and advancing class based advantages in the
education market has been widely considered. In his work (Ball, 2003:83) has
illustrated how middle class parents and middle class schools 'almost always had
relevant social capital to hand'. In my study the middle class schools used personal
contacts to enhance the levels of awareness among the pupils and parents about
universities and university choices. The differential issues and values relating to
'hot' and 'cold' knowledge (Ball and Vincent, 1998) has already been discussed.
Some schools in this study used personal contacts with academics, especially those
in Oxbridge Colleges, to arrange for talks about and visits to the different
institutions, These schools arrange 'Mock Interviews' setting up panels of local
senior managers drawn from a range of national businesses and industry. These
schools also coach their pupils about the interview process, advising them on the
appropriate dress code and the interview format.

> The school has a strong parents committee whose job it is to arrange for
> specialists in a variety of fields to come in and act out interview procedures
> and techniques. On average the school would expect there to be ten
> applications for Oxbridge a year and we advise the girls on their dress and
> conduct during the interviews since this is a significant part of the selection
> procedure.
> (Mrs Jason, Redcoats School)

> I have a friend who is a don at an Oxford College, he comes in to talk to the
> Oxbridge group and they go up to visit and he arranges accommodation and a
> tour and that sort of thing.
> (Mrs Blount, Jenkin High)

Ball (2003) also identified the ways in which some schools had members
of staff who were particularly well placed to help with this preparation for
university. The teacher is able to act as a kind of informal gatekeeper, facilitating
access to key individuals or sources of information. Mrs Ellis has been at the
school for ten years during which time she has built up a large database on
different universities, courses and career options. She also 'encourages' all the girls
who attend university interviews or open days to write up their reflections on the
experience. These written accounts, together with a card index dating back ten
years, detailing the university destinations and course choices of all past pupils
enables her to use her social networks to further inform the pupils choices. Ball
(2003) and Ball with others (including Ball and Vincent, 1998; Ball, Bowe and

Gerwirtz, 1996) has written extensively concerning Bourdieu's concept of social capital and the ways in which its use allows the middle classes to maintain and improve their social positions. He illustrates the ways in which middle class families use ' a place and a sense of place' (Ball, 2003:60) in choosing a school to ensure that they can be confident about what it is that school can offer. Brangwyn Hall offers families additional access to the social networks that will enable them to make clear choices in the higher education market. Mrs Ellis makes use of her social networks to ensure that she has access to 'hot' knowledge about universities and this can be used to supplement the 'cold' knowledge those pupils and their families can seek through the official university networks. In addition former pupils are invited to the school to talk to the girls during the annual higher education convention run by the school. Mrs Ellis illustrated the extent to which social capital can be used to maintain social networks:

> I keep a running card index on all my girls. I even ring up the mothers of former pupils and say 'oh so and so is thinking of applying to x or y university. I know your daughter went there. What was her experience of the place?' I have a really good university and career advice network set up.
> (Mrs Ellis, Brangwyn Hall)

'For some students, school and family capitals are mutually reinforcing and combine to scaffold aspirations and application' (Ball 2003:87). This is a constant thread running thorough this account and is revisited in later sections of this book. Such high levels of support can be contrasted with some other schools in the study where only a minimal amount of the school's attention is focused on any consideration of choice during the application process.

> For me the week of the A-level results was usually one long headache trying to advise students who missed their grades. Then ringing around and trying to fix them up in other places, going for 'clearing', you know, trying to get a match. But then in 1995, 'clearing' was virtually a non existent task, One of the local 'new' universities targeted all our students who had missed their offers, I received a letter on results day offering places to almost everyone. So I was able to fix them up immediately. We have set up the Compact agreement and I expect to continue that way from now on.
> (Mr Dryant, Argoed College)

Some schools in my study, particularly those in the private sector were able to draw on provide their pupils with access to resources, gatekeepers and institutions in order to enhance their options. Comparative research into schools in the state and the private sectors suggests that parents choosing private schools see them as providing 'the ladder of opportunity to higher education and good jobs' (Edwards, Fitz and Whitty, 1989). Private education has sometimes been described as playing a vital part in the establishment and maintenance of an elite in society (Cookson and Persell, 1985). In her study Roker (1993) found that these schools give pupils an 'edge' when it comes to getting into prestigious universities and onto prestigious university courses. The private schools in my study recognize that there is this vast difference in the specific support and preparation available to pupils:

> It fair makes one wince when one realizes the paucity of provision that is
> made available for students in some other parts of the sector.
> (Mrs Ellis, Brangwyn Hall)

However, whilst they acknowledge this 'edge', they work hard to maintain and develop it.

> It's all about making and keeping contacts, you know. I ring and speak to
> tutors, find out what course options are new, get events organized, talks, mock
> interviews and that sort of thing. I keep ahead of the game really.
> (Mrs Ellis, Brangwyn Hall)

These comments epitomize the extent of the disparity in the higher education preparations offered to pupils across different school types. At the one end of the scale in schools like Brangwyn Hall there are tremendous efforts exerted on the part of the school to ensure that the girls are provided with a range of resources and information to assist them to chose a university best suited to them. At the other end of the continuum, Argoed College and Llanover School make little effort to prepare pupils and make them aware of the range of options which might be available to them, since each is confident in the role of the compact arrangement which operates with local 'new' universities.

In the main, careers guidance is minimal, or non-existent. Rather guidance in the sixth form is limited to coaching pupils, to a greater or lesser degree, through the mechanistic strategies of completing their UCAS forms. Even in this, however, it is argued that there is a definite 'edge' for those pupils whose applications are made as a result of their having been rigorously taken through this process by the school. Data indicate that in 1995 UCAS received 20,000 forms that were either illegible or had been incorrectly or only partially completed each of which needed to be returned to the schools for correction. Chapter 3 has discussed some of the pressures that admissions tutors face. Now only a few universities and a limited number of subject specialities like medicine call prospective students for interview. Most, in response to increased numbers of applicants and time constraints, rely on the UCAS form to select students. Applications will be sifted and filtered by university departments since formula funding and quota systems demand that admissions tutors 'get the numbers right'. In consequence the quality of the completed application form is vital. Data indicate that independent schools are very successful in getting their pupils into elite universities and onto prestigious courses. Whereas less than ten per cent of the age group attend private schools, nearly half the student entry into Oxford and Cambridge universities comes from the private sector (Sullivan and Heath, 2003). They suggest that this can be explained in part by the high level of financial resources available to these schools. Among other things, this allows career planning to 'be undertaken at a very detailed level' (Roker, 1993:129). This attention to detail is clearly reflected at

Brangwyn Hall and Redcoats School where the emphasis placed on completing the UCAS forms can be seen as highly significant in facilitating their pupils' university applications.

> Everyone gets a copy of the form, but no one is allowed to complete it until they have made copies and had them approved by me, their subject teachers and their year tutors. Then, in September, when they are back in Year 13, we expect them to complete the real thing in pencil, and then having had it carefully checked once again they ink it in. In fact our secretary is now something of an expert forger and she is able to do a beautiful alteration if it should be necessary.
> (Mrs Ellis, Brangwyn Hall)

This approach can be contrasted with for example Argoed College and Llanover High where the UCAS forms are handed out and the students asked to 'return them when they are done'. Some schools clearly draw on their social and cultural capital and make use of their social networks to maximize the range of university opportunities available to their pupils. However for pupils in other schools and Sixth Form Colleges in the study careers education has become a low status and soft option, restricted primarily the form filling process. Even at this level though, some schools, as the UCAS survey has indicated and this study illustrates, seem unable, or unwilling to ensure that this is done effectively. Having identified these differences between the schools and colleges in the study, I now want to turn the focus of attention to the family in order to consider the impact of the home background and the role of parents as facilitator of choice.

[Re] Defining the 'Family'

The increasing complexities of modernity have contributed to the restructuring of family roles and responsibilities and the reconfigurations of traditional patterns of family life and decision making processes. The policy initiatives aimed at increasing the levels of participation in higher education have led to concomitant rises in the numbers of young people who remain in post compulsory schooling. But this decision places them in a somewhat anomalous position, although legally they are becoming adults, with adult rights and responsibilities, choosing to remain in full time education, in many instances requires that they remain economically dependent upon their families. Unlike the school choice studies, the 'pupil' in this study is no longer a 'child'.

In attempting to consider the role of the family in the construction and facilitation of choices in the university market places, it is important to consider the ways in which family relationships are constructed and social exchanges are acted out in the private sphere of the home. Decisions about higher education subject choices and institutional preferences require exchanges and negotiations to occur within the family during the adolescents' development. Psychologists have identified this as a period of 'storm and stress' (Douvan and Adelson, 1966;

Coleman and Hendry, 1990) and have argued that it is a time of natural and inevitable inner conflict and behavioural turmoil. It is suggested that young adults naturally begin to distance themselves from the control of the parent (Petersen, 1988; Eriksen, 1968). Sociologically adolescence is seen as a natural period of interpersonal conflict (Aquilino and Williams, 1997). Teenagers often experience conflicting demands and role expectations from parents, peers and school. This is particularly apparent in relation to the transition from school to the labour market (Coffield et al, 1986; Hodkinson, 1998). It has been suggested that much of the debate surrounding the supposed 'tumult' of adolescence is little more than popular myth (Fogelman, 1976). As Delamont (1980:53) has noted, 'studies show that in most spheres of life, clashes occur over trivia, dress and music, not core values'. Nicholson (1980) supports this view, she found adolescents to be more in tune with their parents than with their peers. Similar conclusions were reached by Coffield et al, (1986: 209) who reported that they had found young people to be 'non-political and pragmatic young adults, who were conservative on most issues'. These commentaries challenge the stereotypical imagery of adolescence as a period of rebellion and rejection of adult standards; and led Head (1997) to suggest that the so-called 'rebellious teenage phase' is quite simply the adolescent seeking to establish an identity.

From a sociological perspective there are a number of problems that occur with regard to definitions for researchers who are attempting to research 'family' units. Over recent decades there has been a move away from the nuclear, symmetrical family that has traditionally been taken as the unit of analysis for family studies (Wilmott and Young, 1962; Jackson and Marsden, 1962; Leonard, 1980). As divorce rates and cohabitation have increased, many families now are reconstructed or multi-layered. The use of the word 'family', therefore, involves a somewhat complex terminology (Finch, 1986) and it becomes increasingly difficult to provide an authoritative definition of 'the family'. In spite of some changes which have occurred in the structure of the labour market in relation to women and work (Rees, 1992), the domestic division of labour has remained relatively stable. Although women no longer build their lives around a 'housewife' identity (Harrison, 1988), housework still remains a predominantly female responsibility (Oakley, 1974; Collins, 1985; Adkins, 1995).

The historical changes which have occurred in the nature and role of the family in society have led commentators to stress the need for an awareness of the flexibility of the term 'family' in contemporary society (Morgan, 1988; Harris, 1990). The significance of this was apparent very early on in my study. The initial pupil questionnaire was piloted with a group of 20 pupils in the sixth form of a school that was not included in the main study. As part of the pilot pupils were asked to provide information on the post compulsory education experiences of their parents. Twenty pupils took part in this pilot study and raised issues such as:

Do you mean my real dad, or my dad who lives with us?
(Kerry, sixth form pupil pilot study)

> My mum lives in England somewhere, we don't see her, but Sally, she is my
> dad's girlfriend and she went to university. Shall I put that?
> (Martin, sixth form pilot study)

A number of those surveyed seemed to lack any detailed knowledge or awareness of their parents' history. There was a considerable degree of uncertainty among the group as to what many of their parents had done when they were younger.

> I don't know about my dad, he left when I was small, but Gary who lives with
> us now, well he did a course engineering I think, or something.
> (Lisa, sixth form pilot study)

> I haven't got a clue what they did before they had us. I think my mum worked
> in an office, like she does now, and my dad well he works with the Council,
> but college and stuff? Well I don't know? Would they have needed to go?
> (Ross, sixth form pilot study)

Of the 20 pupils in the pilot study only three lived as part of a 'traditional' nuclear family and only one could identify with any degree of accuracy the educational histories of both biological parents. Their comments illustrate both the varieties of 'family' arrangements (Morgan, 1996) and the methodological difficulties inherent in any questionnaire survey. As a consequence, the data that are reported about each of the families in the study are drawn from the qualitative semi structured, in-depth interviews with the families and from focus groups with the sixth form pupils. With the obvious exception of the single sex schools, I tried to recruit families of boys and girls in each school. A total of 20 families, two from each of the ten different schools and colleges were interviewed for this research. I also conducted 16, school based, focus group interviews.

For the purposes of the study like Edwards et al (1989) I defined 'parents' as those adults who were the primary care givers and significant in 'facilitating' choices. This definition did not preclude step-relationships or couples who were unmarried but living together. Much of the previous research on education markets has related to choice of schools and so in consequence has focused on families with much younger children. Parental influences and involvement in the choice process has been identified by means of one to one interviews, usually with the mother alone, for example David, West and Ribbens, (1994). However in this study because of the ages of the 'children' and the complexities of the ways in which teenagers and their parents engage socially, I was anxious to interview the family as a complete unit. I wanted to capture some of the inter-generation dynamics that occurred during discussions about higher education.

Researching by Class

Given the increasing reliance on market led reforms to shape education policy, Reay is critical of the dominant discourses that assert a classless norm. Rather, she argues in support of the idea of class as a complex mixture of interrelated issues and suggests that 'the logic of markets does not displace the logic of class but rather masks it behind a rhetoric of freedom of choice for all' (1998:262). Research has shown that class based inequalities persist regardless of policies aimed at their amelioration (Halsey et al, 1980; Halsey, 1993; Shavit and Blossfield, 1993). This study aims to contribute to this work, considering the cultural discourses of the market led university challenge. Choices are socially constructed, requiring a level of fluency with the field. Attempting to assign social class to individuals can be problematic, as Crompton (1998) has confirmed. Nevertheless it is helpful to be able to describe family groups according to an accepted class categorisation. In common with others, I have used a number of factors to allow me to comment on the class positioning of individuals and families, including the occupations of the parents and the level of their educational attainment (Halsey, et al, 1980; Bellin et al, 1995). Class categories were then assigned corresponding to the Goldthorpe classification scheme. This was constructed from an aggregation of occupational categories in the Hope-Goldthorpe scale and it aimed to 'bring together within the classes we distinguish, occupations whose incumbents share broadly the same market and work situation' (Goldthorpe, 1987:40). The scale distinguishes between the occupational categories of Service (Classes i and ii), Intermediate (Classes iii, iv and v) and Working Class (Classes vi and vii). Table 4.3 provides an overview of the families in the study.

Table 4.3 Composition of Families Interviewed

SCHOOL	PUPIL	HOUSEHOLD	FATHER'S OCCUPATION	MOTHER'S OCCUPATION	ASSIGNED SOCIAL CLASS
Llanover High	Maria Thomas	Mother, Stepfather	Unemployed	Unemployed	Working Class
Llanover High	Mark Istance	Nuclear Family	Computer Engineer	Secretary	Intermediate Class
Jenkin High	Louise Hughes	Nuclear Family	University Lecturer	University Lecturer	Middle Class
Jenkin High	John Walsh	Nuclear Family	University Lecturer	Civil Servant	Middle Class
Briarwood High	Mena Hussein	Nuclear Family	Consultant Surgeon	Medical Secretary	Middle Class
Briarwood High	Giles Roberts	Nuclear Family	Secondary Teacher	Biochemist	Middle Class
Ysgol Bryn Alun	Rhys Joyce	Nuclear Family	Retired Teacher	Secondary Teacher	Middle Class
Ysgol Bryn Alun	David Jones	Nuclear Family	Haulage Contractor	P/T Civil Servant	Intermediate Class
St Non's	Caitlin Smith	Nuclear Family	Engineer Technician	Mobile Hairdresser	Intermediate Class
St Non's	Alex Smart	Nuclear Family	Secondary Teacher	Nursing Sister	Middle Class
Brangwyn Hall	Joanne Parker	Nuclear Family	Landowner-Farmer	Occup. Therapist	Middle Class
Brangwyn Hall	Amy Hubert-Jenkins	Nuclear Family	Accountant	Orthoptrist	Middle Class
Regent High	Stacy Lang	Nuclear Family	Taxi Driver	Part Time Clerk	Working Class
Regent High	Gavin Hutchins	Mother	University Lecturer	Art College Lecturer	Middle Class
Cardinal Gwyn	Susi Powell	Nuclear Family	Service Engineer	Store Supervisor	Working Class
Cardinal Gywn	Glyn Bateman	Nuclear Family	Unemployed	Shop Assistant	Working Class
Redcoats School	Penny James	Nuclear Family	Secondary Teacher	Secondary Teacher	Middle Class
Redcoats School	Victoria Clarke	Nuclear family	Retired Police Officer	Retired Store Owner	Middle Class
Argoed College	Michael White	Nuclear Family	Unemployed	Unemployed	Working Class
Argoed College	Jason Barry	Mother	Not Known	Unemployed	Working Class

However whilst such categorizations can be useful as social markers, they should not be too rigidly embraced. As Ball (2003:11) suggests when attempting to analyse markets and choice there is clearly 'the need to live with a degree of fuzziness in the categorization of class'. In consequence, considerable significance has also attached to Bourdieu's notion of habitus. This is defined as the socially grounded portfolio of dispositions that are expressed through the various manifestations of cultural and social capital (1990). Although Bourdieu is concerned with what people do in their daily lives, 'he is emphatic that social life cannot be understood as simply the aggregate of individual behaviour' (Jenkins, 1992:75). Rather it is the concept of habitus as a social phenomenon that is used to explain the durability of class based advantage.

Educational research has consistently confirmed the relationship between social class and educational attainment for over four decades (Bernstein, 1975; Bourdieu and Passeron, 1990; Halsey, 1992). The recent shift to a market led philosophy in education policy making has overlaid and perhaps exacerbated differential access to, acceptance by, and achievement in, more or less relatively desirable, secondary schools. In the works of both Bourdieu and Bernstein, central to a conceptual apparatus of privilege is the acceptance of the family as the site of transmission of linguistic and cognitive complexities. These act selectively on children's competencies to decode, produce and attain educational texts and gain educational qualifications. Increasingly the wishes of parents have been given primacy in the political agenda surrounding education. The choices, which young people take regarding their future career pathways are heavily influenced and mediated by their access to information and these choices are locked within the sphere of their cultural experience. The following chapters will continue to consider the role of the school and the family as 'facilitators' in the university challenge.

Chapter 5

Schools and Choice

In the previous chapter, I began to consider the interplay between the social composition of these schools and their engagement with the higher education market. I want to continue to develop this theme in order to explore more fully the relationship between the institutional and the family habituses, and the implications for university choices. The particular combinations of educational opportunities of different social class groups that these schools provide 'constitutes a mechanism of deferred selection' that in turn results in 'an inequality of "level" or success. Concealing and academically consecrating an inequality of chances of access to the highest levels of education' (Bourdieu and Passeron, 1977:158). Case studies will enable me to demonstrate this 'deferred selection' in action, and the impact of inequality of access to information in terms of differential access to university choices.

Market 'Alert' School: Market Placed Well Placed

As might be anticipated both private schools, Brangwyn Hall and Redcoats School, were highly market aware. But a market orientation was also visible in Regent High and Jenkin High. Each of these four schools already occupy a particular niche in the local market and they were all anxious to consolidate and improve on this. The ethos of each was highly visible, and their value systems were reflected in the traditional displays of academic and sporting successes in the assembly halls and corridors. As Gerwitz et al, (1995:127) have note the marketisation of the sector has brought with it 'new semiologies of schooling' and these are reflected in and represented by the overt displays of 'excellence' emphasized by the middle class symbolism. This impression management was further extended to their prospectuses and yearbooks and their overall 'glossification'. A-level successes and university destinations of previous students are prominently displaced in their annual reports with particular emphasis given to Oxbridge entrants. These overt statements of academic success and traditional values has also been noted by other commentators (Fitz et al, 1993; Woods, 1992).

Several of these schools were keen to use my presence in the school as a marketing opportunity. I was invited to speak at a parents' evening at one and at Regent High I was told that the school was 'very keen to foster links with your university' and that the parents would be delighted to know that I had decided to research here. That evening I included my reflections on the visit in my journal.

After the session with the staff at the school today I have a funny feeling that I might well appear in the next prospectus for the school. Possibly under the heading of 'Our university researcher!' The school has a high profile, as one of the few GM schools in the area and it is keen to market itself. This has really worked to my advantage. They're very anxious for me to see what a 'good job' they're doing. They are also very interested in the promise of an evaluative report - again another item for the prospectus perhaps.
(Extract from Field Journal, 2nd February 1996)

At each of these schools' open evenings, there was evidence of a corporate approach towards university applications. The focus was very clearly one of encouraging the pupils to 'make the best possible choices' on the UCAS forms. The emphasis was very much on making parents aware of how they and the school could work as a 'team' to ensure that each pupil should maximize their chances of being offered a place at one of the 'better' universities. School choice is a complex process through which parents seek to confirm or enhance the cultural capital of their children and themselves. Many parents use the schools market in order to play out their aspirations for their children. As Foskett and Hemsley-Brown (2003:205) note parents may justify their choices in 'selfless and positive terms and through simplistic explanations'. Often parents report that they 'simply want their children to have the best chance' and schools are aware of these wishes and keen to facilitate higher education opportunities as a reflection of this 'best opportunity'. They appreciate the importance of working within the UCAS application time frame and the need for the UCAS forms to be accurately and 'engagingly' completed. As the previous chapter has indicated, they devote considerable time and effort to ensuring that this is achieved. The staff at the schools are conscious of the status of the different universities and their league positions. In many cases the families, too, are informed as to the league positions of institutions and conscious of the outcomes and the implications of the Research Assessment Exercise (RAE) and Teaching Quality Assessment (TQA). The staff at the schools commented on how many parents were extremely aware of university status and highly informed about institutional differentiation.

Our parents are very aware of the way the system works and are very clued into the application process and the league table.
(Mrs Lindsay, senior mistress Jenkin High)

The parents appreciate how vital it is to make the best possible choices, that's part of why they choose us. But they are really aware of university status and the like. Well, I mean to say it's all about life chances isn't it?
(Mrs Ellis, Brangwyn Hall)

The pupils and their families also demonstrated their awareness of the differentiated higher education sector and the significance of engaging with the market at this level.

> They [the school] are very keen on getting you to apply to the better universities. They do like you to go to the higher status places particularly at our school. They make a point of saying who goes to Oxford and Cambridge and, you know, that they really want to get the most people possible there.
> (Julia, pupil at Brangwyn Hall)

As Bourdieu (1977a:496) notes it is the investment of time, effort and money on the part of families that enables them to engage so successfully with this institutional hierarchy. He suggests that 'it is as if the investments placed in the academic career of children had been integrated into the system of strategies of reproduction'. This sense of matching institutional and individual habitus was evident as one parent explained:

> My husband did the third year of his course at Cambridge, didn't you? And well he just feels, well we feel really, it would be better for her if she were to go to Cambridge too. We don't think that Welsh universities are very good. I know that's a terrible thing to say, I mean I'm sorry if you're Welsh, but... well that's how we see it. It is just absolutely the right thing for her.
> (Mrs Hughes, Louise, pupil at Jenkin High)

Ball (2003:90) has also reported how 'some parents find themselves responding intuitively and instinctively to certain schools' and higher education applicants reported a 'sense of identification with particular universities'.

To ensure a greater success at A-level, the more market aware school use a variety of different Examination Boards, often entering candidates for examination by several different Boards. Each of these schools actively encourages pupils to make Oxbridge applications and on average, between six to eight pupils at each receives an offer each year. At each of these four schools, the Oxbridge candidates are coached through the application and interview process. Often the schools make use of social networks in order to advise pupils on the colleges to apply to and the best interview strategies to adopt. This proactive engagement by academically successful schools, particularly evident in the independent schools, is recognized by parents and is acknowledged as the most effective way to approach the marketplace. In an interview with the James family, whose daughter Penelope was a pupil at Redcoats School, Mr James indicated how aware the family was of the ways in which the school actively sets about preparing pupils to apply to high status institutions.

> The school is very very good at what it does. That's getting the girls into top places you know. They encourage applications to Oxbridge that's key. Yes, and they place very great store on the Examination Boards they use. The London Board the Oxford Board. It's all about status, all status and getting greater qualifications. And of course they are in a competitive private market. They are marketing the school and so those grades are going to count when it comes to attracting more pupils.
> (Mr James, Penny, pupil at Redcoats School)

The high level of support provided by some schools is recognized by the pupils and their families as a means of maximising their chances of a successful transition to university. This was particularly the case at Brangwyn Hall where Mrs Ellis, the guidance teacher, is extremely proactive in making sure that the sixth form pupils are aware of the wide range of university options and the significance of making appropriate choices. She is also anxious to ensure that they have extracurricular activities to enhance their UCAS applications. Her level of drive and enthusiasm was self evident:

> I like to give them a little nudge now and again, it helps to remind them that they need to do these things. They need to get on and this is *such* an important time. If they tell me that they are thinking of doing a summer job in Macdonald's in Cardiff, I say *'for heavens sake why?* Go to the Paris Macdonald's and brush up on your French. Spend the summer in their Moscow branch and improve your Russian. *Do something different'*. It makes for a better UCAS form and you have a good time.
> (Mrs Ellis, Head of Guidance Brangwyn Hall)

The pupils and their families all recognized the extent of Mrs Ellis' efforts to facilitate their choices. In the focus group interviews the girls told me:

> We had an Open Evening about higher education at school, Mrs Ellis is great, she organized it all. Our parents were invited as well, it was really good and we had other bits that were really good like they had a student there from university, a past pupil, telling us how to get the best out of going to university, that was really good. I think it's important to see how well others have done, it sorts of urges you on.
> (Caitlin, pupil at Brangwyn Hall)

Some studies have indicated that pupils are suspicious of the advice they have received about post-compulsory education in schools (Howieson and Semple, 1996; Kidd and Wardman, 1999), while others suggest that teachers can play a significant role in the process (White et al 1996). However the ways in which the social networks and cultural capital was operating in the choice process within the more elite schools in this study was evident in the attention to detail provided by the staff at Brangwyn Hall. The significance of impression management, used effectively by the school to promote its own image, is used to encourage the girls to provide a high impact on their UCAS forms. They are coached in how to write their personal statements so that they can optimize their appeal for the university admissions tutors.

> She [Mrs Ellis] is really good, she spends ages with us individually and we get shown how to write our 'I am great' statements on the UCAS form so that it doesn't just come across as a long boring list.
> (Julianna, pupil at Brangwyn Hall)

The middle class parents too recognize and value the work that the school does in terms of facilitating pupils' university choices. The combination of social networks and cultural capital of the school and the home allows the girls at Brangwyn Hall to maximize the benefits of their engagements with higher education, both in terms of subject and institutional options. In a family interview, one of the mothers of a pupil at the school commented that:

> I must say the school is very good, we had a sixth form orientation evening and they do a lot of hard work getting them to think about their choices. Not just on what to study, but where to go, they know exactly how to get the best out of the girls and to get them to think about career choices and all that.
> (Mrs Parker, daughter Joanne, pupil at Brangwyn Hall)

Accelerating Amy

This section takes as a case study one of the pupils at Brangwyn Hall in order to illustrate the benefits which are to be gained by the young people who are more privileged in making their university choices. Amy is one of the girls who decide to take up the level three GNVQ Business Studies option that the school introduced at the start of here two years in the sixth form. As has been noted in the previous chapter, GNVQ options are also available at Cardinal Gwyn College, Argoed College and Llanover School. However in each there is a prevailing attitude among the staff and the students that these courses lack the intellectual rigour and hence the academic standing of the more traditional A level courses. The GNVQ courses are regarded as second rate options, A level pupils at these schools speak in a derogatory way about GNVQ options and the pupils who study them and a staff member at Llanover School told me 'it's a course for the thickos'. This attitude is reinforced by those schools in the study which do not offer GNVQ courses because 'it's not for a school like ours, we don't want to go down that road' or 'parents don't want it, we wouldn't get the take up, not here'. Commentators have noted how the academic A-level examination is firmly held to be the gold standard and retains its appeal 'despite the introduction of varieties of new forms of vocationally orientated credentials' (Hickox and Lyon, 1998:35). It was interesting, therefore, to see the commitment with which Brangwyn Hall had approached introducing them. The school has been anxious for the GNVQ strand to be a success and the Head and several senior members of staff have gone to great lengths to ensure that pupils who choose this route are fully supported throughout the course. Some universities have been resistant to receiving applications from candidates with non traditional qualifications and the staff at Brangwyn Hall have been careful to identified the universities that are prepared to consider candidates offering a combination of GNVQ and A-level options. Brangwyn Hall has also been very active in promoting the GNVQ option to both parents and the local business community. Researchers have argued that GNVQ programmes have real potential as useful worthwhile courses that can be highly successful in teaching student autonomy (Helsby et al, 1998). The school has made use of a series of open evenings to allow staff and pupils to demonstrate the various strengths of this course of study.

When I interviewed the Hubert-Jenkins family, both parents admitted that they had initially been uneasy when Amy announced her intention to take the GNVQ Business option in combination with two A-level subjects. They have two older children, a son and a daughter, both of whom have been to university having followed a traditional A level route and, because of this, they were anxious about the perception of GNVQ as a low status option and concerned that it would not allow Amy access to a 'good' university. In the family interview Amy's parents spoke of their initial reservations about the course:

> It's the first year of this advanced GNVQ option and so there has been a lot of discussion going on at the school about it. It began in the early stages you know, because well we were concerned as to its acceptability to universities and all that.
> (Mr Hubert-Jenkins)

> Well I must be honest with you, I mean, we took a bit of persuading at first. You know it's usually seen as well, as another, lesser option, you know something for the not so bright. I'm sorry, that sounds awful I know, but well we were bothered. We had several discussions at the school about it, especially in the early stages. But it has been marvellous for Amy.
> (Mrs Hubert-Jenkins)

Amy herself was full of praise for the various strengths that the GNVQ option allowed her to demonstrate. She was also very aware of the level of support that she had received from Brangwyn Hall generally and from Mrs Ellis in particular and made this plain when we spoke:

> We have had so much help from the school in choosing universities and the right courses and that. I mean they have been brilliant in that respect and my doing the GNVQ has been great. it has really helped me to prepare more. We had an open evening recently for prospective pupils and they also had people from businesses too. There was one man, a director of a big group, and he said he really knew nothing about the GNVQ course. So the next day we phoned his company and said look can we come and talk to your Board about it, tell you more about the course so that you'll know what sort of things we can do. So a friend and I went to Cardiff and we gave a presentation and they were really impressed because all they had heard was bad publicity and so they thought it was a bad qualification. We have now talked to executives at Shell, British Steel and places like that and they all admit that they didn't realize that the course content was anything like what we showed them.
> (Amy Hubert-Jenkins)

Amy's mother reinforced the way in which both she and her husband had reconsidered the GNVQ course once they had been given the opportunity to see it in action, she told me:

> As far as Amy is concerned, it's a form of work and a method of learning that
> suits her. She has done brilliantly and I must say that the school has been
> fantastic in supporting it, you know, and getting it off the ground.
> (Mrs Hubert-Jenkins)

Amy is bright and confident a pro-active student at a 'posh' high status
independent day and boarding school for girls. Allowing her to take a non
traditional course has succeeded in giving her 'the edge' (Roker, 1993). Like
Roker, other empirical data from the UK and Australia support the suggestion that
this type of education can 'make a difference' (Connell et al 1982; Delamont,
1990; 1996). Amy is well placed to make the 'best' choices in relation to the higher
education market. She is well able to promote herself and she benefits further from
the role which both her parents and her school plays in facilitating her choices. The
combination of a market aware family and school has ensured that her university
choices are maximized. As a follow up in the study, I had asked each family for
permission to contact them by telephone, in late August, after the examination
results were published and their university destinations confirmed. I spoke to Amy,
two days before she left Wales to spend a Gap Year working in a school in Peru
teaching English. She had gained distinctions in her GNVQ option and a grade B
in A-level Religious Studies and a C in English. She was taking up a deferred entry
place at the University of Durham, The school obviously has a highly informed
clientele who possess the social and cultural capital necessary to enable them to
make informed choices. Brangwyn Hall offers them more of the same and the
structured and supportive frameworks within the school, the social networks, both
formal and informal allow Amy and others like her to maximize their chances of
success within a highly differentiated higher education section. However this level
of support and structured guidance was not always evident in schools in the study
as the following account indicates.

The Market Sidelines

For pupils in a number of the less market aware schools, there was a limited degree
of support available at either the school or the family level to enable them to
engage fully with the choice process and to negotiate the complexities of the higher
education market. Many of the schools especially where a number of the pupils
were from families where this would be a first time engagement with higher
education, the application process and the admissions systems were not explained
in sufficient detail. As Hutchins' (2003b:101) work shows many young people
from working-class backgrounds lack some of the basic knowledge about post
compulsory education. She suggests that this is largely due to the linguistic
complexities of a system where 'at every level, information about higher education
is not straightforward'. Staff at the Cardinal Gwyn College commented on the
complexity of the system and the difficulties they faced when trying to advise
students:

Well, I mean it's a tough world out there. We do what we can, but I'm not
sure if we get it right you know. After all, the whole thing about applying for
places and going to university is that really it's all something of a gamble.
(Mrs Summner, Cardinal Gwyn College)

There is considerable evidence that schools offer different levels of
support to their pupils (Pilcher et al, 1989; Allatt, 1993). When asked about
organized Open Day visits from the school to some of the larger universities in the
region, the head of Year 12 at Briarwood a socially mixed school told me:

Well we do encourage them to visit the open day at Cardiff, because it is on
hand. But I don't know that many of them do. They most likely see it as an
opportunity to bunk off [go absent] for the day.
(Mr Michael, Briarwood School).

This attitude should be contrasted with the pro-active approach adopted
by the more market aware schools like Brangwyn Hall, there staff simply hire a
coach and take all their sixth form pupils to at least one university Open Day. In a
market led higher education sector, the challenge for schools is to fully inform
pupils of their options and to facilitate their successfully accessing the range of
choices available to them. Data in this and the previous chapter serve to illustrate
the level of difference across the sites. The research enabled a typology to be
developed for each site that indicated the extent to which the various schools
engaged with the higher education process. This is considered fully in Chapter 8. It
indicates that the schools with the most middle class composition, such as
Brangwyn Hall, are extremely market alert and adopt a 'thrusting' attitude towards
facilitating their students' university choices. The schools that have some form of
'value added', for example the Welsh medium school, Ysgol Bryn Alun, are
market aware. They have some level of awareness and appreciation of the
university market and go some why to supporting their pupils and offering
guidance and facilitation in the choice process. However staff at these schools
assume that, having engaged with the market and made a choice of school at
secondary level, parents will then possess the necessary competencies required to
engage with and facilitate choices at the higher level.

You'd be surprised how much they [parents] know. They read about the
different universities, the ratings and that, they see it on the telly [*sic*], they are
really into it. A lot of them know as much as I do about it, more some of them.
(Mr Martin, Head of Sixth Form St Non's School)

Pupils themselves recognized the limitations of the extent to which these
schools could or would, facilitate their engagement with the higher education
market, as Tony, a pupil at Briarwood School noted, 'they are good with helping
you do the UCAS forms. But well that's it really'. While the school would provide
the basic information and facilitate the application process, the rest was down to
the family. Geoff, a pupil at St Non's School, told me:

They get the UCAS forms done and that. Like, they organize that with you. But they don't show you what to do with the database do they? We've only had one lesson on how to look for universities and search for courses and stuff. My dad took me to his school and did it with me there. It was good that, we got it sorted then.

Parents of pupils at these schools also realized that they needed to actively engage in the process if they were to ensure that their children had access to a sufficiently wide range of information to facilitate their choices. As Mr Joyce, the father of Rhys, a pupil at Ysgol Bryn Alun, told me in the family interview:

Well, I mean, I knew what was wanted, so I simply summarized his work experience, his record of achievement. I gave a summary; you know [personal statement on the UCAS form]. He wasn't sure what to put in and leave out etc. There's only a short section on the form anyway, and I know you have to sell yourself to them and he wanted the guidance about it, so I said 'well *I'll* fill it in', and that was that really.

Middle class families have clear advantages in these schools. Many of the parents, like Mr Joyce, have been to university themselves and so are familiar with the UCAS process and know exactly the information that should be include on the application forms. Ball and Vincent (1998) found that middle class parents accessed both 'hot' and 'cold' knowledge to inform their choices of secondary schools. In relation to higher education choices these parents are familiar with the official sources of information. The can use these to supplement both their own experiences and the experiences of others in their social networks in order to inform and facilitate the choice process for their children.

However, as the research found there could be instances when middle class families may not possess the necessary competencies to allow them to engage fully with the process. Having used their social networks to find a 'good school' they may be overly reliant on the school to be much more proactive in their role as a facilitator in the university choice process. In these instances the limited input from the school can have dramatic consequences for the family as the next case study illustrates.

Mena's Drowning Not Waving

Mena Hussein was a pupil at Briarwood School. She was studying 3 A-levels, (English, Geography, and Art) her predicted grades were 3 Bs. Her father is a consultant orthopaedic surgeon from the Arab Emirates; her mother is British and works as a medical secretary at a large teaching hospital. The family lived abroad for a number of years and the decision to live in Wales was made to coincide with Mena entering the sixth form for A-level studies. Although they are an affluent middle class family, their familiarity with the British education system was very limited. Mrs Hussein left school at 16 and Mr Hussein was educated overseas gaining his medical qualifications in Saudi Arabia and the United States. In consequence neither parent was familiar with the A-level examination system nor the UCAS application process in the UK. Their years living abroad further disadvantaged them since they had only a sketchy understanding of the school system in Britain prior to moving here. Their decision to send their two children to Briarwood School was taken based on a limited local grapevine knowledge obtained via the social networks of family in this country. I interviewed the family on a Sunday morning; just one week before the school required Mena to return her completed application form for university. At the beginning of the interview, Mena told me she was thinking of applying for a Hotel Management course at a local College of Higher Education. She appeared somewhat sulky, disinterested and apathetic about the whole process of going to university. Both parents were very unhappy with her choice and this had led to a number of heated 'discussions' within the family. Her father, rather quiet and taciturn clearly disapproved and commented that:

> We feel she is going for something that is not a proper degree and this is well below her ability. That is why I don't think she will be happy.
> (Mr Hussein)

Mrs Hussein was extremely anxious that Mena should be given some clear guidance and advice, but was unsure as to where this could be best found. She told me that she and her husband felt that Mena was making a rash, ill-considered choice, that she would later come to regret. The family made it clear that for Mena the whole of her sixth form career had been an unhappy and stressful period. Mrs Hussein was quite emotional throughout the interview, which lasted for almost three hours, literally wringing her hands at some stages as she told me of her frustration and sense of impotence at her inability to offer any practical guidance or advice to her daughter,

> We didn't have much opportunity to research schools before coming back to Wales. As you can imagine my parents did their very best. But there again they had been out of the education thing for more than 20 years and they live in a different area from us. But they have done their best to ask about schools and areas to live. We didn't know the system here, we tried to find out, we did our very best we really did. We didn't know about sixth form colleges because they weren't around before we went. The only feedback came from one or two friends that advised us against them, because, they said, the kids get away with too much and they don't settle down to work. So I thought 'oh well, better to put them in a "traditional school"'. But now I am here well I am so disappointed. I am really. I mean how much trouble did we have when we first arrived here?

The family was obviously angry and frustrated with the limited levels of guidance and support they had received from the school. They felt that having come through a different education, system they had not had sufficient discussion with the staff at the beginning of the sixth form to fully discuss the range of A-level options and the implications of these choices in terms of university courses and career options. Mena told me:

> This school has really stuffed it up for me as far as choosing is concerned. I *know* that for a fact. I nearly dropped out last year; I was just so fed up with it all. I really had no idea what A-levels I wanted to do, and no help from the school and so I just picked any three.

Her mother was still angry about the lack of support provided in terms of subject choices:

> Yes *and* we had no help over that! I rang the school and they didn't even want me there to discuss it. That made me feel pretty shut out then. I mean to say how can I advise Mena if I don't know myself? I think they have been *worse than useless* especially when parents *want* to be interested and *want* the best for their kids. I think they could have spared me ten minutes! Even if it was just to say 'oh well we can't help you, you have to go here or go there. But they gave me no time, no time what so ever.

The resultant sense of disengagement with the system engendered a feeling of disillusionment with the sixth form that had been compounded over time. In consequence Mena appeared disconnected from the whole process and for her parents, there was a sense of her having 'settled' on a course which led her mother to comment:

> to be honest with you, I don't feel that she is 100 per cent happy with what she is doing. Going in this direction is *not right for her*.

Mrs Hussein, would be prepared to invest time and money in gathering information, but she has found that her social field has been disrupted and she has been unable to utilize her social connections in order to help with the choice process. Ball (2003:161) has noted that there are 'emotional and psychological aspects of the market behaviour of parents and students':

> I mean, we don't even know really what her options are with the A-level subjects she has chosen. I mean, where could she go with them, what could she do?. I mean, we weren't happy with her choice of A-levels at the start, we don't see them as... well to me it's a mish mash of subjects and again we got no advice on them. I feel well angry I suppose, yes very angry.
> (Mrs Hussein)

The Hussein family want to maximize Mena's educational opportunities and Mrs Hussein is keenly aware of what 'people like us' do in terms of their professional lives. She was concerned that a qualification from a local college would not carry with it a sufficiently high credential status. Mena admitted she was very angry and frustrated with the school because she felt that they had not provided her with any real opportunity to discuss her various options.

I am very close to just putting *any course* down [on the UCAS form], any course at all, just to get it done. Just to hand it in and get them all off my back. The whole thing's just so stressful. It really is. I don't know what I'm doing and the school just expects me to be able to deal with it. You know, make the choices, fill in the forms, just like that.

For Mena the decision to apply for the course resulted from her having a Saturday job, as a waitress at a large City centre hotel where she had met several people who had done this type of course and said it was 'a good laugh'.

Increasingly throughout the interview her parents' anger and frustration at not knowing the system became more apparent. There had obviously been a considerable amount of tension in the family regarding the whole issue of university choices over recent months.

The school just said that if she is not going to do medicine at university then it doesn't matter what subjects she takes. That was my whole area of advice wasn't it Mena? That was it that was all I got from the school... But what can you do when you are fighting the system and when you don't know the system? Unfortunately for Mena, she has had such a, well, a rough deal really. (Mrs Hussein)

Mena told me that the course she intended applying for had an entry requirement of two D grade passes at A-level. However I knew that Briarwood staff were predicting three B grade passes for her. I then if she knew any pupils in the school who would be likely to get D grades. I wondered 'would they be people that she would include in her circle of school friends', 'did she get on with them?'.

I think they are OK, I suppose, well sort of, I mean. But well, if you want me to be really honest then I think that they are a bunch of wankers, they're just thick...I don't hang around with them, or have any thing to do with them really. (Mena)

I then asked her why she intended spending the next three years of her life with such a group when she clearly had such a low opinion of them. Gradually with some additional 'probing' during the remainder of the interview Mena said that she had thought about studying Law, but felt that it was now too late to think about applying for a place at Law School. At this point I made the conscious decision to come out of researcher role and told her that she was able to make a later application through UCAS if so wanted, I suggested that she make contact with some of the Law Schools in order to find out about the courses that were available. By the time I left the house the family were beginning to work out a plan of action and Mena had become quite animated about the prospect of pursuing this option and told me:

Well I feel much better now that I have decided to make a decision. It's helped me so much just talking to you because well, you're not biased. You're

> not telling me which course you think I should do, or saying 'oh you should apply here, or there to do this, or that'. You just let me talk.

Mrs Hussein was quite clear about what she thought:

> I know her you see and I knew it. I knew she was unhappy, all it has taken is a mediator. It was enough just having you come and sit there. If she can change her mind that quickly just answering your questions, then let's be fair it wasn't right for her…I feel that you have lifted a weight off my shoulders Just getting her to sit and think it through for herself.

From survey data collected in the spring of year 13, I learned that Mena had applied to six universities to read law and had received conditional offers from four. Following the publication of the A-level results, I telephoned the Hussein family and spoke to a delighted Mena, who had gained the grades required by her preferred university. The outcome however does not detract from the ethical issue raised here about the boundaries between the researcher and the researched in a qualitative study that have been addressed elsewhere (Pugsley, 2002).

Briarwood High School, in common with several others in the study, Ysgol Bryn Alun, Cardinal Gwyn College and St Non's High School cater for middle class families who they perceive as 'market aware'. They confidently expect that these parents will have some level of competency to engage with the post-compulsory market. However there can be problems in terms of accessing information where there is some misalignment in the social networks and hence the cultural competencies of individuals or family groups. This, clearly demonstrates that there are intra class differences which can inhibit engagement with the HE market and the choice process.

Michael and Jason: Regretting, Reserving and Repeating

The research has shown that there is a third group of schools, with a predominantly working-class intake who are 'market inert'. They have proved unresponsive to market mechanisms and are reliant on the 'Compact' agreements that are formed with local 'new' universities. These schools and colleges 'trust' that the transition to university will be a relative straightforward procedure. In the case of both Argoed College and Llanover School the average A-level grades are in the lower banded, C-E categories. As one teacher at Llanover High School noted, 'we don't tend to get the high flyers here'. Nevertheless they are confident that the transition to university will be a straightforward process can be a relatively straightforward one. The families, most of whom have no previous experience with higher education in turn, 'trust' the school to take the lead and provide the necessary advice to enable their children to engage with the higher education market. The irony is that this category combines the worst possible mismatch of families and schools. Ideally, pupils who cannot rely on their parents to negotiate and facilitate the choice process would benefit from the sort of high-powered higher-education advice enjoyed by their counterparts at the type of schools which are considered earlier in the chapter and in Chapter 4. Parents in these schools were unaware of the way in which the university choice and application system operates or of how the school or college was preparing their children to engage with the process. One father commented:

> Our Michael, well he goes to the college. But well as for what goes on there, well we don't know like…and so that's it really, it's down to him.
> (Mr Jones, Michael, pupil at Argoed College)

Focus group interviews indicated that not only did the students lack the confidence to engage with the complexities of the application process, they were also unaware of the range of options available to them. Their horizons of choice were limited, focused only on the local institutions. They argued:

> There is no real motivation here for us to want to go to uni. I mean the way they [the teachers] do it, it's made out to be a long and laborious process, you know and I'm not really clear in my own head about the forms and stuff.
> (Debbie, pupil at Argoed College)

> Well, I don't understand the forms like they are really hard, my form teacher just said to put down Glamorgan, 'cos I could go there and do what I want
> (Mickey, pupil at Llanover School)

The university entrance process is complex and working-class young people recognize this and acknowledge their lack of knowledge about the higher education system (Keen and Higgins, 1992; Connor and Dewson, 2001) and look to their schools and their teachers for information and advice.

Michael and Jason were A level students at Argoed College. Both felt that they had been poorly advised about their choice of subjects and neither had been particularly happy or successful in the first year of study. They had both decided to make new subject choices and repeat the year. The consequences of missed opportunities and wasted time is an inevitable result of a misplaced 'trust' in the system on the part of these working-class families. Not having the cultural capital and therefore the social networks to enable them to access information and advice about the appropriateness of the subjects initially selected, they were reliant on the teachers to facilitate the choice processes. But as Hutchins (2003b:100) points out, 'some teachers make rather negative constructions of working-class young people's potential and as a result fail to supply them with adequate information and encouragement in relation to higher education'.

> I took completely the wrong subjects I wanted Geography and they said 'do English' and they completely misadvised [sic] me on that. I though it would be something completely different from what it was. I took Sociology too because they said it would help with like understanding people and that, because it's stuff like that and the environment, that's what I am most

interested in. But well this didn't help, they said it would and it didn't and so I was really misadvised.
(Jason Barry, student at Argoed College)

This theme of lack of advice and guidance was repeated when I interviewed Michael and his family:

I wasn't told like, about anything. I just went to the college and said 'right well I might as well do these ones'. I like Art, you know drawing and that and so I said I'd do that and well, I mean, I asked them a bit about it and about other things and well that was that really. But they didn't give you any real information, no background on what the courses were about. I mean.
(Michael White, Argoed College)

This class-based lack of awareness of the education system has been perpetuated over time. Researching in the 1950s Jackson and Marsden (1962:134) noted that most [working class] children were as unsure of the future as their parents and as uninformed about the possibilities'. Michael went on to say:

I did the whole year all right, but I decided early on that I wasn't going anywhere with it. So I have started again now. I have dropped the Art, and taken up Law. I think that will be a more useful A level to go to university with.

This lack of advice and support provided here contrasts sharply with the amount of support offered to middle class pupils in the 'better' schools in the study. Roberts and Allen (1997) also found students in colleges of further education (more likely to be working class) less well informed than students in schools. For Michael and Jason this reliance on the college to provide information and the subsequent lack of guidance proved costly both in time and money.

Maria: Last of All in the Sack Race

In some instances misplaced trust in a school to facilitate access to HE can prove even more disastrous than a repeated first year of A-levels. Maria Thomas was a pupil at Llanover High School. The eldest of three children both her mother and step father were unemployed, with no experience of post-compulsory education. Maria had transferred to Llanover High School after her GCSE examinations because the comprehensive school she was attending does not have a sixth form. However the Art teacher there, with whom she had a good rapport, had offered to supervise her A-level Artwork. However, Maria was formally registered at Llanover School where she studied A-level English.

When I interviewed the family, it was apparent that this arrangement had resulted in Maria missing out on a lot of the social and pastoral curriculum provided in the sixth form. Roberts and Allen (1997) suggested that one of the reasons why some working-class young people in further education colleges may lack information is because many of the colleges are on split sites and they may only offer higher education guidance at one of them. This was exactly the situation Marie was in. The two schools she was attending are some distance apart and Maria spent considerable parts of the school day walking between the two sites. This led to her being absent from Llanover High School during the tutorial sessions when the higher education information was provided.

When I interviewed the family in mid October of Year 13 (second year sixth) a few weeks before the completed UCAS forms were due to be returned to the school, Maria was clearly doubly disadvantaged. Her parents lacked any knowledge of the system and Maria was missing out on the limited amount of guidance that was on offer to her working-class peer group at Llanover High School. She and her family were totally unaware of the applications process and lacked the support networks necessary to enable them to access the appropriate sources of information.

> I don't get anything at all about it from my old school, because they don't do it [university entry] there. So I am just there for the Art and by the time I do my work there and then walk to Llanover, I don't really get much time when they are doing the tutorial stuff. It always seems to be done on the same afternoons and because most of my time is spent walking back and fore, well I hardly get any chance to be there. That time when you came to see us, you know to do the questionnaire, well I had only been to a few of those lessons because I am not usually there in time.
> (Maria Thomas, Llanover School)

It was clear during the interview that although her parents had only limited knowledge of post-compulsory education and so were unable to offer any advice to Marie they wanted to support her in whatever she decided.

> As I said to her tonight before you came, we don't really know much about any of this university stuff to be honest. I mean we haven't had much involvement with the school. This is one of the big problems about doing it between the two schools. As far as her education goes while she was at her old school well... we have always taken a keen interest and that. But since she has reached like a certain age and she is in the both schools with the A-levels, well we are dead proud of her and that... but well we don't know what's going on not really.
> (Mrs Thomas)

The families' confusion about the higher education system became increasingly apparent throughout the interview. They knew that university was costly and were anxious about the possibilities of their incurring additional debts. However they were unaware of the local authority maintenance grants (still available at the time of the study), or how they could go about applying for them. They were also unaware of the UCAS process or how the forms should be completed. During the interview Maria told me that if she went on to higher education she knew that she would have to study locally and live at home for financial reasons. She also recognized that she had further limited her range of institutional options by only studying for two A-levels subjects. She had talked to some of her friends about possibly doing some degree courses at one of the local HEIs that has a compact arrangement with Llanover High School. However she was unfamiliar with the full range of options offered there or at either of the other two local university institutes. Marie recognized that she needed to get some additional information and guidance:

> I really need to talk to the teachers about it because I know that I need to make up my mind soon about what to apply for. But really I am behind all the others because they have filled in their forms and I know that some of them have even been sent off. But I need to see someone, I need to get on and make a decision.

It was obvious that her family could offer her with little or no help assistance in the process as Mrs Thomas acknowledged:

> Well, its no good her asking us, she is more capable of filling it in than me. We'll go along with it, whatever she wants. Whatever she is happy with. I mean we are always here but really well she is more capable than me. And she needs to talk to the school really. They'll sort it out I'm sure.

Reay and Ball (1998) have referred to this as a working-class discourse of 'child as expert'. It was clear that the parents felt totally out of their depth. Although very proud of their daughter and anxious to encourage and support her they were looking to her and to the school, to take lead roles in the decision making process. At the end of the interview I asked the family whether they had any questions for me regarding the university entry process. In consequence I then spent some time taking them through the various stages of the UCAS application procedure and ended by suggesting to Maria that she try to make a personal appointment with her tutor when they could discuss her higher education options more fully. However even after having given them what information I could about the system, when I left I felt that the family were still very unclear about the whole process and that they were particularly uneasy about the costs associated with higher education. I wondered if I should have done more and reflected on this later in my research journal:

> I think that the Thomas family is probably the most confused of all the people that I have spoken to. Because of the very peculiar system of effectively being at two different schools, Maria is really missing out because of the lack of a co-ordinated timetable and as a consequence the amount of walking between sites that she seems required ton do during the day. Tomorrow I'll send them the address of the local career guidance office and the booklet they do on applying to university. I don't know if I should call and offer to help her fill out the form. But that is really intervening and ethically I guess not on. I think I have done what I can, I just really hope it works out all right for her.
> (Extract from Field Journal 18th October 1996)

Unfortunately things did not work out well for Maria. Following my interview with the family, Maria did arrange to meet with her tutor, however having spoken to him, she felt he only provided her with a limited amount of advice about her possible options which did not really meet her needs. Thoroughly confused and somewhat disillusioned with the whole idea of applying to go to university she decided not to complete and return the UCAS forms. Nevertheless, she had gained grade C A-level passes in both English and Art. This is equivalent to 12 points in the UCAS system and sufficiently high to allow her to apply for a range of courses at a number of the local HEIs.

Having spoken to her and learned of her success, the entry in my field journal reads:

> I feel really angry at the way in which Maria has been let down by the school. Her tutor didn't seem to have time. But if I'm honest, I'm also feeling guilty that I didn't do more to help. Could I have done something? And really **should** I have? Maria has done really well. It's a brilliant result but seems to have gone largely unnoticed by the school. What will she do now?
> (Extract from Field Journal, 22nd August 1997)

Families like the Thomas', with no prior experience of the post-compulsory sector do not understand the complexities of the higher education market. They put considerable trust in the schools relying on them to provide the necessary guidance and advice to ensure that pupils like Maria can make choices. However the level of career and higher education guidance offered in these schools is minimal, shaped by the limited expectations that these schools have of their students and reliant on the arrangements with local institutions to 'sweep up' the student body.

Both this chapter and the previous one have focused on the role of the school as a facilitator in the university choice process. They have illustrated the different competencies that young people and their families' posses to enable them to engage with the higher education market. The ways in which the 'better' schools provide information and support networks to allow choices to be individualized is contrasted with the limited options offered to working-class young people. Choosing a school is not just about getting the grades, it is also about making the grade in the university challenge.

Chapter 6

Families and Choice

In this chapter the focus begins to shift from the school to the home, in order to explore further the relationship between institutional and family habituses and social and cultural reproduction. Going 'behind the numbers' (Jackson and Marsden 1966) will allow for a better understanding of the 'articulations between sets of social practices across sites of experience' (Aggleton, 1987:37). The narratives that emerge demonstrate how educational inequalities are embedded within individual and family biographies and how they are translated into expressions of market engagements and choice. These data also reveal the levels of registration and gendered decision making that occur within different family structures. Some young people from working class families become the principal players in the choice process. With parents who are either unskilled in, or unaware of the impact of choosing in a highly complex and differentiated university sector, children becomes adept at sharing or withholding key information and at making key decisions themselves. For many middle class families, who are already highly skilled and market aware 'choosers', distinctive roles are assumed by each parent along gendered divisions, in order to facilitate and optimize choices. This chapter discusses these different levels of engagement and considers the role of the parent as agent in the market place. Choices are set against a backdrop of family relationships with parents anxious to 'spoil' and in some instances keep their children close to home (Chapter 7) and teenagers anxieties about transitions and status passage (Chapter 8). Morgan (1996:51) notes that 'in considering intergenerational family relationships we are of course often considering inheritance in all its dimensions'. For some young people, habitus shaped their choices, providing them with the necessary cultural competence to enable them to fully engage with the complexities of the system. As Power et al (2003:82) note this involves 'not only identifying 'the best' but having the confidence to regard it as within reach'. Rather than controlling the selection process, many middle class parents deferred to the wishes of their children, confident in the knowledge that that they could and would make these 'best' choices. The relationship between social class and entry to elite universities has been established (Bourdieu, 1988; Brown and Scase, 1994; Morley, 1997). However this study brings into question the homogeneity of a class system, as illustrated by the experiences of the Hussein family, discussed in the previous chapter.

A 'Need To Know' Basis

Although this cohort of students were the last to enter higher education prior to the introduction of tuition fees, a number of parents were aware of the impending changes and the cost implications. While all the parents in the study were fully supportive of their children wanting to go to university, the parents of both pupils at Llanover School did express some reservations as to the potential benefits of higher education. They exhibited anti education attitudes that were similar to those expressed in a Learning Society project in South Wales (Gorard et al, 1997:31). Here one respondent, a 57-year-old working class man was somewhat scornful when he told the interviewer:

> You said about education about getting qualifications. I might fall into something that I would really love...but you asked me about getting education, which I think, would be a foolish thing for me to do really. It's a waste of time as far as I am concerned. You see them on the news, like that woman of 70 or 80 getting a degree or something. What for like? You know, what for? She has wasted hours. To go and do some thing like that at her age is a waste of a couple of years of her life.

In my study both the pupils at Llanover High School were from working class families and neither set of parents has been in post compulsory education. For both families this was to be the first child to apply to university. Although proud of their children, both sets of parents were sceptical of the employment related 'benefits' of higher education. In the case of the Istance family, that Mark had decided to remain in post-16 education and to apply to university.

> We never exerted pressure on him at all. I never said...well we are rather surprised that he has made the decision to go to university. We thought that perhaps he might not. I wouldn't put pressure on him, no not at all. Let me just say that I am concerned that a lot of time and effort will go into a university education and I am worried that his job prospects at the end of that time will be no better than they are now. As I said before I worry if it's all worth it. I would be content with him not furthering his education at all but getting a good job with prospects somewhere. But having said all that I mean I have never ever suggested to him about leaving school and trying to look for a job mind. If he wants to go on then that's OK.
> (Mr Istance)

Similarly the Thomas family were anxious about the costs associated with higher education and the subsequent graduate career prospects. These fears were coupled with a desire on the part of the mother to take care of Maria, to ensure her safety by keeping her close to the family (Leonard, 1980). This theme is developed in the following chapter. As her mother told me during the family interview:

> Well I don't know about it, I've got mixed feelings. I mean I'll support her whichever way she wants to go well...I don't really know. I mean I haven't

made up my mind whether I'm for or against it really, where would she live
and what about a job after, I mean what would she do?
(Mrs Thomas)

Before interviewing the families, I had amassed a considerable amount of
data on each of the young people. During this study, I had interviewed the staff
with responsibility for HE guidance and careers at each of the schools and colleges
I knew all the pupils predicted A-level grades and what particular expectations
staff had of each pupil. I was familiar with the extent of the HE guidance they had
received and the stage that each had reached with regard to completing the UCAS
forms for university application. From the questionnaire data and from the school
based focus group interviews with the pupils I had learned about their post-18
hopes, plans and concerns. During the interviews with the families it quickly
became evident that much of this information was unknown to parents and what
was known was often limited and lacked any real depth. These interviews
demonstrated the extent to which many of the young people were choosing to
withhold information from their parents (Amato, 1994). Parents have a limited
knowledge about what actually goes on in schools and rely on their children to pass
on information. However as Connell et al (1982:54) noted 'kids may tell them a lot
or a little. If a lot it is of course filtered by what kids think is fit for their parents'
ears. If a little parents have only infrequent contacts with teachers, casual
discussions with other parents and school reports to fill out the picture'. I found
that the young people in the study often 'filtered' information from school before
sharing it with their parents. In some instances this was because they felt it was just
'not worth passing on'. In other cases pupils felt that they were able to make
decisions for themselves and did not require any help, or interestingly, they had
recognized that their parents lacked the necessary competencies to engage with the
choice process and so would not be able to advise them.

During the family interviews parents were asked if they knew the extent
of the HE guidance that the respective school or college provided in order to help
prepare their children to engage with the university choices. The Clarke family is
middle class, Victoria is their only child and a pupil at Redcoats School. The
response from Mr Clarke was fairly typical, reflecting the lack of involvement and
limited awareness of school life that is a common pattern in adolescence

We are not so much involved now, we don't know so much about it no. Not
like when she was at the Blessed Virgin School. When she was there we were
involved with things all the time, but since she has gone to this school, no not
really we are not involved so much no.
(Mr Clarke)

A number of parents saw this distancing as a natural part of growing up,
that young people want to make their own decisions and make up their own minds
rather than involving their parents. In the family interviews I heard from a number
of parents how they were making efforts to allow the 'children' to mature and gain
their independence. These comments reflect this recognition:

We don't hear much about university at all, though, really. And, anyway we have no idea what is going on at school, no idea at all. He's very laid back and I think he feels that the less he can say the better really. It's is very much a case that for him he's been there, done it and got the Tee shirt!
(Mr Jones, son David a pupil at Ysgol Bryn Alun)

Well, Louise doesn't want, well, she doesn't really want help from us. She wants to do her own thing, make her decisions for herself. I know of course that she has got to grow up, got to learn to live by herself, make her own decisions which is what she is trying to do.
(Mrs Hughes, daughter Louise, pupil at Jenkin High)

We are not involved a great deal. I'm not really aware of much that's happening. I don't think that the information comes that readily from her if you get me...I'm sure that if we felt the need to know more I would get my questions answered but well...
(Mrs Smith, daughter Caitlin, pupil at St Non's School)

Really I know only what Joanne has told me. They did have a very good sixth form orientation evening before the sixth form started and we have been to a meeting about higher education. That was very useful, but I will, well we will, back the girls in whatever it is that they want to do. But I feel that I take a very superficial interest in what is offered to them at school because. I know that is what she wants. Joanne has various ideas of what she wants to do and so rather than give a pressured performance for the girls, well we stay back I think that they need to find out about things in their own way.
(Mrs Parker, daughter Joanne, pupil at Brangwyn Hall)

In her study of 'good' schools in the USA, Lightfoot (1983:23) noted that, 'parents were often excluded from high school life because of bureaucratic procedures or their own attempts to keep clear the boundary between home and school. The offspring are typically silent on the subject of school life'. Even when parents are allowed access to some details about the daily life in schools, 'there is disparity in the information and the levels of awareness of different socio-economic groups' (Sidgewick et al, 1994:469). Reliance on parents to be actively involved in the choice process, 'presupposes possession of the correct code' (Bourdieu and Passeron, 1990:51). But as Ball (1994:157) has noted 'if the school is considered as an arena where parents and children compete as teams for scarce rewards, then many pupils are seriously handicapped by the lack of knowledge and expertise, and of interest, of their parents'. When they were attempting to move into the higher education 'arena' I found that for a number of parents even the UCAS process was *terra incognito*. As I heard in the family interviews:

I haven't really thrown my brains at it because I assumed that this is the sort of thing that happened after you obtained the A-level results, I mean I didn't know that this sort of thing had to be done now.
(Mr Bateman, son Glyn, pupil at Cardinal Gwyn College)

> Well we looked at that book [the UCAS handbook]. Yes she showed us that
> and the prospectuses like and well I looked at them until my head was
> spinning, the books and the forms and all that.
> (Mrs Lang, daughter Stacy, pupil at Regent High School)

Allatt (1993:142) has argued that 'privilege is not automatically
transmitted but depends upon purposeful activity directed towards the maintenance
of class position and the prevention of downward mobility'. In my study I found
that some families were making considerable efforts to 'keep up' with the activities
provided by the school to facilitate HE access for their children. I found that the
father frequently emerged as the more dominant facilitator:

> Well, I am very much involved in his A level education, much to Mark's
> annoyance, really, I think. Yes, to his annoyance, perhaps I poke my nose in
> *too* much. But I try to keep up with it all.
> (Mr Istance)

> I do make an effort to keep up with it yea…Yes I *do*. I mean I think it's
> important to know what's what. I make a point of getting to grips with what's
> what.
> (Mr Smart)

Most pupils expressed the feeling that they were not intentionally omitting
to tell their parents about the guidance that they were getting from school. Rather,
they felt either that they could deal with it without involving the family, or else it
was of little relevance to the choosing process and so not worth repeating. In the
interview with the Jones family, David said:

> It's not that I don't want to tell them [the parents] things its just there's not a
> lot to tell really. There is not a lot they can do, so what's the point. But I don't
> think the school is to blame because I don't see that there is much that they
> can really do. You know, I think it's more like up to you, like it's something
> that you have got to get on with. They [the school] are quite good because
> they have the computer set up and you can go to that and find out all about the
> different universities and that.
> (David Jones)

Most of the parents I spoke to saw university as an exciting prospect for
their children. They were proud of their academic ambitions and determined to
support them in their choices. For the middle-class families there were· clear, if
implicit assumptions that going to university was an 'automatic' next step in the
educational pathway, as these fathers stressed:

> I think it's a must in this day and age. In terms of her career and well,
> anything that she wants to do with her life. I mean *these* are the important
> years.
> (Mr Clarke)

Well in some ways it's a natural progression you know. It doesn't have to be but, well, in some ways I would like to see him do it because he doesn't really know what he wants to do with his life. Well I can understand and sympathize with that and I think you know that to have three years sound academic study will be the best thing he can do. I am not keen on these years off to go and find yourself and all that kind of thing. I mean that's my point of view but of course he can do what he feels like...well, whatever he wants to do. If he wants to leave school well, he can leave school, I am not totally given up to higher education. In fact, most of the people in my generation who didn't go on into higher education well they are in far better financial circumstances than I am. But then I am of the valley grammar school ethic you know you keep on going up the ladder until you fall off. But if I look back on the people who were in school with me, those who didn't go on into teaching of one form or another but joined the local council, or became hospital administrators etc. etc. well they are making their fortunes. But, well, he is clever, he is doing double maths and physics so it seems only natural for him to look at universities you know.

(Mr Joyce)

Some lack of involvement with school matters and a relinquishing of control on the part of the parent can be regarded as part of the gradual transition from childhood to adulthood. Social capital is acquired and transmitted through social networks and shared identities that enable access to information and resources and common values within the family. In middle-class families particular emphasis attached to the development of responsibility and individualism in the young person. It seemed to be a strategy that allowed the transference of responsibility from parent to young adult. However 'as well as being graduated, this transfer was set within a framework of shared assumptions, expectations and objectives' (Allatt, 1993:150). In consequence a parent choosing to step back from being actively involved in the HE process would be securely underpinned by a confidence that their child would do the 'right' thing. In some families there were implicit assumptions regarding higher education that served to make choices invisible. For many of the young people in the study, the decision to apply to university has been a taken for granted event which has been 'too true to warrant discussion'. Nevertheless, it has proved to be 'a powerful, if silent discourse which has served to inform coherent meanings' (Douglas, 1975:34). As the focus group interviews revealed:

I think my parents just *expect* it and I've come to expect it as well, if you get me. I mean they spend *so long* saying 'when you are at university' that you don't think that there *is* anything else.
(Lisa)

I think that they want me to be happy. But *they* see happiness as my going to university. Certainly that's *their* happiness.
(Coral)

> It's not like they [parents] pressure you. I mean they don't say 'oh you have to
> go to university'. But it's the *unsaid* pressure, you just know it's there.
> (Felicity)

Barthes (1973:11) would argue that discourses such as these fall into the category of 'what goes without saying'. They are part of the *habitus* for 'people like us'. When interviewed, these parents were sure that they had placed no pressure on their child to remain in post compulsory education or to go onto apply for a place at university. They spoke of the child being free to make his or her own decisions. However, as Allatt (1996:173) points out, this aspect of invisibility, which is 'entwined in the cultural strands of the family history', ensures that the power of the discourse lies in the silence which surrounds it. This is exemplified in these extracts from some of the interviews which I conducted with middle class families, where parents made it quite plain that they could rely on their child to 'get it right':

> Joanna is the youngest of our three girls. The eldest has been to university and
> now the middle one is going to university having had a gap year. I will, well,
> we both will, back the girls in whatever it is that they want to do. But I feel
> that I take a very superficial interest in what is offered rather than giving
> pressured performance for the girls. I mean as far as Joanna is concerned, well
> *she* will decide what's *right*.
> (Mrs Parker, daughter Joanna, pupil at Brangwyn Hall)

Focusing on the attitudes of some middle-class families towards Oxbridge applications, I found that my findings replicated by Power et al (2003:88) who noted that Oxbridge was not only an aspiration, 'but something of a family tradition'. One mother told me:

> Well, we have just always *assumed* that she will go [to university]. My
> husband is in the university, and his father was a professor at the university.
> My husband just assumes that...well, he did the third year of his course at
> Cambridge and he just feels, well we both do, that it would be better for her to
> go to Cambridge.
> (Mrs Hughes, daughter Louise, pupil at Jenkin High)

Ball et al (2003:90) also noted how middle class students reported a sense of identification with particular universities, as one student (Anick) told them:

> I love it and I visited a few universities and also we've got friends there so
> I've been to Oxford. And to be honest it's the only place that I felt I could be.
> I clicked with the place...and it just happens to be Oxford.

For the middle classes, this notion of education as some sort of preordained route beginning at primary school and continuing on through to university is not new. Indeed, one middle class parent in Huddersfield in the 1950s reported to Jackson and Marsden (1962:40) that:

Cambridge has always been in the family somehow,...that's why I wanted Shirley to go. I had an uncle who discovered a star. He used to spend his time lying outside in ditches...and he discovered this star. And they adopted it at Cambridge or something like that - so Cambridge was in the family.

Education can be regarded as a variable commodity, a 'quality' product which can be purchased in order to ensure social and cultural reproduction, (Bourdieu, 1986). However, for the middle class parent, their investment in a 'good education' brings with it an implicit assumption that providing the 'better' start and so enabling the individual to make the most of themselves, demands a reciprocity in terms of effort. As Allatt (1993:153) notes 'individualism was contained, while permitting it to flourish'. As Jackson and Marsden (1962:32) noted in their study:

The parents do not feel that their sons or daughters have to be brilliant intellectuals in order to carry off high educational prizes. They believe that such things are well within the grasp of *any* energetic boy or girl provided that they go cannily and whole-heartedly to work.

Within the current expanded and highly differentiated university sector, 'success' is not only expressed in terms of entry to university but in terms of the status and ranking of the course and the institution selected. Parents are aware of the educational advantages that can be anticipated when they invest in a 'good' school (Walford, 1990; Delamont, 1996). Those pupils in the private schools in my study were conscious of the extent to which their parents had already invested in their education. In the focus group interview at Brangwyn Hall pupils told me:

I think that if parents have paid for your education 'till now, they don't expect you to drop out.
(Helena, pupil at Brangwyn Hall)

People think that because you go to a school like this that you have loads of money. It's not necessarily true. I mean my parents put money away, they saved for this. But they haven't got much *now*.
(Patsy, pupil at Brangwyn Hall)

Yes that's the thing, we are not all well off, and so having struggled to pay the school fees I think they [the parents] would be really upset if I didn't want to go on.
(Jody, pupil at Brangwyn Hall)

For middle class families in the 1950s, there was no need for discussions regarding post-compulsory educational trajectories, as Jackson and Marsden (1962:153) found, 'they [the middle class] had a clear idea of where they were going and how to get there'. More than 40 years on the situation was remarkably similar, as the focus group discussions at Brangwyn Hall indicate:

Really, the expectation and the assumptions are there all along. And that's what you come to see as the norm when you go to a school like *this*

[Brangwyn Hall]. Right from the first year you are aware of the people above you going onto university. It's the done thing, I know my parents would be *really disappointed* if I didn't go. Both my brothers are at university and they just expect that I will follow on.
(Jody, pupil at Brangwyn Hall)

But when you think about it we don't really know anything else do we? I mean we came *here* and *saw* how it was. Our parents clearly knew what they were doing in sending us here, knew what we would achieve. You do your A-levels and go on to university. That's the way it is here.
(May, pupil at Brangwyn Hall)

A number of studies have addressed the ways in which middle class families use 'good' schools to gain educational advantages and to reproduce cultural capital (Delamont, 1984; Roker, 1993; Gewirtz et al, 1995). For those in the working-class, studies have shown how the choice of school can reflect and construct inequality (Ball et al, 2003; Archer et al, 2003). I have discussed the ways in which schools, sixth form and further education colleges can impact on the quality and range of HE engagement and choices in Chapter Five. Jackson and Marsden (1962:131) noted that, even among the working class families with no prior experiences of higher education, 'there was a sense of educational excitement and ambition engendered by the new world of the grammar school'. For the working class parents of the 1990s, as the university becomes the 'new world' the excitement levels remain high even if the ambitions cannot be fully articulated. This came through clearly during the focus group interviews with pupils and in the interviews with the families:

Well my parents are really chuffed about it, they think it's great. I mean they keep on saying to me oh, we want what's best for you, we want you to do all the things we didn't have a chance to do.
(Clare, pupil at Argoed College)

Mine are really keen for me to go, I mean they think uni is a big deal like, but they are pleased, they want me to get on.
(Pete, pupil at Cardinal Gwyn College)

However, while clearly very proud, some parents were a little overwhelmed by the thought of having a 'student' in the family:

Well I am thrilled to bits really that he wants it, amazed like, but delighted that he has got it in him and he wants to go on, its brilliant.
(Mrs Barry, son Jason, pupil at Argoed College)

I'm pleased. Chuffed to death to be honest, because it was something that was never available to me and I would, well I always thought that I would like my children to go to university. So I am pleased. Pleased as Punch that he is going to go. I mean I have been sort of pushing him for it like all the time.
(Mr Bateman, son Glyn, pupil at Cardinal Gwyn College)

In some instances the extent of the parents naiveté about the university system was quite shocking. Yet with little or no knowledge of the sector they were blindly attempting to engage with the access process.

Playing the Game Without Knowing the Rules

During the past 40 years considerable policy initiatives have been implemented designed to increase participation and widen access to higher education. However, my study has found that despite the political rhetoric of inclusivity, there are still marked inequalities both in terms of working class under representation and the patterns of participation. Research has shown that many young people, particularly those from working class backgrounds lack information about higher education (Archer et al, 2003; Connor and Dewson, 2001). In my study in south Wales, I found a number of working-class parents whose attitudes and experiences bear a striking similarity to the working class parents in Huddersfield who formed part of the work by Jackson and Marsden (1962). This study demonstrate the ways in which some families are ill equipped to engage with the rigours of choice in the higher education market. For families engaging with university applications for the first time the process is daunting. Many parents feel that they are out of their depth and in some instances that these matters are best left to the 'experts'. For them, any attempt to engage with the higher education system, however peripheral, is very much a voyage into the unknown. Jackson and Marsden (1962:132) noted that the working-class parents whose children had gone to the grammar school found 'there was a growing sense that the child was out on its own, moving into worlds to which the parents had no access'. This lack of familiarity with the system had serious implications for some pupils as their parents told Jackson and Marsden (1962:153). Mrs Giles said of her daughter:

> She didn't find out till she was in her last year [in school] that she needed this Latin. She'd no idea before then.

and Mr Abbott reported that:

> The master said, he can't go because he hasn't got the Latin. Well nobody knew owt about that until right at the end. He couldn't go. Flat!

Some 40 years on, I found parallels in terms of working class families being unable to make informed choices. For many families perhaps the most obvious way to get advice would be to contact their child's school. In the 1950s, opportunities to visit the schools and speak to staff were only taken up by more middle class parents. As Jackson and Marsden (1962:134) note, it was 'the more prosperous, and some of those who had grammar school experience themselves' who felt confident enough to ask for information. In the previous chapter I have discussed how a lack of any formal guidance led Jason Barry to reconsider his A-level options and repeat his lower sixth year. When I spoke to Jason and his mother Mrs Barry she told me how unhappy her son had been during the first year of his A-level course, telling her from a very early stage that he felt he had taken the wrong options. However, she went on to say:

> You don't like to interfere really, I mean you think that they [staff at Argoed College] know don't you? But well [to Jason] you were so disillusioned like really, weren't you?
> (Mrs Barry, son Jason, student at Argoed College)

Mrs Barry had no experience of post compulsory education and no knowledge of A-level subjects, or the implications of subject choices for university entry. She recognized that she was unable to advise Jason, but lacked the necessary cultural competencies to enable her to engage with staff at the College or to seek information from a different source. Although she had recognized that 'something was wrong', she 'trusted' in the system and relied on the 'experts' at the college to 'get it right'. Where working class parents had attended an open evening at a school or college. it was most often the case that only one parent, usually the mother, had done so. This too is a finding shared with the Jackson and Marsden (1962) working class sample. As I heard in the interviews with these families:

> To be fair to the wife she will usually go to the school, to meetings and parents nights and relay the information back to me.
> (Mr Lang, daughter Stacy, pupil at Regent High)

Many of the young people in the study who were from families making first time applications to higher education were conscious of their parents lack of awareness of the system. As Briony, from Argoed College, commented during a focus group interview:

> I know my mum would like me to go, but I'm the oldest and they don't have any experience of it. I mean, they don't really know anything about it. It's a new experience in our family. They haven't got a clue about what to do. I have to tell them the bits I know.

Similarly Dave, a pupil at Llanover School, recognized that his parents were both proud and perplexed by the thought of his applying to university.

> My parents don't know much about it like, but they are keen for me to go. I mean I'll be the brains of our family, because no one else has been. But they don't really know much about it so it's up to me to tell them.

I saw this mixture of working class pride and bewilderment demonstrated during an interview with the Lang family (daughter Stacy, a pupil at Regent High School).

Mrs Lang: No we haven't done any of that studying like. This is the first one with all the brains aren't you? She is the first of my mother's grandchildren to go to university so we are all really proud of her.

Note the very particular way in which Mrs Lang expresses her pride by locating her daughter within an extended matriarchal framework in order to identify her 'difference'. Working class parents regard a university degree as necessary now because of changes in the labour market (David et al, 2003). As Mr Lang noted higher education would offered Stacy the opportunity to 'better herself':

Mr Lang: I left school as early as I could and then I worked. Well Stacy is keen to go on and study and improve herself and that's great. We are really pleased that she wants to do it. She is the first one in the family to want to go to university and that's a good thing. Really it means she can get on.

Parents, who had not been in further or higher education themselves, were often detached from the decision-making process. In some instances because their children, recognising their lack of competence chose to bypass them and seek other 'more expert' help. But also these working class parents were themselves reticent, apprehensive even, about engaging with the complexities of system in which they were unsighted. Reay (1998:103) notes that 'class does seem to have significant effects and appears to be linked to aspects of cultural capital such as confidence, information about available educational provision, assertiveness and a sense of entitlement'. In my study, neither the White family, nor Mrs Barry attended parent evenings at Argoed College, nor had they been involved in the discussions about subject options and university choices with the personal tutors. Even after it became apparent that Jason and Michael were experiencing difficulties and were unhappy with their subject choices, (see Chapter Five) each family had relied on their son to 'sort it out'. There was a deliberate acknowledged that they were out of their depth and a recognition of the 'child as expert' (Reay and Ball, 1998).

In their study Jackson and Marsden (1962:153) noted that the unfamiliarity of the academic curriculum offered to grammar school pupils ensured that 'many of even the most ambitious [working class] parents had, in a sense, been left behind'. Talking to working class parents some 40 years on it became apparent that they too were totally bewildered by the complexity of an unfamiliar system. This was illustrated during the interview with the Bateman family, they live in a run down inner city area, Mr Bateman was unemployed and Mrs Bateman worked part time in a local corner shop. Their son Glyn attended the Cardinal Gwyn Tertiary College and was studying A-level English, History and Computer Science. I knew from my earlier research that Glyn had discussed his various HE options with his form tutor. He wanted to study computing and had completed a draft of the UCAS form before my visit to the family. He had decided having pragmatically considered the cost implications, to restrict his choices to his own locality. However, during the family interview Glyn's father, Mr Bateman, told me:

We haven't really been involved in it [the UCAS application process]. No, well I, really, uhm I mean basically I know there are forms to be filled in for higher education if you apply for it. Well there's grants to be applied for and all sorts of things. There are all sorts of things to be taken into consideration...I just thought that it was something that you...well, that had to be done *after* he got his A level results and *knew* he would be *allowed* to go to university. You know, if he could be given a place. I didn't expect any of *this*. I didn't know that there was this sort of preparatory work which was all piling up.

(Mr Bateman, son Glyn, pupil at Cardinal Gwyn College)

This sense of almost total bewilderment with the entire university entrance procedure among working class families was also noted by Jackson ad Marsden (1962:154). They noted that,

For many young people progress into higher education occurred from a home in which the elements of sheer ignorance, general perplexity or mere lack of initiative are hard to disentangle.

For them, the consequences were that some students were 'slow in putting in application forms' since 'some families knew nothing of closing dates or waiting lists'. Talking to the Bateman family, it was clear that these same comments could equally well apply to the working class parents in my study in the late 1990s. Yet it is perfectly logical for Mr Bateman should have assumed that he had no need to even consider any of the issues associated with choosing a university *before* Glyn knew the outcome of examinations he was to sit some nine months later. However, this seemingly rational 'common sense' approach to the application procedure is far removed from the reality of the UCAS system, as his son Glyn had already recognized. In the 1950s Jackson and Marsden reported that grammar school staff *assumed* that *all* parents and pupils could access the key information about entry requirements, grants and scholarships. However these first generation working class entrants to university came from families who were unconsciously incompetent. Not only did they not know, but also they did not know that they did not know and so therefore, couldn't ask. The working class pupils who attended grammar schools quickly recognized the educational gulf that was developing between them and their parents. Their newly acquired competencies merely underlined the limited extent of their parents; education. Jackson and Marsden (1962:132) noted of one young man that 'the natural respect which he had for his parents lay uneasily alongside his own clearer mastery of the new skills'. These young people were conscious of the limited role that their parents could play in facilitating their transition to higher education. In my study, a number of young people from working class families found it necessary to by-pass their parents and to rely on the school to play the active part in facilitating their progress to HE. In the interview with the Bateman family, Glyn told me:

Glyn: Well I have done a lot of it by myself, 'cos they [the parents] don't know about it like and Mr Howells, the Head of Careers, well he's good. If we want we can get an appointment with him. I actually had an appointment in, I think it was March and he arranged to help me with it [the application process]. And my form tutor, well, he has been good, he teaches me for computer studies too so that's helped. Well I have put down computer science courses and computer studies with philosophy and another with religious studies. I have gone for the ones at Cardiff and Pontypridd [The University of Glamorgan]. I put Swansea and Aberystwyth but well Aberystwyth is quite far, but well I suppose, really when it came to it, I just put Aberystwyth down as an option. Really, I would prefer to live at home and go to university here or Pontypridd [University of Glamorgan]. I mean, I want to stay at home because, well because I know that financially it makes sense. I would rather stay at home. They [staff at Argoed College] told us generally about things, about how much it all costs, so I know about that. I have got all the forms and that [the UCAS information] upstairs. I know that I can go back to them and look at all the details once I have applied.

LP: Have you shown your parents the forms, and talked it over with them?

Glyn: No they are just upstairs. I mean, I know the ones I really want. I mean the course I would like and I know really that I want to go to university here because, like, I say it makes sense financially. So there is not much to tell them. I have filled out a, well, a rough copy one, [UCAS form] and done my personal statement in section ten so that's all sorted. It's been ready since last week. It's just a case of, well, really, getting it done now. But it's all been done in college, really.

Glyn was conscious of the fact that his parents have no understanding of the procedure for applying to higher education or any real awareness of the higher education system itself. He chose to bypass them entirely and to rely on the advice from his teachers, coupled with his awareness of his family's financial circumstances, which he felt necessitated his choosing to study close to home. Glyn was a 'bright' pupil with predicted grades of an 'A' and two 'Bs' but as Hatcher (1998:10) notes 'the costs of education bear more heavily on working class families and have their greatest effects on transition choices after the end of compulsory schooling'. For some students like Glyn, financial and other external constraints impact on the choice process and 'university is viewed from the outside' (Ball et al, 2002:57) As Glyn told me during the interview:

I did look at the massive book from UCAS, you know and then I looked at another book, I think it's like a potted guide. But really, because I am staying in Wales, well that wasn't a great deal of use because it focused on different areas. I will stay here, I want to stay in Wales, well in Cardiff really. I'll keep my part time job and stay with my family. It's much cheaper that way, living at home like and not having the expenses. And I would want to keep my job with Sainsburys when I was in university and get some money that way.

These attitude contrasts with those of more middle class families where the parents are 'used to presenting themselves and evaluating others through talk' (Ball, 2003:64). They are prepared to visit schools and challenge the staff about educational decisions. This level of social confidence was illustrated by Jackson and Marsden (1962:45) who noted that Mr Chapman, one of the fathers in their study, was not prepared to accept the decision that his daughter could not study O-level maths. His daughter Helen recalled his telling her:

> You've got to do maths. Absolutely necessary. You go back and tell the headmistress that you are doing it.

In the 1990s, talking to families about possible disagreements with the schools, one middle class father told me,

> If ever there is a problem at school with any member of staff it's me isn't it? I'm the guy to see to it. She knows I'm the more forceful character. *I'll* hit the nail on the head.
> (Mr James, daughter Penny, pupil at Redcoats School)

Changing to Stand Still

This chapter has begun to identify the different ways in which class membership can enable [or not] family groups to work with school in order to facilitate and maximize university choices. Identifying inequalities in the patterns of participation in education is not a new phenomenon. Despite an expansionist agenda over the past 50 years, successive studies have 'confirmed the continuing, indeed increasing overall dominance of the middle classes in HE' (Ball et al, 2002:53). Whilst this book aims to provide some illustrative accounts of the ways in which families and schools are instrumental in shaping and facilitating choices, it is important to stress that middle and working class categories and characteristics are neither homogeneous nor mutually exclusive. Rather the study seeks to demonstrates the fuzziness that exists in relation to the educational experiences and the market competencies both inter and intra social classes. While class based typologies of both families and schools are developed in order to consider the ways in which choices are informed (Chapter 9) like Gewirtz et al (1995:24) my intention is to illustrate the ways in which 'class is an indicator rather than a determinant of family traits'. The impact of individual social and institutional biographies is explored further in the next two chapters. In both the focus is on the gendered nature of the family in the choice process and the ways in which cultural capital is utilized and transformed in order to produce or reproduce educational advantages and privileges. While the mother adopts a more the supportive role, it is the father who becomes more significant as a facilitator in the choice process. In the following chapter, the 1960s research on the families in South Wales (Barker, 1972; Leonard, 1980) is considered in light of these new data on higher education choices. It is argued that the strategic decisions by parents to 'keep close' and 'spoil' their children identified then have been replicated in relation to post-18 choice now and have class based implications in terms of social reproduction.

Chapter 7

Parental Roles, Locality and Choice

The interconnectedness of the family and educational achievement has been well documented (Halsey, Heath and Ridge, 1980) as has the impact of education reforms on parental involvement and choice (Edwards, Fitz and Whitty, 1989; Coldron and Boulton, 1991; Gewirtz et al, 1995; Ball, 2003). However where researchers have considered the role of the parents in relation to school choice, either the parental roles have been undifferentiated and the research has located parents as an 'ungendered category' (David, 1993:158) or the focus has been on the mother. I want to consider the way in which the roles, actions and activities of parents involved in the higher education choice process are gendered. I want also to explore the relationship between social class, localism and the HE market continuing to theorize through the work of Bourdieu (1977) on cultural capital and habitus between family groups. The work of Basil Bernstein (1977) on 'personal and positional' families is also helpful in exploring the differences in parental roles. These are viewed in relation to the ways in which different groups of parents are able to engage with the process and successfully facilitate access higher education choices, while others are left floundering, with little or no options for choice. The data in my study suggest that, at the level of engagement with the HE market, the father assumes a more prominent role than has been previously identified in the school choice research. The mother, while still visible, takes on more routine roles, often researching options and driving the young people to university open days. These roles are discussed later in the chapter.

Urban sociology, as it developed in the 1960s, owes much to the tradition of the Chicago School and the work of Burgess, Park and Wirth. Studies have observed the close family networks and patterns of social and economic mobility, which occur within communities. Areas of study have been diverse and include intergenerational relationships in Italy (Pitkin, 1985), kinship patterns in east London, Willmott and Young (1962) and the Inuit in the Canadian northern territories (Kleinfeld, 1979). In South Wales, the tradition of urban sociology developed through the community studies research which came out of the 'Swansea School' and the work of Rosser and Harris (1965) which focused on the effects of urbanisation and social and economic change in the Swansea valley. Leonard (1990:39) has criticized the cosy 'cereal box' imagery portrayed in much of the early family studies work suggesting that:

> Marriage was seen as normative and inevitable and seemingly there were no homosexuals to be found in any communities in the British Isles from 1930 to 1970.

However these studies did provide us with snapshots of family life and allowed for intergenerational relationships to be made visible. A number of changes in gendered relationships and gendered expectations have occurred over the past three decades and I want to consider the impact of these changes on family practices and compare parental attitudes then and now in relation to decision-making and leaving home, relating it to contemporary issues of HE markets and university choice.

Keeping Close: The Norms of Locality

The notion of 'home' takes on a wider and stronger definition than simply that of the place where the young person lives. It is not merely an address, the town, the region or the country where one is born and raised. Home is an emotive term, representative of a complex relationship between family members, their norms and values. Children's leaving home is a complex business and 'often does not entail a complete once and for all break' (Morgan, 1996:181). In the late 1960s a study of families in the Swansea valley disputed the widely held assumptions that teenagers then were economically well off, sexually permissive and anxious to break their ties with home and family, preferring to live independently (Barker, 1972; Leonard, 1980). Her study found that rather than being anxious to leave home at the earliest opportunity, the majority of young men and women (86 per cent and 90 per cent respectively) continued to live with their parents until they married. Young people saw home in terms of identity and belonging with 'the norm of locality equal to that of social class' (Barker, 1972:574). Marriage legitimized the act of leaving home, to have moved out before then, either to live alone or with peers, would have been regarded as a sleight on the family. The study, in the 1960s found that even after marriage decisions to live away from the locality were 'exclusively related to the labour market', and young people commented that parents 'are sad to see us go, even though we are bettering ourselves' (Barker, 1972:78).

Even when young people needed to study or train elsewhere, they chose to return to the family home at weekends. Those young people who were students at Swansea University continued to live at home with their parents. Barker noted that while some parents, particularly those from the middle class, expressed values through set phrases such as 'you have to let them go' and 'you can't keep them tied to your apron strings', on balance, the aim was to 'keep them close'. In some instances parents exerted pressure on their children not to accept particular opportunities that required them to move. One women, the daughter of a manual worker, who had studied at Swansea University told Barker (1972:576):

> I had thought of the L.S.E [London School of Economics] but my father went berserk. He would have been very hurt. He thought it very selfish and not good for a girl to go away.

The study of 43 adolescent girls in Swansea (Ward, 1976) mirrored Barker's (1972) findings in relation to parents attitudes to their children and the desire to 'keep them close'. Both studies found that the young people and their parents were anxious to explain and justify the circumstances in cases where this closeness has not happened, or to counter suggestions that the parents were over possessive when it had occurred. The study by Ward (1976) found the parental home was referred to as a known 'territory' and reported (p.33) that few girls had 'any ideas of even wanting to move out into a flat or lodgings'. As these studies show for families where their adult children continue to live at home there is both a dependency and homogeneity in the cultural setting. In the Swansea Valley it seemed that 'educational achievement was valued rather less than affectivity, specifically less than 'keeping close' both before and after marriage' (Barker, 1972:579). Parents utilized a variety of permissive devices in order to maintain these close relationships with their children. These were reflected in their attitudes towards domestic chores, the school leaving age and money financial arrangements. Each of these 'spoiling' tactics resulted in these young people having an economic, social and psychological dependency on the parent. Unlike England Wales does not have a tradition of boarding school education and in the 1960s, most children attended their local schools. With a buoyant labour market, many parents lacked an instrumentalist approach towards post compulsory education, 'spoiling' their children by allowing them to leave school at the earliest opportunity if they were entering employment (Barker, 1972). The spoiling extended to parents' attitudes towards money, with children from a relatively young age being routinely provided with pocket money that they were not required to earn. Parents openly acknowledged their indulgences as Barker (1972:581) heard from one mother:

> Her father gives her some every week, [a few shillings] and if she wanted more she came and asked me. Spoilt she was.

This financial 'spoiling' continued into young adulthood. Unlike families in the north of England (Millward, 1968) which found a formalized situation with regard to wage earning young adults paying for towards their board and loading expenses. In Swansea negotiations took place, usually with the mother, over exactly how much money would be contributed towards the family budget. But the agreed amount was, usually insufficient to cover their living costs and mothers commented that they were helping their children by taking very little money from them. Barker also found that mothers contributed towards the savings of engaged and married couples, frequently loaning their married children money to supplement their housekeeping. The gifting of money from parents to their children at all ages and stages of their lives was a commonly reported 'spoiling' strategy, as Barker (1972:582) heard from one young woman:

> When my sister started work she only got £2.15s [£2.75p] She said she'd give 15s [75p]. My mother told her to go away and live on her £2.15s. So she went to my aunty's. She (the aunt) said she'd want £2.5s[£2.25p]. So my sister came back and gave it all to my mother. She (my sister) knew that she would get it back by the end of the week.

However this South Wales 'spoiling' extended beyond economic help. The gendered nature of domestic labour saw mothers routinely cooking, washing, ironing and cleaning for their families and although girls did more to help around the house than boys even this was relatively little. Young people felt that their parents did not expect them to help with household chores and this contributed to their decisions to continue to live at home. One young man commenting to Barker that 'he knew when he was well off'. Many of these mothers worked part-time which provided them with the money to enable the 'spoiling' to continue. They were at home to look after the family when required but earned sufficient money to spend on luxuries for their adult children. Even after marriage many young couple set up home near their parents and the mother would continue to help with the domestic chores. Rosser and Harris (1965:12) have also typified the Welsh 'mam'. They found that, in spite of increased opportunities for social mobility and economic affluence, after marriage, children continued as extended family units, living in close proximity to their parents and noted that 'it was the her role as the 'mam' to hold them together'. Rosser and Harris also found that the kinship rituals of this valley community reinforced the centrality of the mother figure. Frequent, usually daily, return visits to the family home by the married children, and shared family meals served to reinforce a sense of kinship and close knit unity. However, such protracted levels of contact with children can serve as a double bind, while it ensured companionship for her in her old age, it also successfully 'tied' her to a role of domesticity within the home.

The themes of keeping close and spoiling were replicated some 30 years on when I interviewed families about their HE choices. They were expressed by comments like those of the Lang family when I interviewed them, as their daughter Stacy told me:

> Oh I think I really want to live at home, I mean it's much cheaper and I don't want to leave my mum do I? She spoils me. Well her and my dad they just spoil me whatever I want well it's mine really.

As Leonard (1980) notes, most parents love and care for their children and try to give them what they can. Nevertheless, she found that for the families in her study affectivity, dependency and spoiling were the dominant values. The concept of 'spoiling' was demonstrated through an excessive emphasis on giving at a level of indulgence that was excessive compares with what might reasonably be expected in a child/parent relationship. Rather, Leonard (1980:64) suggests that, 'this 'spoiling' holds the elementary family together at a time of potential schism'. The internal dynamics of the family groups attempting to ensure that childhood dependency continues into adulthood. But such excessive gift exchanges are an effective mechanism of control (Mauss, 1954). If gifts are offered to such an extent that the giving is over and above what might reasonably be expected, then exchange theory could allow that this 'spoiling' in effects provides the giver [parents] some rights [say] in the recipients [children's] lives. This ensures a continued family kinship beyond adolescence and into adulthood for parent, children and grandchildren. Now when the costs of higher education are spiralling, staying on in education places an increasingly high economic burden on many parents. Going to university may become the 'gift' as the child continues to enjoy the parental 'spoiling' in terms of continued financial and emotional support. However, this 'gifting' will become the prerogative of privileged groups since it will be beyond the economic, but not the emotional, means of many parents.

Families, Institutional Awareness and Choice

The fact that 'certain groups in society lack information about the opportunities that are available' (Thomas 2001:135) has already been discussed in earlier chapters in considering the ways in which families engage with teachers and schools in relation to subject choices at A level and the UCAS applications process. A number of those I spoke to, both parents and young people, from working class backgrounds were unaware of the ranking which exists among higher education institutions. In the focus group interviews I asked pupils if they were aware of any differences in the status of institutions and if they knew about league tables. I was told,

> Adrian: What about them? I didn't know they had them.
>
> Dave: What are *they* then?
>
> Sarah: Never heard of them.
> (Pupils at Llanover School)

If pupils from working class backgrounds were aware of rankings, they seemed not to appreciate their significance, as other pupils said:

> Diana: I don't really know about those (university rankings) and anyway I don't see the point in them really.
> (Pupil at Cardinal Gwyn College)
>
> Briony: The whole thing about which university to apply to and all that, I mean its just hard and it's time consuming innit?
>
> Chantelle: Yeah and its so far off, I mean it's a year and a half away.
>
> Briony: Yes and we don't want to have to worry about university and all that, not when we have only just started here in college.
> (Pupils at Argoed College)

In the family interview with the Lang family, their daughter Stacy told me:

> I know that like Oxford and Cambridge are like the top and they want really high grades and are snobby and that. But nothing else really, I think the school

did tell us about the polytechnics changing or something, but I'm not really sure what that means.
(Stacy Lang, pupil at Regent High)

Parents too, particularly those who had not stayed on beyond compulsory education, were also unaware of any, but the most obvious, differences in institutional status. As I heard in the family interviews:

Well, I am aware, I mean I know that there are leagues, obviously, I mean Cambridge and Oxford and that but, well, after that they sort of come down don't they and well they are much of a muchness aren't they?
(Mr Bateman, son Glyn, pupil at Cardinal Gwyn College)

I know about league tables with schools, but I wasn't aware of what they are, for university, well apart from Cambridge and Oxford which I think they have always had the speciality [sic] like you know. The others, well, I'm not sure I understand it all.
(Mrs Smith, Caitlin, pupil at St Non's)

These parents resemble the 'disconnected' school choosers identified in the London study (Gewirtz et al, 1995:45). Disconnected from the market they typically see universities as "much the same". The school choice research revealed those 'disconnected' parents had little awareness of any schools other than those in the locality. In my study some parents, notably working class and first time choosers lacked awareness of the wider market and the implications of choice at university level. They were anxious for their children to attend a local university since the same themes of safety, proximity and spoiling noted by Barker were replicated in my study. Just as one mother in the 1970s responded to the suggestion that her daughter might have moved away to study, telling Leonard (1980:51):

We'd have gone off our rocker, we've put in so much time over her childhood and all that we'd worry too much, be afraid that everything might not go right.

So, too, in the 1990s, working class parents, with no experience of higher education themselves and only limited knowledge of the system expressed similar fears for their children's safety, as they told me in interviews:

I wouldn't want her to go away, I don't know maybe I'm over possessive but I just wouldn't want her to go away. No, the thought of her going away, well...
(Mrs Thomas, daughter Maria, pupil at Llanover School)

You [to daughter] would rather be at home with me wouldn't you? You don't really want to go away from Cardiff at all do you?
(Mrs Lang, daughter Stacy, pupil at Regent High)

Even if parents recognized that part of the 'letting go' would be for their children to live in university accommodation, the local university allows the parents to maintain close contact, as Mr Smart noted:

I know he won't mind me saying this, but he's a little bit immature in the fact that he says 'oh I don't want to leave all my friends, the kids I hang around with'. Some of them are in the high school and some outside and Oh he loves it in Cardiff and he doesn't want to leave his friends and go to Hull or Plymouth or wherever else. Glasgow, wherever. I mean you can get home sick in some of these places. Whereas if he was in Swansea or Cardiff say then you can have your own flat or be in the hostel or whatever there and you can still get back home within the hour. So that's the way we have sorted out for looking and decided on the prospectuses that we have sent for.
(Mr Smart, son Alex, pupil at St Non's School)

Metz (1986) noted the extent of Black localism in America, with Black American pupils not wanting to attend the integrated Magnet schools. Similarly, many of the young people in this study were resistant to the idea of moving out of the area. This was not a result of any nationalistic attachment to Wales, rather it related to the 'home' region. As some pupils told me in the focus group interviews:

My mother keeps on saying she wants me to go to Cardiff, because she will miss me and she doesn't want to lose her kids, and well I am happy to stay here, 'cos I know the place and my friends are here and that.
(Tim, pupil at St Non's High School)

Well it would be weird, I'd feel odd, uncomfortable like. I wouldn't know people and I'd miss my family, I would want something that was familiar, a place that was right for me, somewhere not too far, somewhere in the area.
(Kerryanne, pupil at Llanover High School)

These sixth form pupils also recognized that living at home while they were at university would allow the 'spoiling' to continue both in financial terms and in the level of domestic support that 'mam' would continue to do for them. As I was told in school and home based interviews:

Well, it's cheaper isn't it? I mean you can live at home and sponge off your parents. Well, what I mean is they will pay the bills and your mum can do your washing and cooking.
(Sarah, pupil at Llanover School)

I don't want to go anywhere to far away from home 'cos I'll miss my mum too much. I don't really want to leave my mum and I want to be able to come home every weekend if I do go away.
(Stacy Lang, pupil at Regent High School)

If you stay in Cardiff and live at home like, it's great, I know my mam'll look after me like and do the washing and that, it'll be great, yeah great, a larff.
(Mark, pupil at Argoed College)

The notion of 'keeping close' and 'spoiling' (Leonard, 1980) also featured as a factor in choosing a local university. In the family interviews, I was told:

Well I mean at the moment she doesn't walk anywhere. Wherever she goes
we know and more to the point we take her if we can and she always gets a lift
home. I drive my taxi at night and if I can't pick her up then one of my mates
will. So she is used to being taken care of.
(Mr Lang, daughter Stacy, pupil at Regent High)

That is the main thing for us, she must be safe. Wherever she goes, she must
be. And we must feel confident that she is in the safest possible place.
Always.
(Mrs Smith, daughter Caitlin, pupil at St Non's School)

The idea that 'home' is a region was reinforced in the interview with the
Joyce family. They family are middle class and speak Welsh as their first language.
Rhys told me that he intended to apply only to Welsh universities and particularly
wanted to go to either Cardiff or Bangor. In the interview I heard:

Mr Joyce: My wife's mother, my mother in law, lives in Caernarfon and all
our holidays are spent there, so we are back and fore to Bangor. My wife, well
the family, has a farm in Llanfair PG which is about ten miles from Bangor,
so we are back and fore all the time and so that makes it a base really a...

Mrs Joyce: Well, it's a home from home really. And I think that Rhys is a
home bird, the sort of boy, well who doesn't particularly want to go away
from home. I think that if he was given the opportunity he would just stay at
home and stay on at school.
(Mr and Mrs Joyce, Rhys, pupil at Ysgol Bryn Alun)

Rhys agreed with these comments and acknowledged that he had made his
selections of institutions based on a combination of factors. Proximity to home,
institution and Welsh language options. Although wanting to be close to home he
also recognized the institution hierarchy within the federal university in Wales and
was instrumental in his choices.

I do want to stay close to home and Cardiff seems ideal, it's got a good
reputation, it's a Welsh uni, and offers me what I want in subjects without the
rubbish and worry of being away from home.
(Rhys Joyce, pupil at Ysgol Bryn Alun.)

The categories of selectors which I have found (see Chapter 9) correspond
well with the typologies identified in the school markets studies, which depicts
'disconnected choosers overwhelmingly working class' and the 'privileged/skilled
choosers overwhelmingly middle class'. In my study of higher education choice,
middle class parents knew about university rankings and were aware of their
significance and the hierarchy of status between the universities. In many cases
parents had briefed their children on what to look for and which questions to ask on
open days and visits to institutions. They were 'clued in to' the market and aware
that in many instances it would be advantageous to make application to a
institutions dependent upon status factors rather than proximity to home. Rather for

these families, choices were made in relation to social and cultural classifications and associations, choosing places for 'people like us'. Middle class parents also regarded moving away from home as the ideal way for young people to gain psychological, economic and social independence. They saw the move to university as the initial loosening of parental ties. This attitude was evident in the conversations I had with the Walsh family, whose son John is a pupil at Jenkin High School.

> Mr Walsh: I think he should be encouraged to leave home.

> Mrs Walsh: Oh yes that is part of it really isn't it, part of the experience.

> Mr Walsh: Yes we both did it. We felt the benefits of going away from home when you are 18 or 19. You don't want to be on top of your parents. So I can see why he wants to go away and we would encourage it.

For the middle classes choices are much more about the appropriateness of the university and the benefits to be gained from the whole experience. Distance was neither a threat to the safety of the young person nor a challenge to the stability of the family unit, as these quotes illustrate:

> Mr Clarke: She is not tied to our apron strings, uhm she was in India for two months in July and August. I mean we don't keep her wrapped up. I mean we are quite au fait with the idea of her going off to do her own thing. So if it means going to Newcastle or wherever, then that's fine.
> (Mr Clarke, daughter Victoria, pupil at Redcoats)

As the conversation with Gavin and his mother indicates, parents are anxious to stress that proximity to home should be neither a determinant nor a deterrent in the choice process.

> Gavin: Well as long as it's not right the way up in Scotland say, I mean I don't want it to be too far away because then I wouldn't be able to afford to come up and down a lot. But it would most probably be out of Wales, certainly away from Cardiff.

> Mrs Hutchins. That's fine I'm all for it. I would be quite happy if he went to Scotland (she laughs) no I would really. I think it's wonderful. I think the kids ought to go away. Tim, his elder brother, is up at Manchester and that's fine. The other two are younger, so there is time yet for them to choose. But that's what it's about really they must choose, do what they want, what's best for them.
> (Mrs Hutchins, son Gavin, pupil at Regent High)

Joanne is a pupil at Brangwyn Hall and for the Parker family choice would be unproblematic in terms of distance and financial costs as Mr Parker explained:

We don't mind where she goes, whatever is best. We will organize it, the getting her there and what not. It may be a bit of a juggling act with the time, because we are both working, but the cost is not the issue here.

Gewirtz et al (1995:25) note of the privileged/skilled choosers in their study that they tend 'to be orientated to high status, elite 'cosmopolitan' schools. This orientation continues as their children move on up to the university sector. The next section continues to focus on the family and to consider the ways in which gendered activities come into play as parents take on university challenge and act as facilitators in the choice process.

[Some] Fathers Know Best: Positioning the Parents

As has been noted earlier, the body of work on parental involvement and school choice has been largely ungendered. Where distinctions have been made these have focused largely on the role of the mother (David, 1993; Reay; 1998; Reay, 2000). In the previous section I have considered one way in which some working class mothers can play a significant part in influencing and restricting choices in terms of attachments to locality. However it is also useful to consider some other roles that may be cast for both fathers and mothers set against the issue of social class and access to information about higher education markets. As this and other work has shown, many working class young people lack information about higher education. In this study many are first generation university applicants whose families lack both confidence and competence to access such an unfamiliar field. In contrast many from middle class families who are familiar with the system, have access to the necessary social networks, competencies and skills to make informed choices. The family practices and spheres of influence are crucial since 'it is in the inter-linking of the domestic sphere with public institutions that the work of social reproduction, closure and exclusion gets done', Ball (2003:76). Table 7.1 shows a breakdown of the level of parents' post compulsory education related to their involvement in HE process for their children. In the majority of cases, where one or both parents have been to university their levels of involvement are high. They are already familiar with the field and this experience places them in a position of influence. They are confident players who understand the discourses and the processes of choice and are well able to facilitate and so maximize the field of choice for their children.

Table 7.1 Parents' Visibility in the Choice Discourse

SCHOOL	FAMILY	Educational Qualification FATHER	Educational Qualification MOTHER	Visibility in the facilitation process FATHER	Visibility in the facilitation process MOTHER
Llanover	Thomas	None	None	Minimal	Minimal
Bryn Alun	Jones	None	None	Minimal	Minimal
Argoed	White	None	None	Minimal	Minimal
Regent	Lang	None	None	Minimal	Minimal
Argoed Cardinal	Barry	None	None	None	Minimal
Gwyn Cardinal	Bateman	None	None	Minimal	Minimal
Gwyn	Powell	RAF	None	Moderate	Minimal
St Non's	Smith	BTech	None	Moderate	Minimal
Redcoats	Clarke	Police Force	None	Moderate	Moderate
Llanover	Istance	HNC	Secretarial	Moderate	Minimal
Jenkin	Walsh	Degree	Degree	High	Minimal
St Non's	Smart	Degree	Nursing	High	Minimal
Briarwood	Hussein	Doctor MD	Secretarial	Minimal	High
Regent	Hutchins	Degree	Degree	High	Minimal
Bryn Alun	Joyce	Degree	Degree	High	Minimal
Briarwood	Roberts	Degree	Degree	High	High
Redcoats	James	Degree	Degree	High	Minimal
Brangwyn	Parker	Degree	Degree	High	High
Brangwyn	Hubert-Jenkins	Degree	Degree	High	High
Jenkin	Hughes	PhD	PhD	High	Moderate

One exception in terms of the relation between parental participation in higher education and their involvement with the choice process can be seen in the Hussein family. As the previous chapter has shown regardless of his own experiences of higher education Mr Hussein lacks an awareness of the UK system and becomes somewhat 'invisible' in the choice discourse. However during the interviews with the other middle class families, the father emerged as a key player in relation to university choices.

> If I want advice then I suppose, well yes, I would go to my father. I think because we are more similar. I suppose we get on because we are very similar but also, well, the way in which we have been brought up dad is the head of the family. And I respect that and him. Not that I, well, no disrespect to mum, but I respect what he says a lot. So he would be the person to ask.
> (Joanne Parker, pupil at Brangwyn Hall)

> Well, my dad's like trying to do a lot to help me. He has been phoning up the school and asking to see the teachers about me making my choices for higher education. I know that if he doesn't help or I don't take his help then I'll end up without any information and then just going for a university that I'm not sure about. Like my dad gets all the stuff done, I mean he can get all the information about what colleges [Oxford] to choose for economics.
> (Gavin Hutchins, pupil at Regent High)

Similarly, in some of the focus groups held in the schools I was told:

> Well my father works in the Engineering department of the university and they have just had their TQA and so he said it would be a useful point of comparison if I look at different university departments.

> My dad knows quite a bit about the different universities, and my sister is at Oxford, so they (parents) are already quite clued up and into the system.
> (Pupils at Redcoats School)

Interestingly the fathers' own accounts reinforced the suggestion that they were key informants:

> Well, I know quite a bit about the process. I mean I am doing most of it now. I have got the prospectuses for the universities and the careers guidance books, well I brought these home for him. I'm the one who seems to be plodding through them.
> (Mr Smart, Alex, pupil at St Non's School)

> If he wants to know anything about the forms, university and that he always asks me. You did ask me things about the UCAS form the other day to do with the choices you are going to make didn't you?. You wanted me to do research on the Internet. John wants to do a specialist type course [Dentistry], so ranking is not an issue for him. But I would certainly give him my knowledge of the sector if he were thinking of making applications more generally. I would tell him which are the *better* universities and they tend to be the old ones. It's typical I think that you can identify the better ones in terms of age. I mean I *wouldn't* choose the places that were former polytechnics, I think they have got all sorts of problems with the courses, the status and of *course their funding*. I wouldn't recommend it to John that he apply to those for a number of reasons. But as it is they don't offer what he wants anyway, so it doesn't apply.
> (Mr Walsh, son John, pupil at Jenkin High)

Most significantly, irrespective of their own level of education, the mothers, too, tended to cast the husband and father in the more positional and informed role. Mrs Hutchins is divorced from Gavin's father, a university lecturer but their relationship is amicable and Mr Hutchins is in regular, frequent contact with his children couple. Although Mrs Hutchins is herself a college lecturer she told me:

> If the truth must be known then I am probably not as much part of it as I ought to be. I mean I am fortunate that Gavin's dad is doing an awful lot to help and so it has allowed me to step back. If he is doing it then that's just great. He knows what's what much more than me and that's great and so I have stepped back and perhaps haven't done as much as I could have done.
> (Mrs Hutchins, son Gavin, pupil at Regent High)

It is interesting to note how this authoritative key informant status is automatically ascribed to the father. Even in families like the Hughes' where both parents have a doctorate and both are university lecturers at the same institution, the father was deferred to in matters of university choice.

> Well, she [Louise] is fiercely independent, but she would go to her father to ask about something to do with choices and of course he knows all about the university stuff.
> (Mrs Hughes, Louise, pupil at Jenkin High)

> Yes I suppose that's right I would ask dad I guess. I mean if I really need to know something, get some information then yes you're right I would go to dad, it's silly really I suppose, but then
> (Louise, pupil at Jenkin High)

Where the mother *had* been involved in the choice process, the decision was reached because the family saw her as having some particular expertise, as in the case of the Roberts family. Mrs Roberts works as a senior biochemist at a chemical plant and her husband is a Chemistry teacher at a city comprehensive school. In the family interview I was told,

> Giles: Well I think the personal statement on the UCAS form is the tricky bit. When it comes to that then I think I would ask mum, because she is really good at that sort of thing.

> Mrs Roberts: Well, I interview people at work, and I think that when you have been on the receiving end of the application forms you know what absolute no no's there are. I mean it's a selling game really isn't it, the form I mean, and you can sell yourself short if you are not careful. You need to say that you are better than the next person and it's a very hard concept because you try to bring people up to think of equality and fairness of opportunity and yet when it comes down to it you want the better choice and the most opportunities and so you have to do the best possible job on your own behalf.

During the in depth interviews with the families the role of each parent in the HE process was explored. The key facilitator in each family emerged as a result of self nomination or nomination by other family members. Table 7.2 lists the family groups and identifies both the 'self' nominated and 'other' nominated facilitator in each family. From this it is possible to identify the degree of facilitation offered by each parent in the choice process and to note the congruence in the perceptions between parents and young people as to these roles.

Table 7.2 Parents' Gendered Roles and Choice

SCHOOL	FAMILY	PCE FATHER	PCE MOTHER	Father says	Mother says	Child says
Redcoats	Clarke	Police Force	None	Both	Both	Both
Brangwyn	Parker	Degree	Degree	Both	Both	Both
Brangwyn	Hubert-Jenkins	Degree	Degree	Both	Both	Both
Bryn Alun	Jones	None	None	Father	Father	Father
Cardinal Gwyn	Powell	RAF	None	Father	Father	Father
Jenkin	Walsh	Degree	Degree	Father	Father	Father
Bryn Alun	Joyce	Degree	Degree	Father	Father	Father
Llanover	Istance	HNC	Secretarial	Father	Father	Father
St Non's	Smart	Degree	Nursing	Father	Father	Father
Regent	Hutchins	Degree	Degree	n/a	Father	Father
Redcoats	James	Degree	Degree	Father	Father	Father
Jenkin	Hughes	PhD	PhD	Both	Father	Father
St Non's	Smith	BTech	None	Both	Father	Father
Briarwood	Hussein	Doctor MD	Secretarial	n/a	Mother	Mother
Regent	Lang	None	None	Mother	Mother	Mother
Briarwood	Roberts	Degree	Degree	Mother	Mother	Mother
Argoed	Barry	None	None	n/a	Child	Child
Llanover	Thomas	None	None	Child	Child	Child
Argoed	White	None	None	Child	Child	Child
Cardinal Gwyn	Bateman	None	None	Child	Child	Child

However, as Gewirtz et al (1995:38) note 'the role of decoding is fundamental to the relationship between class and choice that is evident in our study and others'. This takes time, patience and know how, as I heard during some family interviews:

> Oh I spent hours and hours and hours going through the UCAS books you know. Trying to sort of look for things and we had the maps out because originally Amy said she didn't want to be more than two hours away. I think she has come round now to thinking it doesn't matter where she is, in fact one of her choices is Durham, and you can't go a lot further than that without actually going to Scotland. But it did take hours and hours going through all the stuff and trying to sort out which ones would take religious studies as a main subject or which did general primary education.
> (Mrs Hubert-Jenkins, Amy, pupil at Brangwyn Hall)

In the case of the Parker family, I was told by Joanne:

> Well, I went around a number of universities, Nottingham, Birmingham, places like that. Mum took a car full. But I just basically went for the courses. Then we compared notes later, didn't we?
> (Joanne Parker, pupil at Brangwyn Hall)

In the focus groups, too, middle class pupils reported on the amount of effort their parents (usually the mother) put into researching options:

> Well my mum has made an effort this year to find things out. She has asked people she knows about different universities and courses and she says that we must ask more questions and find out things about the different universities. We have started to get some prospectuses and looking at those.
> (Bev, pupil at Jenkin High School)

> I've got a load of prospectuses and information on courses and jobs. My mum is great like that she will write off to places and ask people for information, she happily spends ages going through the books, you know sorting things out.
> (Penny, pupil at Redcoats School)

For the working class families, unfamiliar with the sector, a lack of knowledge and a lack of self confidence inhibited their involvement. As Mrs Thomas told me:

> I mean I can't help, how could I? I wouldn't know where to start. I mean I couldn't just talk to them [university admissions staff]. I mean what would I say?

The use of social networks for the transmission of both actual and symbolic information is reliant on a similarity of 'taste', a case of moving in the same circles and aspiring towards the same goals of membership (Bourdieu, 1986).

This is an approach similarly identified in accounts from the more 'skilled/privileged' choosers in the study by Gewirtz et al (1995:38) where parents like Mrs Brent made use of social networks and told the researchers:

> We tried to find as many people as possible who had children at the various schools, yes, we did discuss it with friends and neighbours.

In my study one of the pupils at Brangwyn Hall girls told me:

> My mum 'phones around universities and well, like she does absolutely everything. If I say I have just the vaguest interest in something, somewhere, then I only have to say it and when I get home from school she will say 'oh I have just 'phoned these ten universities to get information from them and I have spoken to the admissions tutors.' It's awful. Sometimes I think she is interfering too much, and when I get in that is all she wants to talk about. But I suppose I am quite glad, really, that I have found out so many things about the course that I want to do. There are things which I know now that I wouldn't have known otherwise.
> (Patsy, pupil at Brangwyn Hall)

Deciding which universities to apply to can be a complex and time consuming process. I found that the idea of 'spoiling' in the families in the 1990s could be related to the amount of time and effort which parents were prepared to expend on this task on behalf of their children. During both the family interviews and the focus group discussions it emerged that many (middle class) families invested considerable amounts of time and effort in seeking out information and accessing social networks in order to identify the most suitable course and institutional options. However it was notable that these tasks were in the main gender specific. The data reveal that mothers were prepared and in some cases even eager, to spend a considerable amount of their time, sending for university prospectuses and then sifting through these and other information booklets in order to identify the various course options. In a number of cases mothers acted as chauffeurs taking groups of young people to university open days. Allatt (1993:143) has used Bourdieu's concept of emotional capital in order to consider mothers' involvement and investment in their children's futures. She suggests that in addition to 'emotionally valued assets and skills' emotional capital includes 'the apparently gratuitous expenditure of time, attention, care and concern'. Reay (2000:583) has further developed this theme and suggests that 'the concept of emotional capital is useful in unravelling some of the confusing class and gender processes embedded in parental involvement in education'.

Family, Discourse and Choice

Although the sample is small and so does not allow definitive claims to be drawn from the study, it does appear that, at this level of choosing, there are very different discourses at family level from those shown in studies of school choice. It is important therefore, to consider the extent to which families have accessed information on which to base higher education choices. The data in this study illustrate three significant findings, of which two have firm historical roots and one is new. Firstly, comparisons made with the work of Jackson and Marsden (1962) reveal class inequalities in educational decision making that are durable across time. These data bear a striking similarity to those of Jackson and Marsden, since in terms of missed opportunities, anxieties and frustrations some pupils and their families remain as disadvantaged in the education system now as then. Unable to negotiate the complexities of the market, they see higher education as an undifferentiated system, a degree course *per se* as a mark of excellence.

Secondly, there are distinct comparisons with issues of locality and regional identity both now and those in the Swansea Valley of the 1960s (Leonard 1980). This study presents data which are unique in their focus on higher education choices in south Wales. However in common with the studies by Ball, Gewirtz and Reay and their research on local markets and choice in London, would suggest that there is a resonance and a transferability of the themes to a wider more generalized population. In considering higher education markets and choice, this study challenges the taken for granted assumptions implicit in the recent educational reforms which sees 'parents' as an homogeneous entity Rather by making visible the micro-politics of choice within the family, this research demonstrates a range of competencies both inter and intra social class groups.

Leonard's (1980) study found that young people made choices which were constrained by the 'pull' of localism. This still persists. The desire which many of the young people in the study expressed to apply to local institutions has almost nothing to do with nationalism, rather it expresses the significance of 'home' not 'Wales'. Some parents in the 1990s are anxious for their children to engage with a local market in order for them to 'stay close'. At the time of this study 1995-98, it was too soon to gauge the full implications of the introduction of tuition fees and patterns of participation. Now however there is evidence that greater numbers of students are opting to study nearer to home, if only purely for economic reasons (UCAS, 2000; THES, 2002).

However there is also a modern theme which involves issues of emotional capital, gender and power in relation to choice and higher education. Research shows that mothers feature firmly as the significant parent in school choice (David et al, 1997). Even when choice is exercised in respect of post-16 education mothers' still play a more active part in the process than fathers' (Macrae et al., 1996). However, when decisions are to be made about higher education choices, these data indicate ways in which the father is now clearly visible as part of the decision making process. The middle class families in the sample all have some working knowledge of the university system, since one, or both of the parents have been in higher education. Parents and children refer to individual and specific competencies as a means of determining which parent is best equipped to assist with and facilitate their university choices. Frequently, even when both parents have a degree, or as in the case of the Hughes family, where both mother and father have a doctorate, the father is much more visible in the choosing process (see Tables 7.1 and 7.2).

Edgell (1980) identifies the ways in which decision making is 'shared' in marriage. The study found that some decisions are made jointly and others are split between husband and wife. There was a high degree of consensus among couples as to which were 'important' decisions and while these occurred less frequently, were always regarded as husbands' responsibility. In contrast, wives were responsible for the more frequent, and therefore more mundane decisions in family life. Even in families where both husband and wife had full time jobs, the men were seen to have the most important careers. A number of sociological and anthropological studies have theorized men and women's differential location in 'public' and 'domestic' spheres. In the Isle of Sheppey study (Pahl, 1984) found that there was a gendered division of labour in the family. Women were regarded as responsible for domestic chores, washing, cooking, cleaning, child care while men undertook 'male' jobs like car maintenance, gardening and decorating. There was a lack of equality within the home which did not end with the domestic division of labour but, rather, extended to include decisions regarding the family budget. The power differential in relationships were very marked. As Delphy (1984) notes, there is evidence that the husband sometimes 'decides' not to make a decision, and in so doing allows his wife to be responsible for something he regards as not worthy of his consideration. This was especially marked in the study by Pahl in respect of financial decisions made in the home. Pahl's (1989) study found that while the husband may delegate control of the household budget to the wife, the dominant decision making remains as part of the husband's domain. Decisions about weekly shopping and choice of brands, or cuts of meat are seen as decisions which remain within the domestic sphere. On the other hand, these studies suggest that important decisions which require the family to invest a large amount of money, such as moving house, or buying a car, were made by the husband, without reference to his wife. It can be suggested that, given the increasing costs associated with going to university, the father needs to be visible in and engaged with the process if he is to finance the degree.

It may be that the market place is perceived as a masculine, public sphere, where fathers are construed as 'experts'. Shifting the decision making away from mothers, who assumed responsibility for choices at school level may be theorized with regard to notions of public and private spheres. School and schooling fall within the private sphere of the home and family and so become feminized in consequence. It becomes possible to theorize the roles of parents and children making reference to Bernstein (1977). In his work on language and socialisation he has identified variants of speech patterning and codes which he relates, broadly, but not solely, to social class groups. 'Restricted' and 'elaborated' codes are framed within a linguistic construction and the selective access to them is one means of maintaining different value systems in society. While Bernstein (1977) argues that social classes cannot be differentiated into homogeneous groups in contemporary society, he maintains that distinctions can be made between family types and their communication patterns. While these social class categories are not discrete and each class contains elements of the different family types, those which he describes are shaped by their different capacities to maintain their boundary procedures.

In a family where there are strong boundary controls which maintain specific roles for each of its members Bernstein suggests that there is a clear hierarchical ordering of authority. In this 'positional' family there is considerable emphasis on status and social identity, which serves to fix and formalize relationships. In families where there are weak and consequently, flexible boundaries, there is a considerable degree of blurring as far as issues of status and authority are concerned. Such families acknowledge the competencies of each of their members and roles are fluid, accommodating and assimilating the various individual attributes of each, irrespective of age or gender. These 'personal' families undergo a constant programme of adjustment in order to accommodate new skills and qualifications in its members. The individual is valued for their contribution to the family and although there are opportunities for increased autonomy for the individual, there is a more closed value system, than that found in the positional family. Here we see less autonomy, but a greater sense of social identity. It may be that in relation to university choices there is a frame change within the 'personal' family, with the young adult dictating the process of choice. Possibly it might be the case that within a, 'positional', family school choices are made and the wishes of the parents over-ride those of the child, a case of 'go because I say so'. But at the level of university choice, it can be suggested that there is a change in frame, because now it is the 'child' who more frequently holds the power which resides in knowledge of the system, while parents merely hold the purse strings. So the code remains constant, but there is a shift in the framing which allows the father to 'negotiate' with the child. In the following chapter this theorising on family and schools continues and a typology of family and school are developed which allows for a theoretical analysis of the HE choice process.

Chapter 8

Myths, Monsters and Moving On

In this chapter I want to continue to focus on the family but to move the discussion somewhat from the market and issues of choice. Rather I want to consider some of the implications of choices for the families in terms of transitions and the anxieties experienced by these young people as a consequence of their decisions to go on to university. Learning to make choices and take decisions, right or wrong, is an important aspect of becoming an adult (Gardener, 1987). Childhood is usually constructed as a deficit model, where the wishes and the needs of children are often subordinated to meet the desires and wishes of adults (Archard, 1993; Butler and Williamson, 1994). For example, in terms of educational choices, Alderson (1995) has suggested that it is adults who are the real consumers and the young people in this study, whilst rapidly approaching adult hood, often looked to their parents for information, guidance and support. With a few exceptions the families are solidly middle class or socially mobile, having experienced some improvements in their material and social situations. For the children of middle class families clearly going to university is the 'obvious' next step (Connell et al, 1982; Roker, 1993; Pugsley, 2003). Even for those families still in the process of upward mobility, entry to university is seen as both appropriate and desirable. For the most part then both parents and offspring saw this as 'an idea they appreciated and accepted as part and parcel of how things were' (Quicke, 1993:112). There is evidence in the previous chapters to support the suggestion that parents still play a significant role in facilitating the choice process for their children. There has also been some discussion about 'hot' and 'cold' information and the ways in which decisions are made through the dispositions of habitus.

The qualitative data also revealed some of the anxieties and concerns that young people have about making the transition from school to higher education and the ways in which these concerns are often not expressed, or not heard, within the context of the family. The home is the site of family practices and clearly conversational practices will feature as part of the family routine. Whilst there is a difference between discourse in the public and the private sphere, recognition of the different ways in which the social actors within the family construct, or understand situations differently remains an important one. A distinction needs to be made between the ways in which family members can 'hear' information without necessarily 'listening' to or 'understanding' the subtleties that underpin it. Anxieties are an integral part of any transitional process but in many instances these concerns remain *sub rosa* (Best, 1983; Pugsley et al, 1996). This discussion below draws on both the qualitative data, focus groups and interviews and the questionnaire data to consider some of the myths and misapprehensions held by young people and their families as they contemplate the move from secondary school to higher education.

A number of issues of concern were identified in the initial questionnaire survey sent to pupils in the lower sixth (or equivalent) year. These areas included financial, academic and social factors. Of the total number of those surveyed (n=711), 661 pupils (93.2 per cent), intended applying for university entry. Most of the remaining seven per cent were either pupils at Llanover School or students at Argoed College. Of this group, the majority was intending to look for work immediately after finishing their present courses of study. Some felt that they could 'work and train on the job' others though reported that they 'had done enough studying and just wanted to get a job'. It can be suggested that they have been pragmatic in their decision-making and opted for rational career choices 'partly governed by emotions and embedded in habitus, with the decisions bounded by their horizons for action' (Hodkinson et al, 1996:123). Of those surveyed only 17 said that higher education was 'too expensive' and that this was a barrier to their applying. Interestingly these young people were part of the last cohort for whom a university education would not require them to pay tuition fees. Now at the time of writing when there is considerable political debate about top up fees and variable rates, it would be interesting to survey current sixth form pupils to compare these levels of concern. Only ten students felt that they were 'not clever enough' to go to university, possibly a decision made in response to their construction of what universities and university education is like. This theme of the social construction of knowledge about university life is one that will be explored, in greater depth in a later section.

Some pupils (n=140) indicated their intentions to defer entry for a year. They planned to use the 'Gap' year as an opportunity for travel, further study and or employment in order to finance their university plans. The majority of these pupils were from the two independent schools, both of which encourage their pupils to consider this year out option before university. Unlike Redcoats and Brangwyn Hall, the other schools and colleges in the study had no formalized 'Gap' arrangements. These two schools regard the year out as a positive experience for pupils, whereas most of the staff in the other schools and colleges regarded the costs associated with taking a year out as prohibitive for most of their pupils' families.

Home or Away: Region and Choice

As part of an initial survey, conducted in the second term of the lower sixth year, the students were asked to indicate any regional influences on their university choices. In total 56 per cent of those surveyed said they would include *some* Welsh universities in their choices. Interestingly corresponding data indicate that 58 per cent of students domiciled in Wales were attending Welsh universities (HEFCW, 1997). A third of the respondents indicated a preference for studying at universities within a convenient radius of home, while 43 per cent said they would consider any location. This sense of opportunity to choose any location may have been symptomatic of the time when the data were collected. Tuition fees had not yet come into play and the real significance of student hardship and graduate debt had not been perceived as either a barrier to participation or a restriction of institutional choice. It is important though to make the distinction between the significance of region and that of 'home'. In the focus group interviews I conducted with pupils I asked if they felt any inherent sense of 'Welshness' and if this would be a significant factor that would influence their choices and would make them want to continue to study in Wales. The large majority of those interviewed said that they did feel a need to study at a university that was within 'reasonably easy access of home'. This confirms the suggestion that students are more influenced by issues of localism and 'home' rather than 'Wales' an attitude noted in the research into the Women's Road Show (Pilcher et al 1989). In this study of schoolgirls in Wales, they said specifically that they were intending to apply only to Welsh universities. However the focus group data in my study indicated that for some young people from working class families there was a misunderstanding as to the full range of their university choices. Pupils, who were intending to study Welsh to degree level, *said* that they had no option *but* to make applications to local (Welsh) institutions.

> Oh I do [want to stay in Wales] I want to apply to Cardiff and Swansea, those are the ones I want to go to.
> (Lisa-Jayne, Cardinal Gwyn College)

> Yes but you are doing Welsh and you want to do a Welsh degree don't you. So you are bound to go one of these for that in any case.
> (Gaynor, Cardinal Gwyn College)

> Yeah, there is that I suppose. I guess you're right. I mean, if I am doing Welsh I really don't have a choice. Yes I suppose that's true.
> (Lisa-Jayne, Cardinal Gwyn College)

> I think I have to apply for Swansea. I don't think I can go anywhere else. Not to do Welsh and Welsh History that is.
> (Martin, Llanover High)

However that is *not* the case, Welsh and Welsh studies are not only offered in all the higher education institutions in Wales, but are also offered in Queen's University Belfast. What this does indicate is a lack of awareness of where to seek information and a lack of guidance from the school to provide advice. A number of pupils said that they would prefer to go to universities in England 'for a change':

> Living in Wales is not at important, not important at all. No definitely not important, I want to get away, you know go over the bridge. [The Severn Bridge separating Wales from England.]
> (Tony, Briarwood High School)

Well I want to get away, live a bit. I mean it *does* depend on the course but there are places outside Wales that I would look at first. I would prefer to go to England, it's growing up, moving on, isn't it?
(Harry, Regent High)

For some, university allows an escape from the family. Becoming a student legitimizes leaving home and moving away from parental 'care'.

Well I don't want to stay here. I don't want to be near my parents, I don't get on with them at all. This is the first opportunity for me to get away from them. I mean I wouldn't mind going to Cardiff University but I wouldn't stay at home. I would still want to live out, you know live away, even if I went to Cardiff.
(Ian, Regent High)

Oh I can't wait to go, I want to live on my own, you know with no 'olds' bossing you and that. It'll be great at uni, I'm going to apply away from Cardiff and that's definite.
(Pete, St Non's High School)

For the middle class family, having a child move away to attend university is part of the 'natural order' (Allatt, 1993). It is has traditionally been seen as an integral part of the value system of this social group. However the sense of 'home' and 'family' are non the less bounded by intimate and complex emotional links that many young people recognize and wish to maintain. There was evidence of this desire both to 'keep' and be 'kept' 'close' that Leonard (1980) had first identified and discussed in connection with the families in the Swansea valley (Chapter 7). But this was also mediated by an economic pragmatism, awareness that location and distance could be an added expense to what was likely to be an already costly experience as I heard:

I don't especially think, 'oh I am Welsh, so I must pick a Welsh university.' But at the same time I wouldn't want to go say to London, because it's too expensive and I wouldn't want to be too far to say the north of England either because of the cost of travel.
(Lizzie, Jenkin High School)

I agree, I don't feel the need to go to a Welsh university especially. But I will consider them because they are convenient and the costs are so high anyway.
(Elise, Jenkin High School)

I am actually looking at Swansea and Cardiff Universities. Swansea because it's got a good reputation for Geography, which is what I want to do and Cardiff because it's a good insurance policy if I don't get the grades I need. My parents can't afford thousands for me to go away, so I'll live at home and Cardiff is a nice city. But the Welsh element is not important although I like Cardiff. But I don't feel that's a Welsh thing.
(Felicity, Redcoats School)

Clearly in this study there was already an awareness of the financial implications associated with going to university. The 'choices' offered by an expanded sector and a market philosophy are being curtailed by the financial restrictions that have been and will continue to be imposed. As the pupils told me in the focus group interviews:

> I will stay here, but it's not to do with being Welsh. It's because I can't afford to go far. I don't feel particularly Welsh, I mean living here, being in Cardiff like, well, it's not like being from the valleys or something, it's not like being properly Welsh. But it's just too expensive to go to university and live away from home.
> (Briony, Argoed College)

> Well I'm definitely looking local, it's cheaper isn't it? And that's what counts.
> (David, Llanover High School)

> Yes I'll be looking local too, my parents just couldn't afford for me to go away in any case.
> (Joe, Llanover High School)

The living costs and the additional travel costs associated with attending a university that was a distance from home was a cause for concern for more than half the students in this study. Choosing to apply to local institutions may be seen to be a rational economic decision which some pupils, most particularly those who were working class, were seriously considering. It also demonstrates one of the ways in which choice is exercised within a restricted field. How it is embedded in a complex pattern of family demands and structural limitations that is both explicit and implicit, as these pupils from working class families noted:

> It makes sense, I don't want to be in debt and my mother can't afford a lot, so it makes sense to stay at home
> (Karen, Llanover High School)

> Yes I don't want to give up my Saturday job, I can still carry on working and live cheaply if I stay at home. There is no point in getting into debt if you can avoid it, and I would miss my family as well.
> (Sian, Llanover High School)

> Well I think it's easier if you are an only child. A lot easier. I mean I have got two younger brothers and so mine [parents] can't be expected to save for my brother while they are paying for me and then when he goes [to university] my other brother will be needing them to get ready to pay for him to go.
> (Alice, Llanover School)

> Well I want to live at home because my parents are not going to be able to afford me going to university. And the grants and that won't cover paying for me to live away and I don't want to go getting in to debt, taking out loans or anything like that at this age. If I have to, then I have to, but I would really like to avoid that.
> (Chantelle, Argoed College)

Well I will definitely have to take a loan, my family haven't got any money so that's it. When I look to see where I will apply I won't go so far as Birmingham say. But then I won't limit myself to Cardiff. I will look at Swansea and Glamorgan. But it's not fair that the government doesn't give more money. I mean they used to pay for it all and now they say that we are supposed to be able to go into higher education and get the grades and all, no matter what social class you are in. But they are not giving us the money are they? So it's still only the people who have money who are able to go to university and get the good jobs. It means you get stuck in the same class as you started in.
(Briony, Argoed College)

These concerns about the costs and the demands on the family budget, expressed by the young people in this study are similar to the issues raised by young people and their families in Huddersfield in the 1950s (Jackson and Marsden, 1962). I surveyed the pupils again during the second term of the upper sixth year, three months before the start of the A-level and GNVQ examinations. A total of 531 pupils completed the questionnaire and of these 87 per cent had applied through UCAS for university places. These pupils were asked to rank, in order of preference, the institutions of their choice (see Table 8.1 below).

Table 8.1 Pupils Preferred First Choice of Institution

INSTITUTION	% of PUPILS
University of Wales Cardiff	17.5
University of Wales Institute Cardiff	8.2
University of Cambridge	5.0
University of Wales Swansea	4.5
University of Bath	3.9
University of Bristol	3.0
University of Nottingham	3.0
Oxford University	3.0
University of Glamorgan	2.8
University of West of England	2.4

From this it was possible to identify the most popular choices in terms of preferred geographic region and institutional 'type'. It is significant to note that, despite reservations expressed a year previously about attending a local institution, both the top two universities that were nominated as the preferred choice are in Cardiff. The inclusion of Oxbridge as a preferred first choice is explained by the elite nature of these institutions. For the young people in the study, indicating a preference does not allow for this choice to be automatically met. But what is significant is that with the exception of two universities each of the others in the list are all within a 100 mile radius of the research site. This preference for a relatively localized market is highly significant for the 'Producers', the institutions themselves in relation to their marketing strategies and target areas for recruitment. It becomes an increasingly significant issue as costs continue to rise.

Gambling on UCAS

The questionnaire revealed that the greatest source of anxiety experienced by pupils was related to their getting the necessary grades required by their preferred institutions. Of those surveyed 81.8 per cent felt 'very concerned' about the outcome of their examinations. These quantitative concerns about applications pre A-level were reinforced in the focus group interviews. These findings are significant in light of the ongoing debate of the merits and demerits of pre and post A-level applications (Higgins, 1994; Smith, 1997). Pupils in all the focus groups felt that not only would it be more logical to make applications on the strength of qualifications already gained but would help to alleviate much of the stress relating to the university application processes. The expansion of the sector and concomitant institutional hierarchy that now exists exerts tremendous pressure on pupils who apply to the high status institutions with their higher grade entry requirements. The extent of the middle class family's 'investment' in education can exert pressure on their children via implicit expectations as has been discussed in the previous two chapters. These young people feel particular anxieties, as they told me in the focus group interviews:

> I think the worry is that you might get high predictions and then offers and you might not get the grades and so end up well with nothing at all. It's a real pressure and a worry because it's all about doing it on the day.
> (Morag, Brangwyn Hall)

> I'm worried about getting the grades. I really worry about not doing well enough to get in.
> (Julian, Jenkin High School)

> It's not just getting them [the grades] in the exams, it's making sure you keep them up when you get there, that you well let yourself down.
> (Katy, Jenkin High School)

> There is a lot of pressure with these predicted grades and UCAS and all that. I didn't realize how much there would be, and I think the whole thing's just so scary.
> (Meryl, Briarwood School)

> It would be better if we did the A-levels first and then applied wouldn't it? I mean it would be better than all the worrying about it wouldn't it? I mean I am thinking about the grades that I need all the time. Am I going to get them, or not? I mean every year around the A-level results time you hear these reports of people topping themselves. It's just all the stress.
> (Hilary, Briarwood School)

> But it's not worth it is it? I mean it's not worth it.
> (Geraint, Briarwood School)

> To you, maybe not. But it's surprising the pressure some people feel. To them, going to one *particular* university must be *the* most important thing in the world.
> (Justin, Briarwood School)

These fears must be acknowledged and systems put in place to support pupils in the choice process and to extend that support through to publication of the A-level results and beyond. Better still a reworking of the system such that the points lottery is ended and the applications are made once the examination results are known.

This idea that the real university challenge was in being able to 'suss out the system', so that the 'right' choices were made was a commonly recurring theme throughout the study. The initial questionnaire revealed that 80 per cent of those pupils surveyed (n=711) were very anxious about their ability to choose the 'right' courses and the 'best' university. Here 'best' is referred to in terms of what will be most suitable for them and where they will 'fit in', rather than best in terms of league tables. Interestingly league tables hardly featured in the discussions with any of the groups or the families in the study. These concerns need to be considered in relation to the career education and higher education guidance that is provided for these young people in their schools and colleges and considered in the previous three chapters. These chapters highlight the ways in which information may or may not be accessed by social groups and how class based competencies can inform choices. Nevertheless even among for the most 'privileged' chooser (Gewirtz et al 1995) there are still 'risks' associated with any market engagement. As Giddens (1991:32) has noted 'even risk assessments within relatively closed settings are often only valid until further notice'. Many of the young people in my study were aware both of their own limitations as 'informed selectors' and of the problems associated with making wrong choices. This became a cause for even more anxiety, particularly among the young people who were first generation university applicants, as I learned during focus group discussions:

> I do worry about getting it right. I mean, even if you get there [to university] then what? What if you don't like it? You hate the course, or you can't do it, or it's not what you thought. What do you do then?
> (Molly, Cardinal Gwyn College)

> Well you can leave I suppose, but then what do you do? I dunno, I worry as well about getting it right you know?
> (Chloe, Cardinal Gwyn College)

> Well my sister dropped out. She went to do a course that she hated after about the first two weeks, she stuck it until the Christmas and then came home. She tried another one this year but she is not too keen on that, but I think she is

stuck with it now, I mean she can't stop again, the 'olds' would go spare and what else would she do anyway?
(Barney, Llanover High School)

But it's fair enough that innit? I mean how are you supposed to know what it's like? I think it's hard to know if the course is what you want. How do you know?
(Mitch, Llanover High School)

As Ball (2003:100) has noted 'information is a key dynamic in the workings of all markets and has been a particular focus and a powerful mechanisms in the reform of education systems'. It has been argued that working class young people lack information about higher education and this has been offered as an explanation for their low levels of participation. This notion that 'certain groups in society lack information about the opportunities that are available' (Thomas, 2001:135) is an integral factor in restricting choice and limiting opportunity.

Counting the Costs

The expansion of the higher education sector has led to an increase in the financial demands placed on students and as Hesketh (1996) notes, students' attitudes towards debt are complex and multifaceted. Over 70 per cent of the young people in my study were concerned about the financial implications of going to university, even prior to the introduction of tuition fees. The first Blair Government, elected in May 1997, introduced tuition fee payments from the start of the 1998 academic year. Since then students have been required to contribute up to £1,000 per annum towards their tuition costs. At the time of writing this is set to increase, with proposals aimed at allowing universities to charge differential fees. The implications for further stratification in the sector and differential access are vast. Most of the pupils and their parents in my study were uncertain of the actual costs that would be involved. However all the families expressed concerns about the anticipated expense of university courses and the potential level of debt that could accrue. Cost has been identified as the greatest barrier to increased working class participation in higher education (Lynch and O'Riordan, 1998.) Where the financial implications of higher education do not actually deter entry, choice can be critically compromised for young people from working class backgrounds. Glyn Bateman for example, a student at the Cardinal Gwyn Tertiary College decided to apply only to the local institutions in order to continue living at home in order to save money. Many of the young people I spoke to had, like Glyn, not even discussed the matter with their parents, but concerned about the financial implications of further study had taken this decision to restrict their choices to local universities. Of those surveyed over 80 per cent had some part time paid employment. All the pupils I spoke to felt that they would need to continue to work during their time in university and for the majority, this would mean working during the term time as well as in the vacations. These indications are confirmed by recent studies which show that more than 40 per cent of students have term time jobs (THES, 2002) and that it is those students from poorer backgrounds who are the most likely to be in term-time employment (Humphrey, 2001). Most pupils expect to contribute towards the costs of university themselves, either through taking a student loan, or by working part time, or both.

> Well my parents want me to have a year out and go to work to save money. They will help, but they want me to help pay for myself. So hopefully if I can get work for a year then I can go into higher education with some funds myself.
> (Huw, Ysgol Bryn Alun)

> I know my parents will feel it financially, but like my mum is really pleased with what I want to do and she will really encourage me. She wouldn't want to put me off by saying 'oh we can't afford it', but I'll need to keep my job too, and that'll help.
> (Hilary, Cardinal Gwyn College)

More than half the young people I surveyed were very worried by the prospect of their parents going into debt to support them through their degree. Clearly with the real cost implications now more apparent these concerns would be expressed by a greater number of young people and their parents. This concern was common across each of the schools and colleges in the study. However, those pupils at the Independent schools were aware of the levels of financial 'investment' which their parents had already put into their education (Allatt, 1996; Gewirtz et al 1995). During the focus group interviews some of the girls at Brangwyn Hall talked about the ways, in which education had been 'planned for' and included in the long term budgeting of family finances.

> Helena: Well, they [parents] have planned for it. I mean, they knew that it would be like six or seven year here and then say another four at university. Yes I think they have organized it to pay for it as it comes, really, it's what they want, what we all want.

> Jonquil: Yes I think they are happy to go on paying for my education. Also my dad says he will give me extra money at university, like a student loan only at cheaper interest rates than the government. but I will have to pay him back. I think they would only start objecting about the cost if they could see that I didn't do any work and I was failing and they thought that they were going to have to pay out for years and years.
> (Pupils at Brangwyn Hall)

There was a general agreement in each of the focus groups in the fee-paying schools that parents would continue to provide financial support at university. But for some girls there was an indication that financing higher education might not prove that easy, or that the money would not be given unconditionally.

Yes, but I think that the money thing is well, that's a bit of how the pressure works though isn't it? I mean, they are paying for us and like now my mother will say 'Have you done your homework?' and if I say, 'well a bit, but I'm not doing it tonight' then she will say 'Well it's up to **you**.' But I know she would be mad if I didn't do it at all and well if they pay for university they can expect us to work at it can't they.
(Felicity, Brangwyn Hall)

Ruth: I think they are bothered about the cost, but they don't really say much about it. But they do bring it into the conversation that when I go to university then, 'the money will have to be used to do this and this and this, so you don't want to be going too far away because of the cost of travel there and back.' They have said that they will send me so much money each week and that will be all I have, so I will have to be careful what I spend as I won't have a lot of money.

Myra: Actually I think that most probably I am quite different from a lot of the people here. We **had** money, but well. So what I mean is that our parents have got enough to get us all through private education until we are 18 but then, you know, although we have got some, it's not much and I expect I will get a grant. My sister is at Oxford and she has got a full grant and my parents pay for her accommodation and food, which is less than it costs in fees for me to come here. But they don't give her anything else.
(Pupils at Redcoats School)

Patsy: People think because you go to this school that you have loads of money. It's not necessarily true. My parents put money away for this but they haven't got much now so I'm not in for any boozy student lifestyle.

Caitlin: Yes, people are always assuming that we are rich. I mean I can't get an assisted place here because they know that my dad has got a big house. But the truth is that **we** haven't owned it for three years. But they think we have loads of money. They don't believe what we earn. My dad drives a big car, but that is because he spends money that we haven't got. But because we have these illusions [sic] of money we won't get a grant. They simply look at the address and assume that we are rolling in it, but the bank has owned it for years now. So paying for university will be up to me really.
(Pupils at Brangwyn Hall)

Claudia: Well, I know that my parents will throw me into university and say 'Survive, we have paid for your accommodation and fees and that and now it's up to you to survive'. I know they want me to go, but they don't want to make it too easy.

Petra: Yes, my dad says that they will help, but it's up to me to get a part time job and organize my money.
(Pupils at Redcoats School)

In the focus group interviews, a number of pupils, particularly those in the lower social class group with no family history of higher education, noted that their parents had little or no information, or idea about the likely cost implications.

> I think my parents are worried about the cost I mean, my dad is retired and they know a bit about grants and that but not about how much they will need to pay. They keep saying 'don't you worry, we have kept back some money to pay for you when you go to university' and I know they really want me to go, but it's still a problem and a real worry.
> (Charlotte, Regent High)

> I am worried for my parents, you know the costs and that. I don't want to put too much financial pressure on them and I'm just really scared.
> (Hilary, Briarwood High School)

> It will be touch and go with the money really. Because while I know that my parents will find a way to get me to any of the places that I decide to apply to. But at the end of the day, it would be a hell of a lot easier and less strain on them if I was to study say at Cardiff. But they know that's not what I want to do and so they say, 'that's OK, we'll find a way'.
> (Tom, Jenkin High)

> It's a real worry, my parents say that we will have to struggle to do it. Like they want me to go and that, but I know that it will be difficult financially.
> (Gaynor, Cardinal Gwyn College)

> Well my parents say they know it's a lot of money, but they are prepared to do anything for me to go to university. Work all the hours God sends. Whatever.
> (Millie, Cardinal Gwyn College)

> Well I'm not going away because I know that my parents can't afford it. Like my father's unemployed and OK, so I know I would probably get a full grant, but then I still wouldn't have enough to live on as it is now. If I go outside Cardiff, then this would cause a lot of problems. I would like to better myself and go, but financially I know it's going to be awkward, so I am applying to Cardiff and I will live at home. It has some beneficial sides, I will be better off and it won't be quite such a struggle for my parents. But of course I can't party as much (laughs) but, still, that's the way it goes.
> (Maread, Cardinal Gwyn College)

> I haven't had the finances explained to me, no, but I have heard other people speak about them. I got chatting to a teacher at the school who has a son or daughter or whatever in the third year at university and the sort of figures that he started quoting me per year made me even more worried than I was up till that point. But I have got no hard information about it. I mean, up to this moment I don't think that I have ever said in Mark's hearing that I am concerned about meeting the cost, because I didn't want to worry him. He must do what he wants and we will meet the cost, yes, I mean that. But I think that when the time comes, I imagine it will just be a case of meeting each bill as it comes along somehow and calculating how much pocket money and that

he needs you know. Perhaps that's the wrong phrase, but he is obviously going to need cash in his pocket.
(Mr Istance, son Mark, pupil at Llanover High School)

Mr Walsh, a university lecturer, whose son John a pupil at Jenkin High is applying to study dentistry was more familiar with the higher education. process but still uncertain regarding some more specific points, as I heard when talking to the family:

Mr Walsh: Yes of course it's a problem and it's going to become an increasing problem too isn't it? But we will find what money he wants. I mean, we know that with dentistry in particular we are looking at a four year course.

John: Six years! It's six years for dentistry.

Mr Walsh: Is it heck, you had better get a paper round then son. I think I am rapidly going off the idea. (The family laugh at that point.) No I'm joking, of course we will fund it.

I have considered the different types of decision making that occur within families when they are engaged in negotiating and facilitating university choices here (see Chapter 7) and elsewhere (Pugsley, 1998:2003). Mrs Walsh illustrated the different degrees of information held within the family in her lack of awareness about the funding arrangements and the potential costs to the family associated with this course of study.

Mrs Walsh: But what are we talking about? How much is it? I really have no idea of the costs involved.

Mr Walsh: Well, for a start we have to pay for him to live.

Mrs Walsh: But don't they get all that? Isn't that part of it? How much are we talking about in say a year?

Mr Walsh: Well I reckon that it will be between say £3,000 to £4,000 a year. Well at least that is what we tell our students.

Mrs Walsh: Oh well that's all right then. If that's all it is. I thought it was going to be a lot more than that. That's fine that's not too bad is it. Well I have never thought about it. I mean I think that I must live in the past really. I mean you and I well we went through university when it was all given to you. So presumably what you are now saying is that whatever he wants *we* have to pay for it. Is that it?

Mr Walsh: Well, unless you want him to sleep in a cardboard box yes. That's what it really boils down to.

This is a classic example of the husband as 'head of the house' controlling the family budget (Pahl, 1990). Mrs Walsh, despite having been to university, appears totally unfamiliar with the financial implications of higher education. Mr Walsh in contrast has identified his role and his superiority within the family and, as Morgan (1996:58) notes in relation to middle class families, 'it is not gender simply, but gender mediated through patterns of domestic arrangements that are important'. For the Walsh family, their 'domestic arrangements' cast Mr Walsh as the financial controller.

The [Not So] Flexible Friend: Student Loans

Going to university raises concerns about the level of student debt and the survey indicated that the prospect of student debt was an alarming one (see Table 8.2).

Table 8.2 Anxiety and University Debt

CAUSE OF ANXIETY	% VERY CONCERNED
The extent of the debt at end of course	71.6
The possibility of being in debt in University	67.3
Meeting living expenses during University	62.6

While the majority of students knew about the Student Loan, they seemed generally ill informed about the amounts involved or the ways in which the Loan Company operates. Nevertheless, they were anxious about the prospects of being thousands of pounds in debt after their degree and this became apparent in group discussion:

> Claire: I don't know much about it, but I do know that I am going to try really hard not to get one. I mean, once you have got a student loan or whatever, then you are just going to have more and more debt. It's all going to pile up. It's frightening really.

> Ruth: I can't think about it, it's too far off, **and** it's too scary.
> (Pupils at St Non's High School)

> Suzanne: I think it's terrible, I mean after you finish at university you are still paying for your education. Then if you don't get a job you are stuck with the debt and you just get more and more short of money. You have to pay it back someday so it's like a vicious circle. You need money to pay off the loan, but you haven't got a job and you get more in debt then you need a job, because of the debt, then you think 'Oh my god what am I going to do'. It's just so much stress.

Alice: I know that I will have some debts after university, but what I'm saying is that I can't afford to have say thousands of pounds owing. It's a real worry.
(Pupils at Cardinal Gwyn College)

Adrian: The idea of a loan is not very appealing. But I think I would take one if it was necessary. I mean I wouldn't think, oh goody, a free £1,000 or whatever, but if I needed it, then.
(Pupil at Llanover School)

A study of 72 students at Lancaster University also found that, prior to beginning their courses, many were strongly opposed to the idea of a student loan. As one student told Hesketh (1996:77), 'I just didn't like the idea of taking out a student loan, because it meant taking out debt long term.' For some students in the study this attitude persisted throughout their undergraduate career and one noted (p.78), I've never used a student loan or even a small overdraft, because I just haven't really had the need to. However Hesketh reported that some students quickly found that they would be unable to survive without getting into debt, as one said (p.57), 'look, there's just no way you can make ends meet without an overdraft and student loan. You'd be living pretty much on the street'. In the Lancaster study, students reported different parental perceptions regarding the idea of a student loan. While some 'warmly embraced' the idea (p.30), 'I think I, and more, my parents, saw student loans as 'respectable' because they are interest free. It just struck us all as a good idea to use them. In contrast, others were 'deeply suspicious' of the role of the student loan and told Hesketh (p.30), 'my parents gave me the full contribution plus the amount that I would have taken out as a student loan. The agreement was that I would not use an overdraft, as my parents could not deal with the idea of my being in debt'.

In my cohort families were split on the issue of student loans and student debt. Some saw the idea of new graduates being in debt as something that should be avoided wherever possible. This was particularly the case with those families who could be classified as being in the intermediate social category, the Jones, the Smith and the Istance families. Mr Jones a haulage contractor told me:

Well, I have got to be honest, I don't really want him to borrow money. I mean, if we are in the position to put him through his education without him borrowing then that's what I would rather do.

His son was also of the opinion that it was best to avoid student debts:

I don't like the prospect of me or my parents being in debt because of my going through university
(Mr Jones, haulage contractor, David, pupil at Ysgol Bryn Alun)

Similarly comments came from both Mr Smith and Mr Istance who told me in their family interviews:

> I would rather they pay us back if they need more [money], than be in debt
> anywhere else. But I don't think the system is fair, they shouldn't be put in
> debt it's not right.
> (Mr Smith, daughter Caitlin, St Non's High School)

> I mean until this moment in time I don't think that I have ever said in Mark's
> hearing that I am concerned about meeting the cost, because I don't want to
> worry him, you know, but the idea of debt is all wrong.
> (Mr Istance, son Mark, Llanover High School)

In contrast, some middle class families felt that the opportunity to borrow money,
particularly through the student loan scheme, with its preferential rates of interest,
as a very sensible means of meeting some of the costs associated with university as
I heard in other family interviews:

> Well I would be happy about her taking a loan yes, yes I would. I mean I have
> read some stuff and, well, the way I took it was that you could borrow so
> much in the first year and borrow so much in the next and so on. But you
> started paying back when you got a job *and* it's all interest free, or if not then
> very cheap. So it's a good way of getting money I think.
> (Mr Clarke, daughter Victoria, Redcoats School)

> Well Clare, our elder daughter is in her first year at university and is intending
> taking out the maximum loan. She's still got about half her first year loan left
> and she will take the second and third. I mean it's the cheapest form of
> borrowing you can do.
> (Mr Hubert-Jenkins, daughter Amy, Brangwyn Hall)

But there was still some disagreement even within families as I saw with the Walsh
family:

> Mr Walsh: Well, I would encourage him to do it [take out a loan] because
> that's the way to do it. You can borrow the money at the best rates of interest
> you are ever likely to get so I think that's the way to go. Having said that I
> wouldn't want to see him getting horribly into debt But it's a different world
> now they most certainly do have to start off in debt. The students I see almost
> all of them have got debts. They need money, most of them, just to make ends
> meet.

> Mrs Walsh: But why do you think he needs to get involved in this loan
> system? I thought we were having to find all the money? I thought that was
> what you said we would have to do. You know find the money to support him.

> Mr Walsh: We don't *have* to do that. We haven't *got* to fork out anything. I
> mean, it depends on what he actually *wants* and what he *needs* and what we
> decide we want to do about it.

This comment by Mr Walsh reinforces the research on the ways in which
money is managed within marriage (Pahl, 1989; 1990). While Mrs Walsh may be
in charge of the 'purse strings', Mr Walsh is the key financial adviser and controls

the major budgetary decision making. Some parents may choose to contribute some level of financial support but may decide that, over and above that, it is up to the 'child' to fund the process. While the level of maintenance grant is means tested against parental income, there is no obligation for parents to meet any shortfall (Hesketh, 1997). Many of the parents in the study said that they would leave the decision about taking out a loan to the individual child, regardless of their personal feelings about debt. Over the past five years levels of debt have risen and students are faced with hardship during their studies and high levels of debt on graduation (THES, 2002).

The Stress of Being There

In a political climate of mass participation in higher education, going to university is regarded as a 'really good thing'. Little attention is paid to the affective aspects of the choice process and the various anxieties that can attach to making choices and leaving home to go to university. The initial questionnaire survey, conducted when the cohort was in the first year of sixth form study, indicated that their anxieties extending beyond the mechanics of the choice process, entry requirements, and costs. Almost 60 per cent said they were 'very concerned' about being able to cope with the level of work once they were at university. In focus group interviews these fears were further developed and somewhat focused on the sense of 'other' that exists in the identity of university students. People at university 'would be really clever', it would be a problem to 'keep up'. Some of the conversations included comments such as:

> I think that one anxiety is well it's to do with the panic that everyone else will do better than me, be brainier and that I won't be able to cope with it all.
> (Meryl, Briarwood School)

> Well, I'm worried about fitting in you know when people talk about being like the stereotype of being a student and that. I think well, I don't match up to that at all.
> (Maria, Llanover High School)

Missing family and friends and having to fend for oneself were caused some level of anxiety for at least 40 per cent of those surveyed. In the main missing friends was more of an issue that missing family. However, 42 per cent of the respondents were very anxious about their ability to make new friends and fit in which was a common concern that cut across social boundaries.

> There is the worry of moving away, you lose the security of family and friends. You have been to school and lived around here and you know the teachers and you have got your friends, it will be strange starting again.
> (Helena, Brangwyn Hall)

And not knowing where you are on the first day, you know, and just being stared at, it's like being 11 again and coming here, ugh it will be awful, scary. (Angelique, Redcoats School)

I worry about fitting in. I mean, I have been here since Form One. I know everybody. All the teachers, everyone. I can find my way about easily, I worry about making friends and just getting on. I have loads of friends here now, it's going to be well just so strange. I am looking forward to it, but well it will be so strange.
(Stacey, Briarwood School)

The dangers of being forced into proximity with peculiar or frightening strangers were vivid for some of my respondents. They might be 'odd' types who possess characteristics which might relate to ideas of pollution and, so, possible danger (Douglas, 1966). She argues that we need to organize our environment and so classify as 'dirty' anything that is either out of place or out of control.

Jo: What really scares me is the idea of going into a flat say and sharing with people who are really weirdos.

Amanda: Its awful really just think, you might get stuck with quite horrible people. (Pupils at Regent High School)

Mena: Well, as I said, I didn't want to go into Halls [student accommodation] I don't like that communal thing and I think that some student halls, well the ones I have seen, they live like pigs.
(Pupil, Briarwood School)

Living accommodation is a very significant means of identifying and establishing individual tastes and norms of practice. These in turn create territorial boundaries. Fears of these set boundaries being breached leads structural anthropologists like Douglas to suggest that individuals fear a defiling of their territory. Individuals use their own standards in order to classify others and make sense of any enforced associations with strangers (Delamont, 1987). Another possible way of explaining this attitude to shared accommodation could be through the need to protect reputation. Studies of female subcultures indicate that girls and young women are aware of the double standards relating to codes of dress, language and sexual behaviour held by boys and young men (Willis, 1976; Wilson, 1978; Smith, 1978; Lees, 1986; Pugsley, 1995). The lack of social sanctions or imposed discipline and order which young adults associate with university were also expressed as a cause of concern:

Jason: Yes, the one bit is that, well, there is not much supervision here in College, but think what uni must be like. I bet you can get away with murder there. Yeah I think you can get away with a lot more at university and I think you need a lot more self discipline really you know, to attend the lectures and that. But that's just one aspect, I mean, I would have to get up and get on with

it. If I was going to suffer all that studying and that then I would make sure it was worth it and all. I mean, I wouldn't go and mess up.
(Pupil, Argoed College)

Meryl: I think it's weird having all that freedom, you know it will be down to you then. I mean here, well, you have to turn up and there is the register and all that and your mum does things and tells you what to do and all that. It will be odd being on your own. Making your own decisions, it's kind of weird.
(Pupil, Briarwood School)

The school and the family serve as sites of formal regulation of the body (Kirk, 1993), they effectively provide a framework for control of the young adult. This serves a dichotomous function. While it can be regarded as constrictive and prohibitive, its regulatory presence is also clearly valued. However, there are other aspects of family life, which do not have such a positive impact on the young adult. This is the sense of responsibility which some of the pupils I spoke to expressed about their parents and their future life together once the children had left home. The following section considers these emotional concerns in relation to university choices.

Who Needs a Menopausal Mum?

Some of the pupils at Brangwyn Hall, one of the Independent schools, in the study indicated how the transition from school to university can be a traumatic period for parents, perhaps in some instances more so than for their children. With changing patterns in families and breakdown in relationships and marriages, many of the girls sensed that the timing of their leaving home was rather bad in terms of their parents' relationships with each other.

Julianna: Well I am worried about my parents I mean, I don't really know what my mother is going to do after I have gone [to university].

Ruth: Yes, me too, I don't know how my mum will cope, or what she and my father will do. Well, I think really that mine will just split up with nothing to talk about once I have gone.

The ways in which different actors construct social realities can shape their perceptions of events and clearly all accounts are partial (Denzin and Lincoln, 1994). But it must be stressed that those actors who have been engaged in these local lived processes have constructed these accounts. As such the anxieties that they talk about and the concerns that they raise need to be acknowledged.

As Julianna told us during the focus group interview;

Julianna: I mean I think about going away to university, but then my mum has just split up with her boy friend and I seem to have to spend my whole time looking after her and I agree with you lot. I think that my mum is really going mental as well! Then I have my younger brother who won't even have done his GCSEs when I go away. He will be in the fourth year and he'll just have it dumped on him. My parents don't live together so it will just be him and my mum. I don't think he will be any good with her because my mum gets so upset because my sister never phones her, but she is always e-mailing my dad. So I know that when **I** go to university I will have to make so much effort to make sure that I show her as much attention as possible. I know that I will have to phone her twice a week and write to her, just because my sister doesn't do it. I think my mother feels very vulnerable. I mean a couple of weeks ago, I think she was joking about it, but she said that when I leave home she will probably kill herself (there is general laughter around the group at this point).

Ruth: Yes, I've had that one too. (She joins in the laughter.)

Caitlin: I think that a lot of the time it's the kids that keep their parents together you know.

Harriet: Yes, because my mum said the other day, 'What are your dad and I going to talk about when you two have gone?' (Harriet is one of twins). 'We have nothing in common'. I thought 'Oh my God! It's true'. I mean I'm a real mediator in all their arguments, I sort it all out. I don't know what they'll do.

Julianna raised an interesting point about the significance of choosing a university that is any distance from home.

Julianna: It means that when you choose a university you are torn between going far away because **you** want a change you know, a break or staying near to home, because you want to be there to look after your mum.

Cherie: The thing is you can't live at home for ever, so they are going to have to get used to it, and if they *are* going to separate…well.

Attempting to put the whole debate into some sort of perspective, Caitlin told the group:

Caitlin: Yes I agree with Cherie. It's university for Gods' sake, not emigrating to Australia! I have enough to worry about now what with sitting my A-levels and getting the grades, I could do without a menopausal mum thank you!

In the study of the Emma Willard School in New England (Gilligan et al., 1990) a number of girls also reported that their mothers confided in them about their marital problems. Salzman (1990) noted that these concerns made them highly vulnerable vis a vis their parents and the family relationships. These findings do seem to be reflecting a specifically female pattern of discourse, and it seems unlikely that a group of boys would have spoken in this way. However, one rather emotional episode did occur in relation to a male pupil and his concern for his father. In one of the family interviews, Mark Istance, a pupil at Llanover School admitted to feeling stressed about the prospect of taking his examinations and needing to get specific grades. However, he said that he was experiencing even more stress because:

> I'm stressed about the grades, but its more than that really. It's that combined with the fear that I'm going to be disappointing my dad.

His father was clearly quite moved to hear his son say this and became visibly distressed. It was evident that Mark had never expressed either his concerns about his examinations or more significantly perhaps his determination not to 'let his father down'.

> Mr Istance: What's that? Well. I mean he has never said that before, never. Well we should discuss that sometime a bit later, because you wouldn't, you couldn't disappoint me no matter what you do. Never. In fact, if anything, I am more worried about you maybe disappointing yourself.

Some parents admitted to a sense of anxiety about their inability to engage with the application process fully and to act as a skilled facilitator in the application process.

> I think that when it's the first time that you are filling out the form and trying to advise your children, then, it's a real worry. It was really difficult to do the UCAS forms. I felt that we needed a degree to even begin to try and understand them. You know what I mean? Just to look at the relevant notes in the book was an almighty task. I think that things could be set out in a plain and straightforward working manner for everyone to understand.
> (Mrs Smith, daughter Caitlin, St Non's High School)

Mrs Hussein summed up the sense of commitment that these parents feel towards their children and their determination to do their best to help and support them:

> It's not that we think you are sponging on us, we want to do it, don't we. We don't want you to worry about the money, we don't want you to worry about any thing. Don't you worry, we just want you get to university, to enjoy it and to do the best you can. I mean you will pay us back a hundred fold by letting me go and see you have your degree you know. Oh I would be so proud in my new suit. I would just be so proud. I would want to cry for her.
> (Mrs Hussein, daughter Mena, Briarwood High School)

Know Fear and Do It Anyway

The impression is frequently given that 'going to university' is an unproblematic process, regarded with eager anticipation by the young adult and pride and satisfaction by the family. However, during discussions with young people and parents in this study a number of issues were raised which indicated a variety of anxieties and anticipations associated with this transition. The magnitude of this move to university was in some respects class related. Going to university, 'moving on', has long been the 'expected' middle class route (Halsey et al, 1980; Halsey, 1993; HESA, 2000). However, for working class families, where this is their first experience of higher education, the whole process is a giant step into the unknown. Societies rely on a variety of signs in order to classify and identify groups within them. Membership of any particular group is achieved through a status passage which requires the 'novice' to undergo some formalized '*rites de passage*' in order to move from one setting into another. Glaser and Strauss (1967:86) suggest that the transitional period follows a 'prescribed institutional sequence'. Studies of transfer from primary to secondary school have shown that pupils, while recognizing that they have outgrown their present setting and are ready to move are still anxious about the unknown, (Bryan, 1980; Measor and Woods, 1984; Delamont and Galton, 1986; Pugsley et al, 1996).

Researchers have looked at the anxieties and anticipation experienced by college students in the USA (Becker et al, 1968; Moffatt, 1989). However in Britain we lack the richness of ethnographic data of school to university transfer and the accounts of the 'folklore' or 'mythology' associated with it. As higher education becomes a 'mass' experience we need further work to encapsulate this highly significant period. Parents and young people in relation to accessing higher education expressed various anxieties. Included in these are issues of localism, pre-A-level applications and grade requirements. Earlier sections of this chapter looked at anxieties relating to money with particular reference to the prospect of debts and student loans. The later sections focused on anxieties related to academic work and issues of homesickness and friendship groups. Possibly one of the most surprising and unanticipated causes of anxiety among some of the young women I spoke to was the level of responsibility that teenagers feel they have towards their parents. They recognized that their 'moving on' will require adjustments in their parents' lifestyles as well as their own. In some cases the young people I spoke to were anxious, concerned that these changes might not prove positive in terms of their parents relationships with each other. However, their responses also indicted other fears which related to the 'scare stories' which they had heard passed on from earlier cohorts of university students. These were to do with fitting in and making the 'right' kind of friends. Change is often accompanied by a sense of ambivalence, excitement and fear can feature equally in the process. The anticipation and the anxieties that have been expressed in relation to moving 'up' from school to university are remarkably similar to those in primary to secondary transfer. Delamont (1989) identified five major recurrent themes associated with school transfer anxiety; the lavatory, shower myth; the laboratory rat myth; the five mile run myth; the violent gang myth; the weird or strict teacher myth. The spheres of anxieties are set out in Tables 8.3 and 8.4 and serve to compare the anxieties experienced by school pupils at age 11 with those expressed by prospective university undergraduates at age 18.

Table 8.3 Anxiety and School Transition

ANXIETY at 11	FOCUS
Institutional change	The Terrifying Teacher
Curriculum	Rat Myth
Pollution	Lavatory Myth
Fitting In	Violent Gangs
Growing up	Five Mile Run

Table 8.4 Anxiety and University Transition

ANXIETY at 18	FOCUS
Choosing	Institutional change
	Course and subject choice
Academic	Getting the required grades
	Keeping up with the work (curriculum)
Fitting In	Bullies
	Pollution - sharing living space
Independence	Accepting responsibility
	Homesickness
Financial	Student loans
	Managing money
Family	Parents relationships
	Possible divorce/marriage breakdown

They indicate the similarities of fears at 11 and 18. The first four anxieties in Table 8.4 compare with anxieties at age 11. The financial implications and concerns about family are new. As these tables indicate young adults about to enter university, are experiencing the fears of going to 'big school' all over again.

Mulling It Over

This chapter has demonstrated ways in which young people, making application to university are faced with a great deal of stress and anxiety. While these young people were among the last of the cohort of students in the United Kingdom who entered higher education under the Robbins (1963) principle, of access to free tuition, much of their concern is centred around money and the financial implications associated with attending university. Changes in funding arrangements and charges to students that have occurred since this study fuelled the debate that we still have a university system based on wealth and social class and figures indicate that working class groups continue to be under represented in higher education. At the time of writing, there are further changes proposed, in the form of the higher education bill currently limping its way through parliament that will likely sharpen the debate still further. The location of the institution, already seen to be a significant factor in the choice process, is likely to become increasingly relevant. It may well be that the trend, which has been demonstrated in this study, towards a more localized market may be increased. In consequence, the more geographically isolated institutions may well lose out in the race for students as the introduction of tuition fees accelerates the trend for study close to home.

All the pupils in this study reported some level of stress associated with making university choices. However, issues of class and region exacerbate these concerns. All of the families were supportive of their children's ambitions to go to gain a place at university. However as this and the previous chapter have shown, the level of parental involvement in the process varies substantially. In some families the support may well prove more emotional than practical. Some parents are able to engage with the process as active facilitators, their involvement with the process relieving much of the stress associated with completing the application. Cultural resources and past knowledge of the sector, either through their own, or older offspring experiences, can provide some parents with levels of competencies which others lack. The ability to provide financial backing makes the choice process a less stressful one. But pupils from all social class backgrounds still experience levels of anxiety about achieving the necessary grades to allow them to go on to the university of their choice. The choosing process is clearly fraught with anxieties and a lack of proper communication with parents can serve to exacerbate these issues. Previous chapters have shown how pupils are making assumptions about their parents' willingness and, or their ability to meet the costs of university and are making choices accordingly, without discussion.

The influences and impact of social and cultural capital in allowing informed decisions to be made and information to be accurately and competently accessed are clearly significant factors that underpin the discourses. The ways in which families discuss and negotiate the choice process and share common experiences and expectations can influence the ways in which they access information and make informed choices. Throughout this chapter what has been clear has been the ways in which anxiety and uncertainty are an inherent part of contemporary family life. What it not clear is what strategies these family units adopt to ameliorate some of these concerns.

Chapter 9

Exploring Choice

The earlier chapters of this book have traced growth of higher education in the UK and identified the political changes in welfare benefits and the implications for youth employment and patterns of participation in post compulsory education. These changes have all occurred within a political discourse of widening access and increasing participation in higher education. However within the rhetoric of this expansionist agenda there has been a persistent trend to recruit from the middle classes. The emphasis on free market principles, linked with a continued manipulation of the funding mechanisms and the introduction of loans and fees has been such that certain groups and sections of the community have been effectively discriminated against.   This monograph considers some of the factors that influence and facilitate young people in their university choices The data have enabled me to theorize on three key concepts, of which two have firm historical roots and one is new. First is the durability of class based educational inequalities that are revealed by making comparisons with the Jackson and Marsden (1962) study. Second is the emergence of kinship, identity and anxiety comparable with the study in the Swansea Valley in the 1960s (Barker, 1972; Leonard, 1980). The modern theme is concerned with the emergence of gender specific roles within the family and the prominence of the father in the university choice process. The narrative accounts of parents, students and teachers are presented within broad theoretical perspectives since theory 'allows us to de-familiarize present practices and categories of experience' (Ball, 1995:266). The work of Bourdieu has clearly underpinned the analysis and has been used to consider the implications of class in terms of social and cultural reproduction in education. In addition I have drawn on the theorising of Basil Bernstein in order to explore the ways in which decision making is negotiated within families and used the traditions of social anthropology to allow me to demonstrate the affective significance of family and localism. In this final chapter I will revisit these themes in order to develop some typologies of both the schools and families in the study. I will offer some additional theorising on the data in order to underscore the complexities of social class and higher education choices in order to comment on the very real class based university challenge.

Central to Bourdieu's thinking is the concept of social practice and practical logic. He uses the 'field' as a metaphor for 'the structured system of social positions the nature of which defines the situations for their occupants' (Jenkins, 1992:85). Certain institutions and individuals possess a practical logic that gives them a feel for the game that reproduces rather than reduces differences between social groups. The higher education market is highly stratified and the process of selection and application complex. Knowing which qualifications to seek and where to acquire them 'are dimensions of cultural competence most readily available to applicants from educated homes and schools with the know how to read the system' (Power et al, 2003:82). The role of the school as a key facilitator in maximising academic success and entry into middle class occupations has been well-documented (Brown and Scase, 1994; Ainley, 1994). Similarly studies have shown the inequalities that exist in terms of patterns of participation and the under-representation of working class groups in higher education (Archer et al, 2003; Halsey et al 1980). This can be explained in terms of 'deferred elimination', since pupils from working class backgrounds are 'more likely to enter those branches (establishments or sections) from which there is least chance of entering the next level of education' (Bourdieu and Passeron 1990:42). The ways in which the school system perpetuates class inequalities is summarized in Table 9.1 below.

Table 9.1 Education and Reproduction: The Five Levels of Practice

Level 1	For under-privileged young people there is a lower success rate. GCSE passes are fewer and the average A level points per pupil are lower. Expectations of HE destinations are adjusted accordingly, and become part of the habitus.
Level 2	Where some success is attained, under- privileged young adults (and their families) tend to make the 'wrong' option choices.
Level 3	Learned ignorance of school and selection agents - recognising only those who recognize them. Implications for UCAS applications and choice
Level 4	Denigration of the academic - preference of style over content.
Level 5	Devaluation of certificates in favour of habitus. Where selection now turns on habitus (style, presentation, language etc.) these things then become a form of symbolic capital, which acts as a multiplier of the productivity of educational capital (qualifications).

(Adapted from Harker, 1990)

These five levels seem to be a suitable framework for theorising the class inequalities which are evident in the data on the role of each of the schools and colleges as Facilitators in the choice process. At Level One schools 'naturalize' the culture of the dominant group, immediately disadvantaging children whose habitus is different from that of the school and the school would be those young people's only route into the habitus of the educationally successful middle classes. Level Two provides a double bid, firstly because working-class pupils have a lower educational success rate and secondly they and their parents frequently make the 'wrong' choices in terms of subject options. At Level Three, we meet what Bourdieu refers to as a 'learned ignorance' exhibited by pupils as they get older. Schools and selection agents become progressively less able to recognize any merits in them that are not central to the dominant habitus. At Level Four schools and colleges doubly disadvantage certain pupils by evaluating those with the appropriate attitudes and style as more naturally brilliant, compared with the more plodding, pedantic even academic styles of other cultures. In the final stage at Level Five examiners and higher education admissions tutors look for style and a 'goodness of fit' between the institution and the individual, over credentials, thereby ensuring that social capital multiplies educational capital. In this study Level Two processes can be seen to come into play for both Michael and Jason, both of whom achieved a number of passes at GCSE level, indicating their ability to continue in post compulsory education. However, this 'success' led them to make uninformed choices as to where and what to study at post compulsory level.

The 'Good' School: Typifying Choice Facilitators

In earlier chapters notably Chapters 4 and 5, I have considered the ways in which the different schools and sixth form colleges in the study have engaged with the higher education market and worked with pupils and their families in order to optimise [or not] their choices. A differentiated and hierarchical system has emerged across the sector in relation to the levels of facilitation afforded to pupils in respect of their career and higher education guidance. The data from the study have been used to illustrate the causal relationship between inequality and class and have allowed me to construct typifications 'intended to capture the key features of a given phenomenon without necessarily displaying all the particulars of individual cases' (Coffey and Atkinson, (1996:143). These typologies are not intended to be all-inclusive but rather are used as heuristic devices to illustrate the range of facilitation that can be found in and between schools. The variations between schools have clear implications for young people in relation to post 18 trajectories. For some their choices are determined as a consequence of rigorous coaching and vigorous engagements with the higher education market. As Power et al (2003:83) note there is a 'close alignment of high entry scores with high proportions of middle class and privately schooled students'. In contrast schools that have a less informed, less proactive and less well-structured approach to the HE market may leave some young people and their families feeling isolated and ill equipped to engage with the choice process. The characteristics of each school or college in the study in respect of their levels of awareness and engagement with the HE market have been typified as 'Thrusting', 'Trying' or 'Trusting'. The categories and the sites can be readily identified with reference to Table 9.2.

Table 9.2 School Typologies and Choice

THRUSTING	TRYING	TRUSTING
Brangwyn Hall Redcoats School Regent High School Jenkin High School	Cardinal Gwyn RC College Ysgol Bryn Alun St Non's CW High School Briarwood High School	Argoed FE College Llanover High School

These typologies reflect the level of expertise that each of the schools and colleges has in terms of market awareness and their approach to facilitating the choice process. The schools in the 'Thrusting' category all have middle class students, the category includes both Private Schools, the Grant Maintained School and the comprehensive school in the most middle class catchment area. They each ensure that their students are successfully steered through the complexities of the higher education marketplace in order to enable them to choose the 'best' universities. Here 'choice of university is a choice of lifestyle and a matter of taste' (Ball et al, 2002:53). Progress is heavily monitored throughout each stage of the application process, different Examination Boards are selected in order to maximize examination successes and students are coached in the UCAS procedure and the Oxbridge interview. These schools are 'ranking active' (Ball et al, 2002) and students are encouraged to make strategic choices to optimise their advantages. With a rapidly expanding graduate work force and in the absence of objective ways of comparing graduate qualifications, Bourdieu's 'dominant groups' are best served by choosing and being chosen by the 'best' universities (Morley, 1997).

Schools that are in the 'Trying' category do their best to facilitate choices. With the exception of Briarwood School, each of the schools in this category have some element of 'value added' in terms of the Welsh language or a particular religious affiliation and parents will have made choices at secondary level in opting for one of these three. However, the pressures of the A-level curriculum and the marginalization of guidance programmes can sometimes serve to limit the effectiveness of their institutional habitus. Although many students do choose successful, others like Mena slip through the net and are disadvantaged choosers. As Power et al (2003:157) note 'contrasting individual experiences at the 'same' school highlight the importance of home backgrounds'. Trying' schools rely largely on the family to reinforce and supplement the information that they provide and since many of these families are middle class, this strategy is often highly effective. Where there is dissonance and the family habitus cannot assist or inform choice, then slippage may occur. This in part explains the lack of homogeneity within class groups.

In contrast both Argoed College and Llanover School are located in working class areas and both fit the 'Trusting' typology. Both have highly successful Compact arrangements with 'new' universities locally and this is reflected in their approach to the UCAS process. Both Argoed College and Llanover School know that these two HEIs will accept the majority of their applicants and this negates the need for any real engagement with the market. Rather 'perceptions and expectations of choice are constructed over time in relation to school friends and teachers views and advice and learning experiences' (Ball et al, 2002:58). The teachers at both Argoed College and Llanover School suggest to many of their students who are predominantly working class, moderate achievers, that they are 'well suited' to the local institutions. In common with Ball et al (2002) I do not want to suggest that 'new' universities are second best, nor that every working class student attends a 'new' institution. Indeed it may be argued that, given the costs associated with higher education, these choices will be more easily affordable and may also provide these students with greater levels of academic success. However 'Trusting' institutions lack the initiatives and the competencies to facilitate choices and so enable the middle classes to 'continue to dominate the elite routes within higher education in order to ensure the reproduction of class privileges' (Archer et al, 2003:201)

Bernstein's (1975) notion of 'classification' and 'framing' also proves helpful in considering how the different institutions structure and organize sessions to prepare students to make higher education choices. In a 'Thrusting' school like Brangwyn Hall that is characterized by strong classification and framing, higher education guidance is taught as a separate subject, by a specialist teacher and is given time and status within the syllabus. Choices are individualized to maximize a successful outcome as students are coached through the application process. In contrast Llanover High, a 'Trusting' school has both weak classification and framing. University and career guidance is delivered as one part of a broad PSE syllabus. The school is reliant on Compact agreements with 'new' universities and it is left to the family to explore other choices. But unfamiliarity with and fear of the university system frequently results in a paralysis of activity for these families.

Theorising On Family and Choice

I have noted that at this level of choosing, that the spheres of influence and the roles adopted within the family are very different from those identified when researching school choice (Gewirtz et al, 1995; David et al, 1994). These studies found the mother to be central in the decision making process. In contrast at the level of choices for higher education in some families the father assumes prominence. The data on the families (Chapter 6, Chapter 7 and Chapter 8) consider the ease with which some young people can access information about higher education the extent to which parents are able to facilitate choices. These data indicate how working class students recognize that their parents, not having been to university themselves, know little about the system and can offer little practical help since they are uncomfortable in this new milieu. In consequence these young people look to schools for information and guidance about the HE process. If the schools fail to provide sufficient levels of support and encouragement then this group will see higher education as an undifferentiated sector and a degree course *per se* as a mark of excellence. A lack of information may inhibit any engagement with the sector at all so that 'not going to university becomes part of a "normal" biography' (Ball et al 2002:54).

By way of contrast the middle class families in the study, where one or both parents have been to university, are on familiar territory. They know the process and the range of skills and competencies that are required in order to make informed choices. Interestingly though, even in families where both parents have a degree (the Walsh family) or even where both have a doctorate (the Hughes family), the father is much more visible a facilitator (see Tables 9.3 and 9.4). This apparent gender shift is not immediately theorizable. However allowing for the small sample size it seems that at this level of choice there is a shift from the domestic to the public sphere. When a secondary school is chosen the criteria for choice are essentially domestic, the journey to school, the uniform and the happiness of the child (Coldron and Boulton, 1991; David, 1993; David et al, 1997). While the power of the husband in western families has proved 'an extraordinary resilient form of social relationship (Bell and Newby, 1976:166) at this level of choice the fathers' authority is not noted. However it may be that while the mother 'appears' to be making the choices, these choices may be constrained within a decision-making framework that has been predetermined by the father. To that end the father will make all the decisions 'even if his choice is simply to follow tradition and continue as before, or to allow the decision to be made by someone else in the household' (Delphy and Leonard, 1992:137). The choice of university however is more about status, career trajectories and money and so the discourse moves to the public (male) sphere. It can also be argued that given the escalating costs of higher education, that the father is positioned, or positions himself prominently in response to this financial investment. Studies show that while control of the household budget is usually delegated to the wife, the dominant decision making remains part of the husband's domain. It may be that the HE market place is perceived as a male preserve and fathers are cast as 'expert' in the field. Shifting decisions away from mothers, who assumed responsibility for choices at the level of the school market, may be theorized with regard to notions of public and private spheres. Issues relating to schooling fall within the private sphere of the home and family and become feminized in consequence.

It may be that the emergence of the father as the more significant player at this level is an artefact of the methodology. The school choice research, in which the mother is central to the decision making, is often based on interviews with one parent, usually the mother. For example Gewirtz et al (1995) conducted interviews with 137 parents of which 82 were mothers only, 20 fathers only and 34 with both parents. Similarly 70 per cent of the interviews conducted by David et al (1994) were with the mother alone. By way of contrast, I interviewed 20 families in total and in all but two of the interviews both parents, or primary care givers were present. The exception being mothers who were divorced or living apart from the fathers. Interviews conducted with both parents may have resulted in the full extent of the father's involvement being known. Seen as a unit, families may chose to rehearse their 'traditional' roles and so place the father central in the discussions. Or perhaps researchers on school choice have over emphasized the role of the mother set against an 'invisibility' of the father. In either case future researchers may wish to compare data gained by a variety of interview techniques and recruitment strategies.

It is possible to further theorize family roles again making reference to the work of Basil Bernstein (1977). He maintains that distinctions can be made between family types and their patterns of communication. In the 'positional' (middle class) families there are strong boundary controls, specific roles are identified and a clear hierarchy maintained. This contrasts with the working class 'personal' families where boundaries are flexible there is a considerable degree of blurring in terms of status and authority. These families acknowledge the competencies of each of their members and roles are fluid, accommodating and assimilating the various individual attributes of each, irrespective of age or gender. These families undergo a constant programme of adjustment in order to accommodate new skills and qualifications in its members. At the level of university choices this frame change is evidenced with young people cast as experts in the process. For 'positional' families, school choices are made and the wishes of the parents often over-ride those of the child, a case of 'go because I say so'. However university choices lead to a change in frame, with young people more aware of and involved in the decision making process while parents merely hold the purse strings. So the code remains constant, but there is a shift in the framing that allows the father space to 'negotiate'.

Throughout I have considered the ways in which choices are informed by both the institutional and the family habitus and the characteristics and typologies developed for the schools (Table 9.2) can be equally applied to the families (Table 9.3).

Table 9.3 Family Typologies and Choice

THRUSTING	TRYING	TRUSTING
Louise Hughes	Giles Roberts	Maria Thomas
John Walsh	Caitlin Smith	Michael White
Joanne Parker	Gavin Hutchins	Jason Barry
Amy Hubert-Jenkins	Penny James	David Jones
Rhys Joyce	Victoria Clarke	Susi Powell
Alex Smart	Mark Istance	Glyn Bateman
		Stacy Lang
		Mena Hussein

In the 'Thrusting' families, social capital is brought into play and social networks used in order to maximize choices. Familiarity with the field means an awareness of credential values in a highly stratified sector. These families can be contrasted with those in the 'Trusting' category where, in many cases, the children are first generation university entrants. Parents who have no experience of the higher education process are somewhat in awe of the academy and are hesitant to take on the 'challenge' fearing their own incompetence. They are reliant on schools to provide information and guidance and on their children to relay this knowledge to them. Here choices are constrained by a sense of what is 'culturally permissible' for 'someone like me' (Bates, 1993). The 'Trying' typology depicts families with some level of awareness of the educational market and the university sector. The Clarke family for example, have already engaged with the school market, their daughter Victoria attends private school, however as first time users of higher education, they are consciously incompetent, aware that options exist, but restricted by their habitus and unable to engage with choice at this level.

Merging the two sets of typologies of the level of institutional and family facilitation (Table 9.2 and 9.3) enables me to demonstrate the ways in which these habituses combine to reinforce the social patterns that both constrain and enable choice. In Table 9.4. it is possible to see how the interplay between the types can ensure 'success' or 'failure' or something in between. The Hughes and the Walsh Families, whose daughter Louise and son John, respectively, attend Jenkin High School and the Parker Family and the Hubert-Jenkins Family whose daughters Joanne and Amy attend Brangwyn Hall, exemplify 'Thrusting' families in 'Thrusting' schools. This is clearly the best of all combinations to ensure successful facilitation of higher education choices. These young people have the most leverage in the current HE market. By way of contrast, a combination of Trusting families and Trusting schools delimits 'opportunity structures' (Roberts, 1993). The Compact agreements act against the expectations of the market and ensure these young people go to one of the 'new' universities on the local 'circuit' (Gewirtz et al, 1995).

Table 9.4 Intersecting School and Family Typologies and Choice

		SCHOOLS		
		THRUSTING	**TRYING**	**TRUSTING**
FAMILIES		Brangwyn Hall Redcoats School Regent High Jenkin High	Cardinal Gwyn Ysgol Bryn Alun St Non's High Briarwood	Argoed College Llanover High
THRUSTING	Louise Hughes	X		
	John Walsh	X		
	Joanne Parker	X		
	Amy Hubert-Jenkins	X		
	Rhys Joyce		X	
	Alex Smart		X	

TRYING	Gavin Hutchins	X		
	Penny James	X		
	Victoria Clarke	X		
	Giles Roberts		X	
	Caitlin Smith		X	
	Mark Istance			X
TRUSTING	Stacy Lang	X		
	David Jones		X	
	Mena Hussain		X	
	Susi Powell		X	
	Glyn Bateman		X	
	Jason Barry			X
	Michael White			X
	Maria Thomas			X

A real implication of these groupings can be seen in a comparison of post-18 destinations (Table 9.5 and Table 9.6.) These illustrate the combined effectiveness [or not] of the institutional and family habituses as mediators of choice. Considering the 'best' and 'worst' combinations of school and family allows comparisons to be drawn between school choices, higher education and markets.

Table 9.5 'Thrusting' Families and Post-18 Destinations

PUPIL	DESTINATION
Louise Hughes	Oxford University Jesus College
John Walsh	Nottingham University
Joanne Parker	Goldsmiths College London
Amy Hubert-Jenkins	Durham University

I am suggesting here that these destinations are the 'best' options for each of these students. The combined forces of school and family has ensured that for each of these young people there has been an opportunity to explore choices and make rational decisions based on 'what is best for me'.

Table 9.6 'Trusting' Families and Post-18 Destinations

PUPIL	DESTINATION
Michael White	Third year of A level study (repeated 1st year)
Jason Barry	Third year of A level study (repeated 1st year)
Maria Thomas	Did not apply to HE – no real plans

These 'destinations' are the result of misplaced trust, a belief in others to know 'what is best for me'. For the young people in these two categories and others like them, these destinations demonstrate 'the opposition between the tastes of luxury (or freedom) and the tastes of necessity' (Bourdieu, 1986:178).

The Bernsteinian notion of classification and framing explored earlier in this chapter has a clear congruence with the theorising of Douglas (1973) in that they 'share their explanatory potential and empirical problems' (Delamont (1989a:37). Douglas suggests that the exclusivity of a 'group' is maintained by its entry requirements, so for example, elite institutions such as Oxford and Cambridge can, and do, set very high admissions standards. The degree of social control or regulation which an organisation or group exerts over its membership is then conceptualized in terms of a grid. So entry to university is strongly regulated via the A-level points system and the UCAS applications process. In Figure 9.1, I have adapted the work of both these theorists in order to represent the interface of the habituses of institution and family typologies with levels of market engagement.

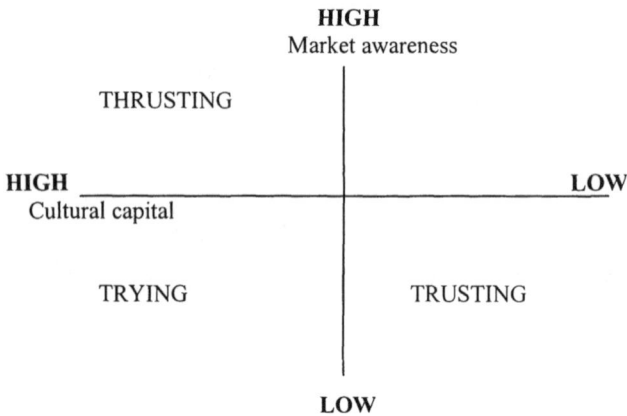

HIGH
Market awareness

THRUSTING

HIGH _____ **LOW**
Cultural capital

TRYING   TRUSTING

LOW

Figure 9.1 Family and Institutional Typologies

Things Not Being Equal

The analysis in this study is broad based and identifies the four different forms of 'capital', economic, cultural, social and symbolic which together serve to privilege, (or otherwise) these young people in their choice of HE. The different expressions of 'choice' that emerge provide an analogous relationship with class analysis. Cultural 'capital' enables some, middle class families to have the necessary competencies required to interpret and engage with the market in ways which yield maximum social educational and financial benefit. These competencies allow for choices to be made as to the 'best' schools and allow access to information and social networks that ensure that successful engagements with HE markets. In an attempt to theorize these findings further, it may be useful to consider Figure 9.2, which is adapted from Harker (1990). Using this model, educational and ultimately career 'success' via educational choices is equated with the 'Thrusting' typology of institutional and family facilitation. In contrast the under-privileged groups, the 'Truster' category, lack the social capital necessary to engage with the market system and are unaware of the implications of choices made within a highly stratified sector.

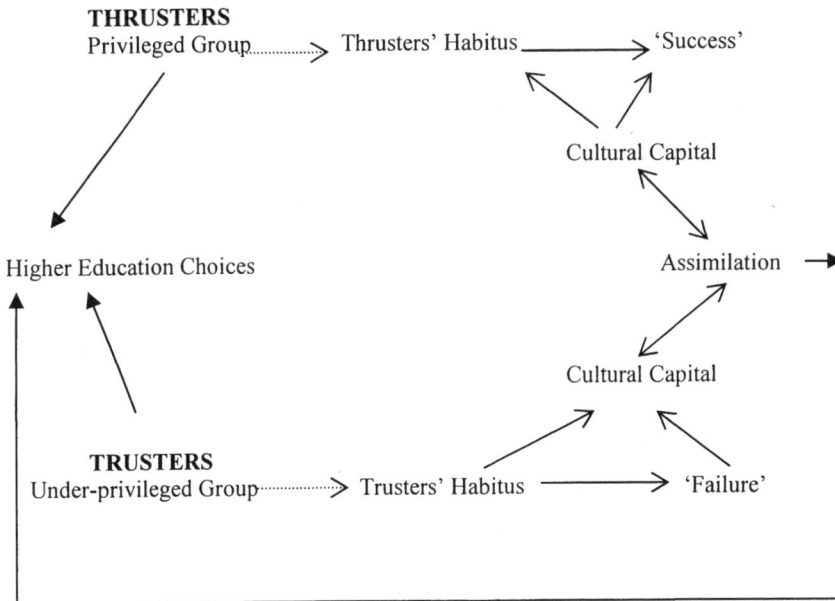

THRUSTERS
Privileged Group ··········> Thrusters' Habitus ─────────> 'Success'

Cultural Capital

Higher Education Choices   Assimilation →

Cultural Capital

TRUSTERS
Under-privileged Group ··········> Trusters' Habitus ────────> 'Failure'

Figure 9.2 Cultural Reproduction and Education Choices

Throughout this monograph I have attempted to demonstrate how sets of ideas feed into normative cultural practices which privilege and maintain the status of dominant groups. Such ideas become so internalized that they are 'taken for granted' and 'social hierarchy dissimulates itself to those it dignifies no less than to those it excludes' (Bourdieu, 1996:x). Focusing on social reproduction within family groups is helpful as 'the reproduction of family habitus would seem to offer the possibility of finer-grained analysis' (Harker, 1990:104). Choices are made within very different 'horizons of action' (Hodkinson and Sparkes, 1997), for many middle class families their tacit decoding of the rhetoric of equality which accompanied the dissolution of the binary divide between universities and polytechnics in 1992, privileges them in the market place. These parents are 'thrusting', proactive and informed as they facilitate their children's choices.

In attempting to draw together the threads of the research the intention has been to clarify, rather than to confuse the relationships between cultural reproduction and social reproduction in the choice of higher education. Overarchingly there is evidence of the persistence of inequality between classes, but there is also evidence of intra class differences. Some middle class families lack a degree of awareness of the field while some working class families can and do, access social networks for information and advice. This has clear implications in terms of class analysis since 'class identification is both a reaffirmation of values, lifestyle and aspirations and a projection towards reproduction or social betterment (Ball, 2003:176). The following is written, not as an act of closure but, rather, in an attempt to summarize the situation so far and consider the way forward for future research. I want to consider the current paradox of widening access and increasing participation set against a fee and loan levy. It is in the nature of this chapter to return to some of the themes identified in earlier chapters and to consider the findings in relation to social justice, social inclusion and citizenship. In what remains of this chapter I will attempt to move full circle returning to the questions which prompted the research and use them as an organisational framework for the discussion.

The data from this last cohort of undergraduates to benefit from 'free' access to university suggest that some 45 years post Robbins, issues of cultural reproduction continue to dominate university access. There are clear implications for Schools and Further Education Colleges, since these data make explicit the variations in the quality of HE guidance provide for students across the sector. Changes in the post 18 labour market and the implications of the National Curriculum have led to a marginalization of the career guidance programmes provided by many institutions. Where the sessions do occur the provision is often piecemeal with a shift in emphasis away from the broadly conceived curriculum of career guidance, into a programme which is firmly focused on the mechanics of the UCAS application process. In the more 'market alert' schools, their 'thrusting' approach is demonstrated in the quality and breadth of the guidance given and the consequent empowerment of the pupils and their families. The process of sifting through the higher education literature is one that many parents and young people find complex and alien. Similarly, the discourses associated with higher education are, in many cases, unfamiliar and serve to constrain choices. Policy initiatives that place relevant information and guidance within a structured framework of delivery in sixth forms would allow for a more equitable engagement with the higher education market. Government has already acknowledged the need for better access to information in the post-16 sector (DfEE, 1998). There is clearly a need to ensure that young people are provided with access to clear and comprehensive information in order to allow them to maximize their options and choose wisely. Paradoxically those young people least well placed to decode the complexities of the market place are often those who are in receipt of the least institutional help. The 'trusting' uninformed parents in this study while anxious to help were ill-equipped to facilitate choices and were reliant on 'trusting' schools to 'do the right thing' and provide options. This is particularly true for working class young people like Michael and Jason who are in the FE sector where information is not readily available (Hutchins, 2003b). These typologies demonstrate how the educational system works to reproduce social inequality. The more 'market-aware' schools have a vested interest in ensuring that their pupils transfer to high status institutions. 'Elite' school practice ensures that university destinations are used as a marketing strategy to attract future 'clients' and ensure cultural reproduction. For those schools with limited market awareness, the over reliance on tracking students to local, 'new' universities, limits their 'horizons of opportunity' (Hodkinson and Sparkes, 1997).

Social Justice, Citizenship and Choice

This research has identified a number of themes and issues in relation to social justice and citizenship, some of which might be considered relevant in the context of post-16 education and 'life long learning'. In contrast to other localities (Macrae et al, 1996) there is a very limited market in the 16-18 age group sector in south east Wales. In this region the majority of young people chose to remain at their original school for their sixth form courses. While some students feel constrained in their subject choices at A-level by the curriculum offered at their school, but see no viable alternative. Providing more sixth form colleges that could recruit more widely and offer a broad curriculum could well provide additional options and widen choices as could comprehensive and individualized HE and careers guidance programmes for all young people, prior to and during their sixth form careers. Political and educational will is needed if the non-traditional routes such as NVQs are to succeed. It will be necessary to implement policies to create a more positive image of these courses and to ensure that they enjoy a parity of esteem with the more traditional A-level courses.

The data have demonstrated and underscored the durability of class inequalities across 50 years of education policy. There is need now for measures to be introduced which ensure much greater equality of opportunity of access to information relating to higher education and the graduate labour market. In line with government 'commitment' to a policy of 'life long learning', citizenship and social justice there is a need for initiatives to encourage full engagement with market choices across the spectrum of class, gender and race. Since 1998, university students have been required to contribute towards their tuition costs. The implications in relation to issues of classed participation are clearly indicated in this levy. Although UCAS data continue to report an increase in the participation rate, the trend for local applications has also increased and the patterns of participation are already indicating a decline in applications by those in the lower income and manual social class categories.

The data illustrate how university choices are mediated and reinforced by class based competencies. Earlier engagements with the education market and school choice by the middle classes ensures that their university choices are well facilitated. In contrast, those families who are unfamiliar with market discourse often find themselves choosing from a limited menu of options, with restricted access to A-level guidance and higher education choices. This can and does lead to disillusionment and disaffection with the HE sector and often results in a rejection of the system 'before it can reject me'. Clearly a marketized higher education sector merely replicates class-based inequalities, successfully polarising rather than up-skilling the graduate workforce (Coffield and Williamson, 1997). This study has served to expose the complexities of university choice and the 'entrenched inequalities in 'participation' in and across HE (Ball, et al, 2002:70). The 1944 Education Act introduced the tri-partite system under the banner of 'secondary education for all', however, the promise of 'parity of esteem' was never realized. Rather, a hierarchical system emerged in which 'pupils of similar social origins had similar educational fates' (Halsey et al, 1980:171). This stratification proved an alienating experience for many pupils (Hargreaves, 1967; Lacey, 1970; Ball, 1981; Burgess, 1983; Brown, 1987) and led Halsey et al (1980:213) to note that , 'this system was neither a class solvent nor an engine of meritocracy: It added educational to class rigidity'. Throughout the '70s, a lack of provision was blamed for the low levels of HE participation by the working classes. Commenting Halsey et al (1980:215) stated that, 'the supply of places is a major obstacle to equalisation of opportunity'. In 1992 the removal of the binary divide led to a massive expansion of the higher education sector, which should have provided the opportunity to address Halsey's critique, offering all students meritocratic access to university. However, the resultant stratification of the sector has done little to ameliorate class inequality but rather has had a significant impact on the patterns of participation, graduate opportunities and destinations (Ainley, 1994; Brown and Scase, 1994). It is the ability to engage with the market, coupled with the ability to pay, which privileges not only access, but also outcome. There is a clear paradox between policymaking and practice in relation to participation in higher education which successive Labour governments have failed to address. While Ministers espouse a commitment to widening access and increasing student numbers, privilege remains the passport to higher education.

In the 1970s Willis asked why working class 'kids' got working class jobs. In 2004 we should question why it is they get working class choices, if indeed they get choice at all, especially when 'the pool of ability is clearly not a limit' (Halsey et al, 1980:215). In terms of social justice and equity, ensuring that real choices are available to all students regardless of their social background remains the real university challenge.

Glossary of Terms

A LEVEL	Advanced Level Examination - university entry
CAG	Computer Assisted Guidance - career / university
ECCTIS	Education Counselling and Credit Transfer System
FE	Further Education
GCSE	General Certificate of Education - precursor to A level
GMS	Grant Maintained School
GNVQ	General National Vocational Qualification
HE	Higher Education
HEFCE	Higher Education Funding Council, England
HEFCW	Higher Education Funding Council, Wales
HEI	Higher Education Institutions
ISCO	Independent Schools Careers Organisation
LMS	Locally Managed School
NUS	National Union of Students
NVQ	National Vocational Qualifications
PSE	Personal and Social Education
UCAS	Universities and Colleges Admissions Service
UCC	University College Cardiff
UGC	Universities Grant Committee
VET	Vocational Education Training
YT	Youth Training
YTS	Youth Training Schemes

Bibliography

Adam, B. (1995). *Timewatch*. Cambridge, Polity.

Adkins, L. (1995). *Gendered Work*. Buckingham, Open University Press.

Adonis, A. and Pollard, S. (1997). *A Class Act: The Myth of Britain's Classless Society*. London, Hamish Hamilton.

Aggelton, P. (1987). *Rebels Without a Cause? Middle Class Youth and the Transition from School to Work*. Lewes, Falmer Press.

Ainley, P. (1994). *Degrees of Difference Higher Education in the 1990s*. London, Lawrence and Wishart.

Alderson, P. (1995). *Listening to Children: Children, Ethics and Social Research*. London, Barnados.

Allatt, P. (1993). Becoming Privileged. In I. Bates and G. Riseborough (eds). *Youth and Inequality*. Buckingham, Open University Press.

Allatt, P. (1996). Consuming Schooling. In S. Edgell, K. Hetherington and A. Warde (eds). *Consumption Matters*. Oxford, Blackwell.

Amato, P. (1994). Father-Child relations, Mother-Child relations and offspring psychological well being in early adulthood. *Journal of Marriage and the Family*. 56: 1031-1042.

Anyon, J. (1983). Intersections of Gender and Class. In S. Walker and L. Barton. (eds). *Gender Class and Education*. Lewes, Falmer.

Aquilino, M. and Williams, S. (1997). From Adolescent to Young Adult. A Prospective Study of Parent-Child Relations during the Transition to Adulthood. *Journal of Marriage and The Family*. 59: 670-686.

Archard, D. (1993). *Children. Rights and Childhood*. London: Routledge.

Archer, L., Hutchins, M. and Ross, A. (2003). *Higher Education and Social Class*. London: RoutledgeFalmer.

Ashton, D.N., Maguire, M. and Spilsbury, M. (1990). *Restructuring the Labour Market: The Implications for Youth*. London, Macmillan.

Atkinson, P. (1990). *The Ethnographic Imagination*. London, Routledge.

Babbie, E. (1992) (6th Edition). *The Practice of Social Research*. Belmont, Wadsworth.

Ball, S.J. (1981). *Beachside Comprehensive: a case study of secondary schooling*. Cambridge, Cambridge University Press.

Ball, S.J. (1994). *Education Reform: a critical and post structuralist approach*. Buckingham, Open University Press.

Ball, S.J. (1995). Intellectuals or Technicians? *British Journal of Educational Studies*. 43 (3): 255-271.

Ball, S.J. (2003). *Class Strategies and the Education Market. The middle classes and social advantage*. London, Routledge.

Ball, S.J., Bowe, R. and Gewirtz, S. (1996). School choice, social class and distinction: the realization of social advantage in education. *Journal of Education Policy*. 11(1): 89-112.

Ball, S.J. and Vincent, C. (1998). I heard it on the grapevine: 'hot' knowledge and social choice. *British Journal of Sociology of Education*. 19:377-400.

Ball, S.J., Maguire, M. and Macrae, S. (2000). *Choice, Pathways and Transitions Post-16: new youth, new economies in the global city*. London, Routledge-Falmer.

Ball, S.J., Davies, J., David, M. and Reay, D. (2002). 'Classification' and 'Judgement': social class and the cognitive structures of choice of Higher Education. *British Journal of Sociology of Education.* 23(1): 51-72.

Banks, M., Bates, I., Breakwell, G., Bynner, J., Emler, N., Jamieson, L. and Roberts, K. (1992). *Careers and Identities.* Buckingham, Open University Press.

Barker, D. (1972). Young People and their Homes: 'spoiling' and 'keeping close' in a South Wales town. *Sociological Review.* 20(4): 569-590.

Barrett, L.R. (1996). On Students as Customers: Some Warnings from America. *Higher Education Review.* 28(3): 70-76.

Barthes, R. (1973). *Mythologies.* Frogmore, Palladin.

Bates, I. (1993). A Job which is Right for Me? In I. Bates and G. Riseborough (eds).*Youth and Inequality.* Buckingham, Open University Press.

Bates, I. and Riseborough, G. (1993). Deepening Divisions, Fading Solutions. In I. Bates and G. Riseborough (eds). *Youth and Inequality.* Buckingham, Open University Press.

Beck, U. (1992). *Risk Society.* London, Sage.

Becker, H. (1986). *Writing for Social Scientists.* London, University of Chicago Press.

Becker, H., Geer, B. and Hughes, E. (1968). *Making the Grade: the academic side of college life.* New York, Wiley.

Bell, C. and Newby, H. (1976). Husbands and Wives: the dynamics of the differential dialectic. In D. Barker and S. Allen (eds). *Dependence and Exploitation in Work and Marriage.* London, Longman.

Bellin, W., Osmond, J. and Reynolds, D. (1994). *Towards an education policy for Wales.* Cardiff, Institute for Welsh Affairs.

Bellin, W., Farrell, S., Higgs and G. White, S. (1995). A Strategy for using Census Information in comparing School Performance. *Welsh Journal of Education.* 5(1): 42-57.

Berdahl, R. and Millet, J. (1991). Autonomy and Accountability in US Higher Education. In G. Neave and F.Van Vught (eds). *Prometheus Bound: The Changing Relationship between Government and Higher Education in Western Europe.* Oxford, Pergamon Press.

Berger, P.A., Steinmuller, P. and Sopp, P. (1993). Differentiation of Life Courses? Changing patterns of labour market sequences in West Germany. *European Sociological Review.* 9(1): 43-59.

Bernstein, B. (1975). (2nd Edition). *Class, Codes and Control Vol. 1.* London, Routledge and Kegan Paul.

Bernstein, B. (1977). Class and Pedagogies. Visible and Invisible. In J. Karabel and A.H. Halsey (eds). *Power and Ideology in Education.* Oxford, Oxford University Press.

Berry, M. (1995). The Experience of Being a Woman Student. *British Journal of Guidance and Counselling.* 23(2): 211-218.

Best, R. (1983). *We've all got scars: what boys and girls learn in elementary school.* Bloomington, Indiana University Press.

Betts, C. (1997). *Funding in Wales.* Western Mail, 21st March, 4-5.

Beynon, J. (1985). *Initial Encounters in the Secondary School.* London, Falmer.

Billis, D. and Harding, M. (1996) (eds). *Voluntary Agencies and Strategic Time Management.* Basingstoke, Macmillan.

Block, M.T. and Hesketh, A.J. (1997). *The Traditional Prospectus - A User Survey.* Orkney Islands, Big Zed.

Boulton, M. (1983). *On Being a Mother.* London, Tavistock.

Bourdieu, P. (1977). Marriage Strategies as Strategies of Social Reproduction. In R. Forster and D. Ranum (eds). *Family and Society. Selections from the Annnales*. Baltimore, Jon Hopkins University Press.

Bourdieu, P. (1986). *Distinction*. London, Routledge.

Bourdieu, P. (1988). *Homo Academicus*. Oxford, Polity Press.

Bourdieu, P. (1990). *The Logic of Practice*. Cambridge, Polity Press.

Bourdieu, P. and Passeron, J-C. (1990) (2nd edition). *Reproduction in Education, Society and Culture*. London, Sage.

Bourdieu, P., Passeron, J-C. and Saint Martin, M. (1994) (eds). *Academic Discourse*. Cambridge, Polity.

Bourner, T. and Mahmoud, H. (1987*). Entry Qualifications and Degree Performance*. London, CNAA.

Bowe, R. and Ball, S.J. with Gold, A. (1992). *Reforming Education and Changing Schools*. London, Routledge.

Bowles, S. and Gintis, H. (1976). *Schooling in Capitalist America*. New York, Basic Books.

Brantlinger, E. (2003). *Dividing Classes: how the middle class negotiates and rationalizes school advantage*. London, Routledge-Falmer.

Brown, P. (1996). The Transformation of Education and Society. In A.H. Halsey, H. Lauder, P. Brown and S. Wells (eds). *Education. Culture, Economy and Society*. Oxford, Oxford University Press.

Brown P. (1987). *Schooling Ordinary Kids*. London, Tavistock.

Brown, P. and Scase, R. (1994). *Higher Education and Corporate Realities: class culture and the decline of graduate careers*. London, University College London Press.

Brunvand, J.H. (1984). *The Choking Doberman*. New York, Norton.

Bryan, K. A. (1980). Pupil Perceptions of Transfer. In A. Hargreaves and L. Tickle (eds). *Middle Schools*. London, Harper and Row.

Bryant, R. (1995). Does being a Mature Student have to be so painful? *Adults Learning*. 16(9): 270-271.

Burgess, R.G. (1983). *Experiencing Comprehensive Education: a study of Bishop McGregor School*. London, Methuen.

Burgess, R.G. (1996). *Working in Border Country. Discussion Paper on Ethnography in Cardiff*. SSSI Stone Symposium. University of Nottingham..

Burnett, J. (1969). Ceremony, Rites and Economy in the Student System of an American High School. *Human Organization*. 28(1): 1-10.

Butler, I. and Williamson, H. (1994). *Children Speak: Children, Trauma and Social Work*. London, Longman.

Bynner, J., Chisholm, L. and Furlong, A. (1997) (eds). *Youth, Citizenship and Social Change in a European Context*. Aldershot, Ashgate.

Callender, C. (2001). Changing student finances in higher education: policy contradictions under New Labour. *Widening Participation and Life Long Learning*. 3(2): 5-15.

Carley, K. (1994). Content Analysis. In R.E. Asher (ed). *The Encyclopaedia of Language and Linguistics*. Ennsford NY, Pergamon.

Clancy, P. (1997). Participation in the Republic of Ireland. *Higher Education Quarterly*. 51(1): 86-106.

Cleaton, D. (1993). *Careers Education and Guidance in British Schools: A Survey*. NACGT:ICG. West Midlands, Institute of Careers Guidance.

Coffey, A. and Atkinson, P. (1996). *Making Sense of Qualitative Data: complementary research strategies*. London, Sage.

Coffield, F., Borrill, C. and Marshall, S. (1986). *Growing up at the Margins*. Milton Keynes, Open University Press.

Coffield, F. and Williamson, B. (1997). The Challenges Facing Higher Education. In F. Coffield and B. Williamson (eds). *Repositioning Higher Education*. Buckingham: Open University Press and SRHE.

Cohen, I.J. (1996). Theories of Action and Praxis. In B.S. Turner (ed). *Social Theory*. Oxford, Blackwells.

Cohen, L. and Manion, L. (1994) (4th edition). *Research Methods in Education*. London, Routledge.

Coldron, J. and Boulton, P. (1991). Happiness as a criterion of parents' choice of school. *Journal of Education Policy*. 6(2):169-178.

Coleman, J.C. and Hendry, L. (1990). *The Nature of Adolescence*. London, Routledge.

Collins, R. (1985). Horses for Courses: Ideology and the Division of Domestic Labour. In P. Close and R. Collins (eds). *Family and Economy in Modern Society*. Basingstoke: Macmillan.

Connell, R.W., Ashenden, D.J., Kessler, S. and Dowsett, G.W. (1982). *Making the Difference. Schools, Families and Social Divisions*. London, George Allen and Unwin.

Connor, H. and Dewson, S., with Tyers, C., Eccles,. J., Regan, J. and Aston, J. (2001). *Social Class and Higher Education: issues affecting decisions on participation by lower social class groups*. Research Report 267, London, DfEE.

Conway, A. and York, D.A. (1991). Universities and Markets. *International Journal of Public Sector Management*. 4(2): 17-35.

Cookson, P.W. and Persell, C.H. (195). *Preparing for Power: America's Elite Boarding Schools*. New York, Basic Books.

Cortazzi, M. (1992). Narrative Analysis. London, Falmer.

Crompton, R. (1998) (2nd Edition). *Class and Stratification. An Introduction to Current Debates*. Cambridge, Polity Press.

Crompton, R. and Sanderson, K. (1990). *Gendered Jobs and Social Change*. London, Unwin Hyman.

Crowley, T. (1992). Computer Aided Career Guidance: an Investigation involving an Artificial System. *British Journal of Guidance and Counselling*. 20(2): 344-351.

Crowther Report. (1959). *Fifteen to Eighteen*. London, Central Advisory Board for Education.

Dabney, J. (1995). Opinion: Stress in Students. *Innovations in Education and Training International*. 32(2): 112-116.

Daniel, J. (1993). The Challenge of Mass Higher Education. *Studies in Higher Education*. 18(2): 197-202.

David, M. (1993). *Parents, Gender and Education Reform*. Cambridge, Polity Press.

David, M., Ball, S. J., Davies, J., Reay, D. (2003). Gender Issues in Parental Involvement in Student Choices of Higher Education. *Gender and Education*. 15(1): 23-36.

David, M., Davies, J., Edwards, R., Reay, D. and Standing, K. (1997). Choice within constraints: mothers and schooling. *Gender and Education*. 9(4): 397-410.

David, M., West, A. and Ribbens, J. (1994). *Mothers Intuition? Choosing Secondary Schools*. London: Falmer.

Davies, P., Wiliams, J. and Webb, S. (1997). Access to higher education in the late twentieth century: policy, power and discourses In J. Williams (ed) *Negotiating Access to Higher Education: the discourses of selectivity and equity*. Buckingham, SRHE and Open University Press.

Daws, P. (1972). The Role of the Careers Teacher. In J. Hayes and B. Hopson (eds). *Career Guidance, the Role of the School in Vocational Development*. London, Heinemann.

de Vaus, D. A. (1994) (4th Edition). *Surveys in Social Settings*. London, UCL Press.

Dearing Committee (1997). Report of the National Committee of Inquiry into Higher Education. *Higher Education in the Learning Society. Summary Report.* London, HMSO.

Deem, R., Brehoney, K. and Heath, S. (1994). Governors, schools and the miasma of the market. *British Educational Research Journal.* 20(5):535-549.

Delamont, S. (1980). *The Sociology of Women.* London, George Allen and Unwin.

Delamont, S. (1984). The Old Girl Network. In R.G. Burgess, (ed.) *Fieldwork in Educational Settings.* London, Falmer.

Delamont, S. (1987). Clean Baths and Dirty Women : Pollution beliefs on a Gynaecology Ward. In N. McKeganey and S. Cunningham-Burley (eds). *Enter the Sociologist.* Aldershot, Avebury.

Delamont, S. (1989). The Nun in the Toilet: urban legends and educational research. *Qualitative Studies in Education.* 2(3): 96-119.

Delamont, S. (1989a). *Knowledgeable Women.* London, Routledge.

Delamont, S. (1990) (2nd Edition). *Sex Roles and the School.* London, Routledge.

Delamont, S. (1996). *A Woman's Place in Education.* Aldershot, Avebury.

Delamont, S. (2002) (2nd Edition). *Fieldwork in Educational Settings.* London, Routledge.

Delamont, S. and Galton, M. (1986). *Inside the Secondary Classroom.* London, Routledge and Kegan Paul.

Delamont, S. and Rees, G. (1996). *The Sociology of Education in Wales: A Future Agenda. School of Education Working Paper.* Cardiff, University of Wales.

Delphy, C. (1984). *Close to Home: A Materialist Analysis of Women's Oppression.* London, Hutchinson.

Delphy, C. and Leonard, D. (1992). *Familiar Exploitation A New Analysis of Marriage in Contemporary Britain.* Cambridge, Polity.

Denscombe, M. (1995). Explorations in Group Interviews. *British Educational Research Journal* 21(2): 131-146.

Denzin, N. and Lincoln, Y. (1994) (eds). *Handbook of Qualitative Research.* London, Sage.

Department for Education and Employment (DfEE) (1994). *UK Participation Rates in post-compulsory education. Statistical Bulletin 10/94.* London: DfEE.

Department for Education and Employment (DfEE) (1998). *Higher Education for the 21st Century. Response to the Dearing Report.* London, DfEE.

Dill, D. (1997). Higher Education, Markets and Public Policy. *Higher Education Policy.* 10(3/4): 167-185.

Dore, R. P. (1976). *The Diploma Disease.* London, Allen and Unwin.

Douglas, M. (1966). *Purity and Danger.* London, Routledge and Kegan Paul.

Douglas, M. (1973) (ed.) *Rules and Meanings.* Harmondsworth, Penguin.

Douglas, M. (1975) (ed.) *Implicit Meanings: Essays in Anthropology.* London, Routledge.

Douglas, M. (1982) (ed.) *In the Active Voice.* London, Routledge.

Douvan, E. and Adelson, J. (1966). *The Adolescent Experience.* London, Fontana.

Edgell, S. (1980). *Middle Class Couples.* London, George Allen and Unwin.

Edwards, T., Fitz, J. and Whitty, G. (1989). *The State and Private Education: an Evaluation of the Assisted Places Scheme.* Lewes, Falmer Press.

Egerton, M. and Halsey, A.H. (1993). Trends by Social Class and Gender in Access to Higher Education in Britain. *Oxford Review of Education.* 9(2): 51-78.

Eggleston, J. (1993). Post 16 Young Black Britain. In A. Fyfe and P. Figueroa (eds). *Cultural Diversity.* London, Routledge.

Eriksen, E. (1968). *Identity: Youth and Crisis.* New York, Norton.

Evetts, J. (1995) (ed). *Women and Career Themes and Issues in Advanced Industrial Societies.* Harlow, Longman.

Fevre, R., Rees, G., Furlong, J. and Gorard, S. (1997). *Patterns of Participation in Education and Training. Working Paper 3.* School of Education, Cardiff University of Wales.

Field, F. (1989). *Losing Out: The Emergence of Britain's Underclass.* Oxford, Blackwell.

Finch, J. (1986). Whose Responsibility? Women and the future of family care. In I. Allen (ed.) *The Future of Informal Care.* London, Policy Studies Institute.

Fitz, J., Halpin, D. and Power, S. (1993). *Grant Maintained Schools : Education in the Market Place.* London, Kogan Page.

Fogelman, K. (1976). *Britain's 16 year olds: preliminary findings from the 3rd follow up of the National Children's Development Study.* London, National Children's Bureau.

Forsythe A. and Furlong, A. (2000). *Socio economic Disadvantage ad Access to Higher Education.* Bristol, Policy Press and Joseph Rowntree Foundation.

Foskett, N. and Hemsley-Brown, S. (2003). Economic Aspirations, Cultural Reproduction and Social Dilemmas - Interpreting Parental Choice of British Private Schools. In G. Walford (ed). *British Private Schools. Research on Policy and Practice.* London, Woburn Press.

Fuller, M. (1984). Black Girls in a London Comprehensive School. In M. Hammersley and P. Woods (eds). *Life in School: The sociology of pupil culture.* Buckingham, Open University Press.

Furlong, A. (1992). *Growing up in a Classless Society? School to Work Transitions.* Edinburgh, Edinburgh University Press.

Furlong, A., Biggart, A. and Cartmel, F. (1996). Opportunity, Structures and Occupational Aspirations. *Sociology.* 30(3): 551-565.

Gardener, R. (1987). *Who Say? Choice and Control in Care.* London, National Children's Bureau.

Gellert, C. (1996). Recent Trends in German Higher Education. *European Journal of Education.* 31(3): 311-319.

Gewirtz, S. Ball, S.J. and Bowe, R. (1995). *Markets, Choice and Equity in Education.* Buckingham, Open University Press.

Giddens, A. (1973). *The Class Structure of Advanced Societies.* London, Hutchinson.

Giddens, A. (1991). *Modernity and Self-Identity.* Cambridge, Polity.

Gilborn, D. (1990). *Race, Ethnicity and Education.* London, Unwin Hyman.

Gilligan, C., Lyon, N. and Hanmer, T. (1990) (eds). *Making Connections: The relational worlds of adolescent girls at Emma Willard School.* Cambridge MA, Harvard University Press.

Ginzberg, E., Ginzberg, S.W., Axelrad, S., Herma, J.L. (1951). *Occupational Choice: An Approach to a General Theory.* New York, Columbia University Press.

Glaser, B. and Strauss, A. (1967). *The Discovery of Grounded Theory.* New York, Aldine Publishing.

Glatter, R. Woods, P.A. and Bagley, C. (1997) (eds). *Choice and Diversity in Schooling: perspectives and prospectives.* London: Routledge.

Goffman, E. (1969). *The Presentation of Self in Everyday Life.* London, Allen Lane.

Goldthorpe, J.H. (1987) (2nd Edition). *Social Mobility and Class Structure in Modern Britain.* London, Oxford University Press.

Gorard, S. (1996a). *School Choice in an established market: families and fee paying schools in South Wales.* Unpublished PhD Thesis. Cardiff, University of Wales.

Gorard, S. (1996b). Stating the Welsh school-effect. *Journal of Education Policy.* 13(1): 115-124.

Gorard, S., Rees, G., Fevre, R., and Furlong, J. (1997). *Learning trajectories : Some voices of those "in transit". Patterns of Participation in Adult Education and Training. Working Paper II.* Cardiff, School of Education Cardiff University.

Guerney-Dixon Report. (1954). *Early School Leaving*. London, Central Advisory Board for Education.

Guri-Rosenblit, S. (1996). Trends in Access to Israeli Higher Education. *European Journal of Education*. 31(3): 321-340.

Gray, L. (1991). *Marketing Education*. Buckingham, Open University Press.

Hall, S. and Jefferson, T. (eds) (1976). *Resistance through Rituals: Youth Sub Cultures in Post War Britain.* London, Hutchinson.

Halpin, D. (1992). Staying On and Staying In: Comprehensive Schools in the 1990s. In M. Arnot and L. Barton. (eds). *Voicing Concerns: sociological perspectives on contemporary education reforms*. Oxfordshire, Triangle.

Halsey, A. (1993). Trends in access and equity in higher education: Britain in International perspective. *Oxford Review of Education*. 19(2): 129-140

Halsey, A. (1992). *Decline of donnish dominion: The British Academic Professions in the twentieth century*. Oxford, Clarendon Press.

Halsey, A.H., Heath, A.F. and Ridge, J.M. (1980). *Origins and Destinations. Family, Class and Education in Modern Britain*. Oxford, Clarendon Press.

Hammer, T. and Furlong, A. (1996). Staying On: the effect of recent changes in education participation for 17-19 year olds in Norway and Scotland. *Sociological Review*. 44(4): 675-691.

Hargreaves, D.H. (1967). *Social Relations in a Secondary School*. London, Routledge Kegan Paul.

Hargreaves, D.H. (1982). *The Challenge for the Comprehensive School*. London, Routledge and Kegan Paul.

Harker, R. (1990). Bourdieu: Education and Reproduction. In R. Harker, C. Mahar, C. Wilkes (eds). *An Introduction to the Work of Pierre Bourdieu. London*, Macmillan.

Harris, C.C. (1990). Reflections on Family, Economy and Community. In C.C. Harris (ed.) *Family, Economy and Community*. Cardiff, University of Wales Press.

Harris, S. (1992). A Career on the Margins? The position of the careers teacher in schools. *British Journal of Sociology of Education*. 13: 163-176.

Harris, S. (1997). Partnership, Community and the Market in Careers Education and Guidance: conflicting discourses. *International Studies in the Sociology of Education*. 7(1): 101-119.

Harrison, M. (1988). Domestic Service Between the Wars. The experiences of two rural women. *Oral History*. 16(1): 48-54.

Hatcher, R. (1998). Class differentiation in education: rational choices? *British Journal of Sociology of Education,* 19(1): 5-24.

Head, J. (1997). *Working with Adolescents: constructing identity*. London, Falmer.

Headington, R. and Howson, J. (1995). The School brochure : A Marketing Tool? *Educational Management and Administration*. 23(2): 89-103.

Heathfield, M. and Wakeford, N. (1991). *They Always Eat Green Apples: Images of University and Decisions at 16.* Lancaster Unit for Innovation in Higher Education, Lancaster University.

HEFCE (1996). *Higher Education Funding Council England, Annual Report*. Bristol, HEFCE Agency.

HEFCW (1997). *Higher Education Funding Council Wales, Annual Report*. Cardiff, HEFCW.

Helsby, G., Knight, P. and Saunders, M. (1998). Preparing Students for the New Work Order: the case of Advanced General National Vocational Qualifications. *British Educational research Journal*. 24(1): 63-78.

HESA (1997). *Higher Education Statistical Bulletin. 1997.* London, HESA.

HESA (2000). Higher Education Statistical Bulletin. 2000. London, HESA.

Hesketh, A. (1996). *Beg, Borrow or Starve? How to finance your degree.* Lancashire, Ampersand Press.

Hesketh, A. (1997). *When Clarity Aint Parity : Mapping young people's perceptions of the Academic / vocational divide.* Paper presented at ECER Annual Conference. Frankfurt Germany.

Hesketh, A. (1998). *GET: graduate employment and training towards the millennium.* Cardiff, Cardiff University School of Education.

Hesketh, A. and Knight, P. (1998). Secondary School prospectuses and Educational Markets. *Cambridge Journal of Education.* 28(1): 21-35.

Hickox, M. and Lyon, E.S. (1998). Vocationalism and Schooling : the British and Swedish experiences compared. *British Journal of Sociology of Education.* 19(1): 25-38.

Higgins, T. (1994). Application Procedures to Higher Education: An Admission of Failure? In S. Haselgrove (ed.) *The Student Experience.* Buckinghamshire, SRHE and OUP.

Hodkinson, P. and Mattinson, K. (1994). A Bridge too far? The problems facing GNVQs. *Curriculum Journal.* 5(3): 323-326.

Hodkinson, P., Sparkes, A. and Hodkinson, H. (1996). *Triumphs and Tears: Young people, markets and the transition from school to work.* London, David Fulton.

Holland, R. (1990). *The Long Transition: Class, Culture and Youth Training.* Basingstoke, Macmillan.

Hoover-Dempsey, K.V. and Sandler, H.M. (1997). Why do Parents Become Involved in their Children's Education? *Review of Educational Research.* 67(1): 3-42.

Howieson, C and Semple, S. (1996). *Guidance in Secondary Schools.* Edinburgh Centre for Educational Sociology: University of Edinburgh.

Hughes, M. Wikely, F and Nash, T. (1994). *Parents and their Children's Schools.* Oxford, Blackwell.

Humphrey, R. (2001). Working is a class issue. *Times Higher Education Supplement.* 19th January 2001.

Hunter, J. B. (1991). Which School? A study of parents' choice of secondary school. *Educational Research.* 33(1): 43-67.

Hutchins, M. (2003). Financial barriers to participation. In L. Archer, M. Hutchins, and A. Ross. *Higher Education and Social Class. Issues of exclusion and inclusion.* London, RoutledgeFalmer.

Hutchins, M. (2003a). Information, advice and cultural discourse of higher education. In L. Archer, M. Hutchins and A. Ross. *Higher Education and Social Class: Issues of exclusion and inclusion.* London, RoutledgeFalmer.

Jackson, B. and Marsden, D. (1962). *Education and the Working Class.* London, Routledge.

James, C. and Phillips, P. (1995). The Practice of Educational Marketing in Schools. *Education Management and Administration.* 23(2): 75-88.

Jarrett Report (1985). *Report of the Steering Committee for Efficiency Studies in Universities.* London, HMSO.

Jenkins, R. (1992). *Pierre Bourdieu.* London, Routledge.

Jones, G.E. (1997). *Policy making in Wales: an historical perspective.* Paper presented at Culture, Curriculum and Community Seminar. Swansea University, November 1997.

Kelly, G. and Slaughter, S. (1991) (eds). *Women's Higher Education in Comparative Perspective.* London, Kluwer Academic Publisher.

Keen, C. and Higgins, T. (1990). *Young People's Knowledge of Higher Education.* Leeds/ Cheltenham, HEIST / PCAS.

Keen, C. and Higgins, T. (1992). *Adults' Knowledge of Higher Education*. Leeds, Heist/PCAS.

Kidd, J. and Wardman, M. (1999). Post-16 course choice: a challenge for guidance, *British Journal of Guidance and Counselling* 27(2): 259-274.

Killeen, J. (1996). The Social Context of Guidance. In A.G. Watts, B. Law, J. Killeen, J.M. Kidd and R. Hawthorn. *Rethinking Careers Education and Guidance*. London, Routledge.

Kirk, D. (1993). *The Body, Schooling and Culture*. Deaking, Deaking University Press.

Kitzinger, J. (1994). Focus Groups: Method or Madness? In M. Boulton (ed.) *Challenge and Innovation. methodological advances in social research in HIV/AIDS*. London, Francis Taylor.

Kivenen, O. and Rinne, R. (1991). How to Steer Student Flows and Higher Education: the headache facing the Finnish Ministry of Education. In G. Neave and F. Van Vught (eds). *Prometheus Bound: The Changing Relationship between Government and Higher Education in Western Europe*. Oxford, Pergamon Press.

Kleinfeld, J. (1979). *Eskimo School on the Andreafsky a study of effective bicultural education*. New York, Praeger.

Kogan, M. (1987). Review of the University Grants Committee: Report of a Committee under the Chairmanship of Lord Croham. *Higher Education Review* 12(3): 225-240.

Kogan, M. and Kogan, D. (1983). *The Attack on Higher Education*. London, Kogan Page.

Kreuger, R. (1988). *Focus Groups*. London, Sage.

Lacey, C. (1970). *Hightown Grammar the School as Social System*. Manchester, University Press.

Lacey, C, (1976). Intragroup Competitive Pressures and the Selection of Social Strategies: Neglected Paradigms in the study of Adolescent Socialisation. In C.J. Calhoun and F.A. Ianni (eds). *The Anthropological Study of Education*. The Hague, Mouton and Company.

Laursen, P. and Foersom, B. (1993). Student Choice: a Model. *Higher Education Review*. 26(1): 64-73.

Law, B. and Storey, J. (1987). *Is it Working?* Cambridge, National Institute for Career Education and Counselling.

Law, B. (1996). Careers Work in Schools. In A.G. Watts, B. Law, J. Killen, J.M. Kidd, and R. Hawthorn. *Rethinking Careers Education and Guidance. Theory, Policy and Practice*. London, Routledge.

Lawrence, D. (1992). Under Pressure to Change: the Professional Identity of Careers Officers. *British Journal of Guidance and Counselling*. 20(2):257-273.

Le Grand, J. and Bartlett, W. (1993) (eds). *Quasi-Markets and Social Policy*. Basingstoke, Macmillan.

Lees, S. (1986). *Losing Out*. London, Heinemann.

Leonard, D. (1980). *Sex and Generation*. London, Tavistock Publications.

Leonard, D. (1990). Sex and Generation Reconsidered. In C.C. Harris (ed). *Family, Economy and Community*. Cardiff, University of Wales Press.

Lightfoot, S. L. (1983). *The Good High School: portraits of character and culture*. New York, Basic Books.

Lowe, R. (1993). *The Welfare State in Britain since 1945*. London, Macmillan.

Lucey, H. and Reay, D. (2002). Carrying the beacon of excellence: social class differentiation and anxiety at a time of transition. *Journal of Education Policy*. 17(3): 321-336.

Lynch, K. and O'Riordan, C. (1998). Inequality in higher education a study of class barriers. *British Journal of Sociology of Education*. 19(4): 445-478.

Mac an Ghaill, M. (1988). *Young, Gifted and Black: Student-Teacher Relations in the Schooling of Black Youth*. Buckingham, Open University Press.

Mace, J. (1996). Contradiction and Conflict. *Higher Education Review*. 29(1): 7-32.

Mackay, L., Scott, P. and Smith, D. (1995). Reconstructed and differentiated? Institutional responses to the changing environment of UK higher education. *Higher Education Management*. 7(2): 193-205.

MacLoed, D. (1997). Taking the High Road. *The Guardian Higher Education Supplement*. 1st July, 1997

Macrae, S., Maguire, M., and Ball, S.J. (1996). *Competition, Choice and Hierarchy in a Post-16 Education and Training Market*. Paper presented at Kings College London Seminar. Summer 1996.

Maguire, M., Macrae, S., and Ball, S.J. (1996a). *Open days and Brochures: marketing tactics in the post-16 sector*. Paper presented at the 1996 BERA Conference Lancaster.

Mallier, T. and Rodgers, T. (1995). Measuring Value Added in Higher Education. *Educational Economics*. 3(2): 119-132.

Mauss, M. (1954). *The Gift: forms of exchange*. London, Cohen and West

McCaig, C. (2001). New Labour and education, education, education. In S. Ludlam and M. J. Smith (eds). *New Labour in Government*. Basingstoke, Macmillan.

McPherson, A. (1973). Selection and Survival: sociology of the ancient Scottish universities. In R. Brown (ed). *Knowledge, Education and Cultural Change. London*, Tavistock.

McRobbie, A. (1978). Working Class Girls and the Culture of Femininity. In Women's Study Group (eds). *Women Take Issue*. Milton Keynes, Open University Press.

Measor, L. and Woods, P. (1984). *Changing Schools*. Milton Keynes, Open University Press.

Metz, M. H. (1986). *Different by design: the context and character of three Magnet schools*. London, Routledge and Kegan Paul.

Moffatt, M. (1989). *Coming of Age in New Jersey: colleges and American culture*. New Brunswick, Reuters University Press.

Molinero, L. H. (1990). Understanding University Undergraduate Applications. *Higher Education Review*. 22(2): 7-19.

Moodie, G. C. (1983). Buffer, Coupling and Brake. Reflections on 60 years of the UGC. *Higher Education*. 12: 331-347.

Morgan, D. H. (1988). Socialisation and the Family. In M. Woodhead and A. McGrath (eds.). *Family, School and Society*. London, Hodder and Stoughton.

Morgan, D. H. (1996). *Family Connections*. Cambridge, Polity Press.

Morgan, D. L. (1997) (2nd edition). *Focus Groups as Qualitative Research*. London, Sage.

Morley, L. (1997). Change and equity in higher education. *British Journal of Sociology of Education* 18(2): 231-242.

Morris, M., Simkin, C. and Stoney, S. (1995). *The Role of the Careers Service in Careers Education and Guidance in Schools*. Sheffield, Careers Service Branch.

Moscati, R. (1991). Italy. In G. Neave and F. Van Vught (eds). *Prometheus Bound: The Changing Relationship between Government and Higher Education in Western Europe*. Oxford, Pergamon Press.

Murphy, R.J.L. (1981). Examinations O level grades and Teacher estimates as predictors of the A level results of UCCA applicants. *British Journal of Educational Psychology*. 5: 1-9.

Neave, G. (1991). The reform of Higher Education: or The Ox and The Toad a Fabulous Tale. In G. Neave and F. Van Vught (eds). *Prometheus Bound: The Changing*

Relationship between Government and Higher Education in Western Europe. Oxford, Pergamon Press.

Neave, G. and Van Vught, F. (1991). Introduction. In G. Neave and F. Van Vught (eds). *Prometheus Bound: The Changing Relationship between Government and Higher Education in Western Europe.* Oxford, Pergamon Press.

Newsom Report.(1963). *Half Our Future.* London, Central Advisory Board for Education.

Nicholson, J. (1980). *Seven Ages.* London, Fontana.

NUS (1993). *Accommodation Costs. Reports 1992/3.* London, NUS.

NUS (1996). *Report on Levels of Student Debt 1995/96.* London, NUS.

Oakley, A. (1974). *The Sociology of Housework.* Oxford, Martin Robertson.

OHMCI (1997). *A Survey of Careers Education and Guidance in the Secondary Schools of Wales. Cardiff*: Hackman.

Pahl, J. (1989). *Money and Marriage.* London, Macmillan.

Pahl, J. (1990). Household Spending, Personal Spending and the Control of Money. *Sociology* 24(1): 119-138.

Pahl, R. (1984). *Divisions of Labour.* Oxford, Basil Blackwell.

Parry, G. (1986) From patronage to partnership. *Journal of Access Studies.* 1(1).

Parry, G. (1997). Patterns of Participation in Higher Education in England: A Statistical Summary and Commentary. *Higher Education Quarterly.* 51(1), 6-28.

Paterson, L. (1997). Trends in Higher Education Participation in Scotland. *Higher Education Quarterly.* 51(1): 29-45.

Paterson, L. and Raffe, D. (1995). Staying on in Full-time Education in Scotland, 1985-1991. *Oxford Review of Education.* 21(1): 3-23.

Peshkin, A. (1986). *God's Choice.* Chicago, University Press.

Petersen, A.C. (1988). Adolescent Development. *Annual Review of Psychology.* 39: 358-367.

Phillips, R. (1997). *Contemporary Education in Wales: Theory Discourse and Research.* Paper presented at the Culture, Curriculum and Community Seminar. Education policy in Wales in the late 20th century. Swansea University, November 1997.

Pilcher, J. and Wagg, S. (1996) (eds). *Thatcher's Children? Politics, childhood, and society in the 1980s and 1990s.* London, Falmer Press.

Pilcher, J., Delamont, S., Powell, G., Rees, T. and Read, M. (1989). Evaluating a Women's Careers Convention. Methods, results and implications. *Research Papers in Education.* 4(1): 57-76.

Pitkin, D.S. (1985). *The House that Giacomo Built.* Cambridge, Cambridge University Press.

Power, S., Edwards, T., Whitty, G. and Wigfall, V. (2003). *Education and the Middle Class.* Buckingham, Open University Press.

Power, S. and Whitty, G. (1999). New Labours' educational policy: first, second or third way. *Journal of Education Policy.* 14(5): 535-546.

Pritchard, R.M.O. (1990). *The End of Elitism? The Democratisation of the West German University System.* New York: Berg.

Pritchard, R.M.O. (1994a). Government Power in British Higher Education. *Studies in Higher Education.* Vol. 19(2): 253-265.

Pritchard, R.M.O. (1994b). Fissures in the Federal Structure? The case of the University of Wales. *Higher Education Quarterly.* 48(4): 256-276.

Pugsley, L. (1995). *Education in Wales: A Suitable Case for Devolution?* Pamphlet University of Wales, Cardiff

Pugsley, L. (1995). *Sex Education: Ideology and Indifference.* Unpublished MSc Thesis: University of Wales, Cardiff.

Pugsley, L. (1996). Sex, Lies and the PSE curriculum. In S. Betts (ed.) *Our Daughters' Land.* Cardiff, University of Wales Press.

Pugsley, L. (1998). *Class of '97: Higher Education Markets and Choice.* Unpublished PhD Thesis. Cardiff, University of Wales.

Pugsley, L., Coffey, A. and Delamont, S. (1996). I don't eat peas anyway! Classroom stories and the social construction of childhood. In I. Butler and I. Shaw (eds). *A Case of Neglect? Children's experiences and the sociology of childhood.* Aldershot, Avebury.

Pugsley, L. (2003). Choice or Chance The University Challenge: How Schools Reproduce and Produce Social Capital in the Choice Process. In G. Walford (ed). *British Private Schools: Research on Policy and Practice.* London, Woburn Press.

Quicke, J. (1993). A Yuppie Generation: Political and Cultural Options for A level Students. In I. Bates, and G. Riseborough. (eds.) *Youth and Inequality.* Buckingham, Open University Press.

Raffe, D. and Willms, J. (1989). Schooling the Discouraged Worker: Labour Markets Effects on Educational Participation. *Sociology.* 23(4): 559-581.

Reay, D. (1995). A silent majority? Mothers in parental involvement. *Women's Studies International Forum*, 18: 337-348.

Reay, D. (1998). Rethinking Social Class: Qualitative perspectives on Class and Gender. *Sociology.* 32(2): 259-275.

Reay, D. (1998). *Class Work. Mothers' involvement in their children's primary schooling.* London, UCL Press Ltd.

Reay, D. (2000). A useful extension of Bourdieu's conceptual framework? Emotional capital as a way of understanding mothers' involvement in their children's education. *Sociological Review* 48(4): 568-585.

Reay, D. and Ball, S.J. (1997). Spoilt for Choice: the working class and educational markets. *Oxford Review of Education.* 23(1): 89-101.

Reay, D. and Ball, S.J. (1998). 'Making their minds up': family dynamics of school choice. *British Education Research Journal.* 24(4): 431-448.

Rees, G. and Istance. D. (1997). Higher Education in Wales: The (Re-) emergence of a National System? *Higher Education Quarterly.* 51(1):49-67.

Rees, G., Fevre, R., Furlong, J. and Gorard, S. (1997). History, place and the learning society: towards a sociology of lifetime learning. *Education Policy.* 12(6): 485-497.

Rees, T. (1992). *Women and the Labour Market.* London, Routledge.

Rist, R. (1978). *The Invisible Children: School Integration in American Society.* Cambridge MA, Harvard University Press.

Robbins Report. (1963). Higher Education. Cmnd. 2154. London, HMSO.

Roberts, D. and Allen, A. (1997). *Young Applicants' Perceptions of Higher Education.* Leeds, Heist.

Roberts, K. (1977). The Social Conditions, Consequences and Limitations of Careers Guidance. *British Journal of Guidance and Counselling.* Vol. 5(1) pp. 1-9.

Roberts, K. (1993). Career trajectories and the mirage of Social Mobility. In I. Bates and G. Riseborough (eds). *Youth and Inequality.* Buckingham, Open University Press.

Roberts, K. (1995). *Youth Employment in Modern Britain.* Oxford, Oxford University Press.

Roberts, K. (1997). Structure and agency: the new youth research agenda. In J. Bynner, L. Chisholm and A. Furlong (Eds) *Youth, Citizenship and Social Change in a European Context.* Gateshead, Tyne and Wear, Athenaeum Press.

Robertson, D. and Hillman, J. (1997). *Widening participation in Higher Education for Students from lower socio-economic Groups and Students with Disabilities.*

Report 6 for the National Committee of Inquiry into Higher Education. London, The Stationery Office.

Roker, D. (1993). Gaining the Edge: Girls at a Private School. In I. Bates and G. Riseborough (eds.) *Youth and Inequality*. Buckingham: Open University Press.

Rosser, C. and Harris, C.C. (1965*). The Family and Social Change : a study of kinship in a South Wales town*. London, Routledge.

Salisbury, J. (1994) *Becoming Qualified: ethnography of a post-experience teacher training course*. Unpublished PhD Thesis. Cardiff: University of Wales.

Salter, B.G. and Tapper, E.R. (1992*). Oxford, Cambridge and the changing idea of university: the challenge to donnish domination*. Buckingham, Open University Press and SRHE.

Salter, B. and Tapper, T. (1994). *The State and Higher Education*. Ilford: Woburn Press.

Salzman, J. P. (1990). Save the World, Save Myself. Responses to Problematic Attachment. In C. Gilligan, N. Lyons and T. Hanmer (eds). *Making Connections: The rational worlds of adolescent girls at the Emma Willard School. London,* Harvard University Press.

Scott, J. (1990). *A Matter of Record: documentary sources in social research*. Cambridge, Polity Press.

Sharp, S. (1976). *Just Like a Girl*. London, Penguin.

Shattock, M. (1994). *The UGC and the Management of British Universities*. Buckingham, SRHE and OUP.

Sidgewick, S., Mahony, P. and Hextall, I. (1994). A Gap in the Market? A Consideration of Market Relations in Teacher Education. *British Journal of Sociology of Education*. 15, 467-479.

Shavit, Y. and Blossfield, H. (1993). *Persistent inequality: changing educational attainment in thirteen countries*. Boulder Co, Westview Press.

Slater, D. (1998). Analysing Cultural Objects: content analysis and semiotics. In C. Searle (ed.) *Researching Society and Culture*. London, Sage.

Smedley, D. (1995). Marketing Secondary Schools to Parents - some lessons from the research on parental choice. *Educational Management and Administration*. 23(2): 96-103.

Smith, L. (1978). Sexist Assumptions and Female Delinquency. In C. Smart and B. Smart (eds). *Women, Sexuality and Social Control*. London, Routledge and Kegan Paul.

Smith, J. (1997). *From FE to HE: the experience of GNVQ students*. College Research, Summer 10-11.

Southall, J. (1990). *Girls, Women and Occupational Choice*. Unpublished MSc.Econ. Cardiff, University of Wales.

Statham, J. and Mackinnon, D. with Cathcart, H. and Hales, M. (1989) (2nd Edition). *The Education Fact File*. Kent, Hodder and Stoughton.

Stewart, D.W. and Shamdasani, P.N. (1990). *Focus Group: theory and practice*. London, Sage.

Sullivan, A. and Heath, A. (2003). Intakes and Examination Results at State and Private Schools. In G. Walford (ed) *British Private Schools. Research on Policy and Practice*. London, Woburn Press.

Super, D.E. (1957). *The Psychology of Careers*. New York, Harper and Rowe.

Swinnerton-Dyer, P. (1991). Policy on Higher Education and research, the REDE Lecture 1991. *Higher Education Quarterly*. 45: 204-218.

Teichler, U. (1996). The Changing Nature of Higher Education in Western Europe. *Higher Education Policy*. 9(2): 89-111.

Thomas, K. (1991). *Gender and Subject in Higher Education*. Buckingham, OUP and SRHE.

Thomas, E. (2001). *Widening Participation in Post-Compulsory Education.* London, Continuum.

Times Higher Education Supplement. (1996). *Focus on Wales.* April 26th: 8-12.

Times Higher Education Supplement (2002). *Poor face a steep climb.* 18th January 2002

Times Higher Education Supplement (2002). *Debts grow even bigger and more painful.* (Findings from the MORI Unite Student Living Survey). Times Higher Education Supplement. 1 February: 6-7.

Trow, Martin (1973). *Problems in the Transition from Elite to Mass Higher Education.* Berkley, C.A, Carnegie Commission on Higher Education.

Trow, M. (1998). The Dearing Report: A Transatlantic View. *Higher Education Quarterly.* 52(1): 93-117.

UCAS, (1996). *Statistical Survey 1996 Report on Qualified Applicants: those who did not enter higher education (1995).* Gloucestershire, UCAS.

UCAS (2000). *Statistical Survey 2000. Applicants to Higher Education by Social Class.* Gloucester, UCAS.

Van Vught, F. (1991). The Netherlands: From Corrective to Facilitative Governmental Policies. In G. Neave and F. Van Vught (eds). *Prometheus Bound: The Changing Relationship between Government and Higher Education in Western Europe.* Oxford, Pergamon Press.

Vincent, C. (2000). *Including Parents? Education, citizenship and parental agency.* Buckingham, Open University Press.

Wagner, L. (1995). A Thirty Year Perspective: From the Sixties to the Nineties. In T. Schuller (ed). *The Changing University?* Buckingham, SRHE and OUP.

Walford, G. (1990). Privatization and Privilege in Education. London: Routledge.

Walford, G. (1992). The reform of Higher Education. In M. Arnot and L. Barton (eds). *Voicing Concerns.* Oxfordshire: Triangle.

Ward, J. P. (1976). *Social Reality for the Adolescent Girl. Swansea.* Faculty of Education, University of Wales

Warner, D. and Palfreyman, D. (1996) (eds). *Higher Education Management: The Key Elements .* Buckingham, SRHE and Open University Press..

Watson, A., Stuart, N. and Lucas, D. (1995). *Impact of New Management Arrangements in Pathfinder Careers Services.* Sheffield, Careers Service Employment Branch.

Watts, A. G. (1988). The changing place of careers education in schools. *Prospects.* XV111(4): 473-482.

Watts, A. G. (1991). The Impact of the New Right: Policy Challenges Confronting Career Guidance in England and Wales. *British Journal of Guidance and Counselling.* 19(3): 230-245.

Weiler, W. C. (1996). Factors Influencing the Matriculation Choices of High Ability Students. *Economics of Education Review.* 15(1): 23-35.

Welsh Office (1997). *School Performance Information. 1997.* Cardiff, Welsh Office.

Westegaard, J. and Barnes, A. (1994). *Inspecting Careers Work.* Chelmsford, TVEI.

White, C., Stratford, N., Thomas, A. and Ward, K. (1996). *Review of Qualifications for 16-19 year olds: young people's perceptions of 16-19 qualifications.* London, Social and Community Planning Research.

Whitty, G. (1997). Creating Quasi-Markets in Education: A Review of the Recent Research on Parental Choice and School Autonomy in Three Countries. *Review of Research in Education.* 22: 3-47.

Whitty, G., Edwards, T. and Gewirtz, S. (1993). *Specialisation and choice in urban education the City technology college experiment.* London, Routledge.

Whitty, G., Rowe, G. and Aggleton, P. (1994). Discourse in cross curricular contexts : limits to empowerment. *International Studies in Sociology of Education.* 4(1): 25-41.

Wilcox, K. (1982). Ethnography as a Methodology and its applications to the study of schooling: a Review. In G. Spindler (ed). *Doing the Ethnography of Schooling.* New York, Holt Rinehart and Winston.

Williams, G. (1997). The Market Route To Mass Higher Education. *Higher Education Policy.* 10 (3/4): 449-496.

Willis, P. (1977). *Learning to Labour.* Farnborough, Saxon House.

Willmott, P. and Young, M. (1962). *Family and Kinship in East London.* London, Routledge.

Wilson, D. (1978). Sexual Codes and Conduct. In C. Smart, and B. Smart (eds). *Women, Sexuality and Social Control.* London, Routledge and Kegan Paul.

Wilson, J., Davies, M. and Preston, D. (1992). Does Accommodation play a part in student choice of university? *Higher Education Review.* 25(1): 57-67.

Windolf, P. (1995). Selection and Self Selection at German Mass Universities. *Oxford Review of Education.* 21(2): 207-231.

Woods, P. (1992). Empowerment through Choice? Towards an understanding of parental choice and school responsiveness. . *Education Management and Administration.* 20(4): 204-211

Youth Cohort Study. (1989). *Youth Cohort Series.* London, DES.

Index